I0824369

ULTIMATE ENCYCLOPEDIA OF Fabrics & Unconventional Materials

SEW WITH 100+ MATERIALS *from* TRICKY TO TAME

Annye Driscoll

FanPowered PRESS
an imprint of C&T Publishing

Publisher: Amy Barrett-Daffin

Creative Director: Gailen Runge

Senior Editor: Roxane Cerda

Associate Editor: Karly Wallace

Technical Editor: Barbara Emodi

Copy Editor: Elizabeth Kuball

Cover/Book Designer: April Mostek

Production Coordinator: Zinnia Heinzmann

Illustrator: Mary Flynn

Photography Coordinator: Rachel Ackley

Front cover photography by Annye Driscoll

Photography by Annye Driscoll, unless otherwise noted

Published by FanPowered Press, an imprint of C&T Publishing, Inc., P.O. Box 1456, Lafayette, CA 94549

Library of Congress Control Number: 2025034417

Library of Congress Cataloging-in-Publication Data is available upon request.

Printed in China

10 9 8 7 6 5 4 3 2 1

Dedication

This book is dedicated to *We Are Paul*. You got me through this one. I love you!

Acknowledgments

Ultimate Encyclopedia of Fabrics & Unconventional Materials was a massive undertaking and, consequently, took a massive amount of help to complete. Thank you to Roxane, Karly, and the rest of the C&T team, who trusted me with this project before my first book had even come out. Thank you to Oliso, Olfa, Stonemountain & Daughter Fabric, Shannon Fabrics, Bernette, Worbla, Wonderflex, C&T Publishing, Greg and Cheryl Paquette, and my dad for providing products to experiment with and photograph. Thank you to the *NoNaNo!* Discord group; the heart reacts on my massive lists gave me life. Thank you to Zeke and Sharon for helping with so many of the pieces of this book, and to Paul S for contributing to a lot of (probably fairly incomprehensible) technical discussions. Thank you to Carol and the rest of the wonderful sewists at Sew-A-Lot in Centerville, Ohio, for answering my extremely esoteric questions. Thank you to specialty materials experts the Wig-Wigs and Snow Dragon for beta-reading my leather and latex chapters, respectively. Any mistakes remaining are my own! Finally, thank you to my incredible guest artists, to their stupendous photographers, and to everyone who helped me find them.

Contents

Introduction 6

Swatching and Practicing 7

The Basics 8

Fibers 8

Plant Fibers 9

Animal Fibers 10

Semi-synthetic 12

Synthetic 12

Atypical Materials 14

Identifying Fabric 15

Weaves 17

Woven 17

Knits 18

Nonwoven and Adhered 18

Parts of a Fabric 19

Fabric directions 19

Sides of fabric 19

Stretch 20

Choosing Fabric 21

Cutting layouts 23

Supplies 24

Machine Feet 25

Machine Needles 26

Stitch Plates 28

Pins 29

Thread 31

Pressing and Ironing 34

Cutting Tools 37

Marking Tools 40

Adhesives 42

Interfacing 44

Commercial interfacing 44

Alternative interfacings 45

Starch 47

The Serger 47

Hems, Seams, and Techniques 49

Stitches 50

Seams 52

Seam Finishes 55

Hems 57

Other Techniques 59

Lightweight and Medium-weight Wovens 63

Easy Sewing 64

Suiting and Shirting 67

Lightweight Wovens 71

Heavyweight Wovens 76

Canvas and Denim 78

Jacquards 82

Textured Heavyweights 86

Classic Knits 89

Sturdy Knits 91

Stretch Knits 95

Sweater Knits 102

Delicates 106

Sheers 107

Shinies and Sleeks 116

Meshes 126

Nets 128

Piles and Naps 133

Cozies 135

Velvet, Velveteen, and Corduroy 139

Stretch Velvet, French Terry, and Velour 142

Faux Fur 144

Embellished and Embroidered Fabrics 148

Embellished 149

Embroidery, Lace, and Eyelet 153

Specialty Fabrics 157

Felt, Boiled Wool, and Melton 158

Leather 161

Tissue Lamé 166

Cork 169

Latex 172

Vinyls 174

Non-Stretch Vinyls 175

Stretch Vinyls 178

Clear and Tinted Vinyl 180

Paper 182

Thin Paper 183

Standard Paper 185

Fabric Paper 187

Thin Cardboard 189

Thick Cardboard 191

Foam 193

Thin Foam 195

Thick Foam 199

Neoprene 202

Utility Materials 205

Nonslip Materials 206

Tarps, Cling Saran Wrap, and Plastic Bags 208

Structural Materials 210

Fabric Encyclopedia 215

Further Reading 271

About the Author 272

Introduction

I want sewing to be fun, but sometimes the fabrics and projects I choose make that difficult. As a cosplayer, my sewing is often off the beaten path: I concoct gravity-defying garments; I expect my sewing machine to handle "armor"; I fabricate my own textiles, textures, and techniques; and I create with a whole heap of pretty weird materials. Whether you're a bag maker, performance apparel creator, cosplayer, fursuiter, home upholsterer, special event garment maker, dabbling sewist, or part of any other of our myriad of incredible sewing sub-hobbies ... I'm with you in the struggle! Sewing is hard, weird fabrics make it harder, and—let's be honest—the textile arts are ancient ones, featuring a whole lot of confusing topics and techniques.

I want you to be able to realize your sewing ambitions. This book will help.

The first chapter, The Basics (pg 8), introduces you to fundamental fabric concepts. Next, Supplies (pg 24) is an overview of everything you'll use when implementing the techniques in this book. Hems, Seams, and Techniques (pg 49) is a high-level overview of stitches, seams, seam finishes, hems, and other techniques referenced in this book, with page numbers leading to their corresponding full tutorials. The information in these sections will cover the basics; when you see these topics referenced in further sections, you will understand when and why to use what you've learned.

In the next chapter, Lightweight and Medium-weight Wovens (pg 63), the meat of the book begins. I've sorted each fabric (and other material!) into a group of shared characteristics, wherein I guide you through:

- What each material is.
- How to prewash and then subsequently care for it.
- How to press it.
- How to transfer patterns to it and cut and pin it.
- How to interface it.
- And how to sew with it!

There are thirteen chapters of this—from quilting cotton to disposable trash bags—and you'll learn a whole lot along the way.

Pillows made of velvet and corduroy and stuffed with two years of sewing scraps

PILLOWS BY ANNYE DRISCOLL
Photo by Annye Driscoll

Finally, the Fabric Encyclopedia (pg 215) offers a concise reference to each material in this book including a short description, basic sewing guidelines, and a cross-reference to its main chapter in the text.

Ultimately, you can use this book one of two ways:

- You can read it end to end, learning about more difficult (and weirder!) materials as you go.
- Or, you can look up your material in the encyclopedia, learn the basics, and then go to its corresponding chapter for more detailed instruction.

QUICK TIP!
Is neither of these strategies quite right for you? Need an idea of the easiest materials to work with? I recommend the fabrics in Easy Sewing (pg 64), Felt (pg 158), and Cozies (pg 135) as great beginner materials.

Either direction you choose is fine; this is a no judgment zone! And on the topic of judgment: I have tried to assume nothing about your level of sewing knowledge in this text. We all learn from different instructions and at different paces. And hey! I sometimes glue my hems, and I encourage you to do it, too. Unless you're actually getting professionally critiqued for the work you're making, no one is keeping score.

Sound good? Ready to learn? Ready to make?! Let's go!

Swatching and Practicing

But first ... we need to talk about swatching. **Swatching**, using a small scrap of your material for experimentation, is always important, but rarely more so than when embarking with new materials and techniques. Always make sure to try the following on an extra piece of fabric before committing to large pieces:

- Washing and drying
- Pressing
- Steaming and otherwise wetting
- Mark-making
- Pinning
- Interfacing (especially if using fusible interfacing)
- Sewing and seam ripping

Swatching conventional and overlock stitches on various fabrics

New materials often mean new techniques. Much like you want to swatch new *materials*, you'll want to practice new *techniques* before starting your actual construction ... especially if you're using expensive materials. You want to secure your skills before committing to the technique, but just as important, you need to make sure the technique actually makes sense and works for the materials you're using. Is that tricky new hem actually going to look good on your deadline-looming party dress? Will your machine even agree to topstitch the sticky faux leather you've chosen for your barstool tops? Make sure you can execute your chosen strategy *and* that your strategy actually makes sense for your project!

Consider that some fabrics cannot easily be altered without damage. Ripping out stitches may leave visible holes or even be impossible without ripping through the fabric itself. Other fabrics, once pressed, cannot be uncreased. Not all mistakes can be corrected during the sewing process.

For that reason, making a mock-up when faced with new-to-you fabric is particularly important. You can always make a mock-up with muslin, bedsheets, or other inexpensive fabric, but you may want to consider purchasing a fabric similar to the one you'll use in your final piece. Consider whether a cheaper version of your specific fabric would allow you to practice and make fit adjustments. You may be able to thrift a similar material you can practice on!

A mock-up marked for reference in the final piece

Button-down shirt made with cotton sateen

GARMENT AND MODELING BY ANNYE DRISCOLL
Photo by Abigail Davidson

The Basics

The following chapter covers some basic terminologies, concepts, and tools that are necessary when learning about the vast array of materials we have at our artistic disposal.

Fibers

Fiber is what a material is made of. A **natural fabric** is one derived from plants or animals like silk, wool, leather, or cotton. Man-made materials are described as **synthetic**; examples of synthetic materials are polyester, nylon, and spandex. A third, much smaller category is **semi-synthetics**, man-made materials made from natural components that undergo chemical processing. The two most common semi-synthetic fibers are acetate and rayon.

Fabrics can be a combination of fibers, including combinations of synthetic and natural fibers; your T-shirt, for example, may be 80 percent natural cotton and 20 percent semi-synthetic rayon. These fabrics are referred to as **blends**.

QUICK TIP!
The following fiber descriptions also include care guidelines. Although each kind of fabric may require specific methods (which you can find in the Encyclopedia [pg 215]), knowing *general* rules for caring for the different fibers will extend the life not only of your sewing projects, but also of your purchased fabric goods.

Fabrics made from different materials:

1. PVC
2. Polyester
3. Silk
4. Cotton, acrylic, and rayon blend

Plant Fibers

COTTON

Cotton fibers come from the seed pod of the cotton plant. Cotton is durable, soft, and inexpensive. It's a particularly breathable fiber. It is extremely versatile; cotton voile is light enough to be translucent, but the heaviest of denims are also cotton. Cotton fabrics include terry, denim, voile, and batiste.

Cotton is fairly durable and easy to care for, but, like all materials, it will break down with repeated washes. If a full wash isn't necessary, consider airing out your cotton piece instead of washing it with water.

Cotton shrinks dramatically; be sure to preshrink cotton fabrics—maybe more than once! After preshrinking, consider washing with cold or warm water and tumble dry on low heat to prevent further shrinkage.

Cotton is easy to press and can tolerate a lot of heat from an iron. It does well when steamed.

1. Quilting cotton
2. Cotton velveteen
3. Cotton poplin
4. Cotton gabardine
5. Cotton denim

LINEN AND HEMP

Linen fibers come from the stalks of linen or flax plants. Linen is strong, smooth, and comfortable. It is matte. Sometimes it has *slubs*: variations in the yarn diameter that create a textured fabric. Because it has low elasticity, linen wrinkles dramatically. Examples of linen are lawn, damask, canvas, and linen jersey.

Hemp fibers are harvested from the stalk of the hemp plant. Hemp is tough, absorbent, and prone to wrinkles. It is breathable and soft. Although it is available in many variations, the most common fabric made from hemp is a simple plain weave called *woven hemp,* which comes in multiple weights. Because hemp requires less water and chemical finishing than cotton, hemp is often blended with cotton to increase the sustainability of the resulting fiber.

Generally, linen and hemp can be washed hot and dried on high heat, and ironed and steamed with high temperatures. Linen and hemp should only be washed using liquid detergent. The relatively loose weaves of fabrics made from these fibers are particularly susceptible to powdered detergent granules getting stuck in the yarns of the fabric, causing damage.

Linen can attract moths and other bugs, but to a much lesser extent than silk and wool. If you'll be storing a linen or hemp piece for a long time, make sure it's clean and in an airtight container.

1. Linen woven
2. 70% rayon, 30% linen woven
3. 6-ounce hemp "denim"

1. Silk chiffon
2. Silk dupioni
3. Silk charmeuse
4. Silk habutai
5. Silk taffeta

1

2

3

4

5

Animal Fibers

SILK

Silk is luxurious, comfortable, and versatile. It has a natural sheen. It is strong and absorbent but has very little natural elasticity. Some silk fabrics are organza, chiffon, and dupioni.

With some exceptions, silk is dry-clean only; even hand washing can damage the delicate material. Iron with a medium heat and a press cloth to avoid scorching it or affecting its finish. Do not steam; silk is susceptible to water spots.

What Is Water Spotting?

Water spotting is staining left behind by water. It has two common causes:

1. In the case of silk, which can be difficult to dye, water causes the dye to run, causing discoloration.

2. Minerals are left behind when the water evaporates, leaving a ring of visible residue.

Water spotting is one reason to always swatch your fabric if you'll be washing or steaming your creation. Take particular care to test when using natural fibers like linen, cotton, and (of course!) silk; because these materials absorb water, they're more susceptible to spotting.

If you do get water spots, the best way to remove them is by entirely soaking your fabric in water. This will cause the entire piece to become "water spotted," removing visible blemishes.

If you choose to machine wash silk, wash it only in a mesh laundry bag with other silk pieces. Otherwise, you risk causing snags on silk's delicate surface. Wash on cool; then lay flat to dry.

Only use liquid detergents when hand or machine washing silk. If powdered detergent fails to fully dissolve, the solid granules will damage your fabric both by causing friction and by leaving residue stains.

Silk attracts moths, which lay their eggs in the fabric. When those eggs hatch, the larvae chew holes in fabrics and garments, ruining them. Because of this risk, silk must be stored in an airtight container. If you do get larvae in your fabric or finished pieces, you can kill the eggs either by heating the fabric (by running it through the dryer on the hottest setting for at least 30 minutes) or by freezing it for at least 72 hours.

WOOL

Wool is warm, breathable, and fairly easy to work with. It's naturally elastic, which means it resists wrinkles. It's very absorbent and insulating. Wool fabrics include felt, flannel, and twill. Many sweater knits—including those made by home knitters and crocheters—are made from wool yarns.

Wool shrinks dramatically; if you'll be washing your wool creation, make sure to prewash it carefully, and follow the label (usually that's in cold water with special detergent made for wool). You can also steam wool to preshrink it. Ultimately, you may want to take your fabric to a dry cleaner to prepare it, especially if it's pricey yardage.

1. Bouclé

2. Melton wool coating

3. 60% viscose, 40% wool boiled wool

Check the Bolt!

When purchasing fabric—especially if it's a sensitive fiber like wool or silk—consider taking a photo of the bolt's information label. Just as the tag on a store-bought garment will explain care instructions, this tag will explain how best to wash and dry your new material.

Generally, you'll want to wash your wool pieces as infrequently as possible. Washing wool incorrectly turns it into felt. (If you actually *want* felt, check out Making Felt, pg 158, for more details on that process!) To prevent wool from felting, avoid hot water and agitation (including wringing). Consider either airing out your wool piece or sending it to a professional to be dry-cleaned instead of washing it yourself.

Lay your wool flat to dry; hanging it will stretch and distort the fibers.

When pressing wool, always use steam or a spray bottle and a press cloth. A dry iron can quickly damage wool.

Like silk, wool is susceptible to moths and other pests. Store wool fabrics and creations in airtight containers.

Kinds of Wools

Particular kinds of wools may seem like fabrics, but they are actually fibers. For example, you can buy merino *jersey* or merino *suiting*—two very different kinds of fabrics made from the same material. There are many kinds of wool, but I've covered common varieties here.

Merino, which comes from sheep, is particularly soft and fairly inexpensive. It's often blended or mimicked by synthetics, so be sure to read the label on anything labeled merino. It is durable, absorbent, and warm.

Mohair comes from Angora goats. It is durable, lustrous, and insulating.

Cashmere wool is also a goat fiber. It is particularly fine and thin when compared to other types of wool, but is still very insulating. It is soft and delicate.

Alpaca fleece is hypoallergenic, warm, and naturally elastic.

Angora is produced by the Angora rabbit (not to be confused with the Angora goat, which produces mohair). Angora is soft, silky, and distinctly fluffy. Angora is both warm and lightweight.

1. 75% polyester, 20% rayon, and 5% spandex sweater knit blend
2. Acetate twill lining
3. Rayon/spandex jersey
4. Rayon challis
5. Ponte knit in a viscose, nylon, and spandex blend

Semi-Synthetic

ACETATE AND RAYON

Acetate is made from manufactured cellulose fibers. It is lustrous, hangs beautifully, and has good elasticity. It is very heat-sensitive; it will melt under a hot iron. Some fabrics commonly made from acetate are gauze, tricot, and lining satin.

Rayon (also known as **viscose**, which is a specific manufacturing method used to make rayon), like acetate, is made from manufactured cellulose fibers. It is soft and breathable, but strong. Materials made from rayon hang nicely and often emulate natural fibers. Jersey and suiting are among the fabrics made from rayon.

Rayon and acetate should be washed using a delicate cycle or hand washed; consider sending a piece with high acetate content to the dry cleaner's. Hang dry. Rayon can tolerate a bit more heat than plastic fibers; ironing on medium heat with steam will be effective. Acetate, though, should only be ironed with low heat and from the wrong side.

1. Cotton, acrylic, and rayon tweed blend
2. Acrylic craft felt

Synthetic

ACRYLIC

Acrylic (also known as **polyacrylic**) is lightweight, warm, and soft. It is durable. Suiting and faux fur are commonly made from acrylic.

Acrylic and polyacrylic can be machine washed hot and then laid flat to dry. They can be carefully ironed with a press cloth.

NYLON

Nylon is smooth and inexpensive, but easily *pills* (gets covered in small tangled balls of fibers and lint). It is durable. Fabrics made from nylon include chiffon, tulle, and velvet.

Most nylon pieces can be machine washed warm or cold. Tumble dry on low heat, hang, or lay flat to dry; then iron on low heat with a press cloth. Counterintuitively, nylon cannot be dry-cleaned—the fibers may get damaged during that process.

1. Nylon tulle
2. 82% nylon, 18% spandex swimsuit fabric blend
3. 80% nylon, 20% spandex milliskin tricot blend
4. 84% nylon, 16% powernet mesh blend

POLYESTER

Polyester is strong, durable, and cheap; for that reason, it's often blended with other fibers to increase strength and reduce price. It is not breathable but is easy to care for. Common polyester fabrics are chiffon, organza, and knits.

Polyester can be machine washed hot and machine dried on low heat. It can be ironed with steam using a low- to medium-heat iron.

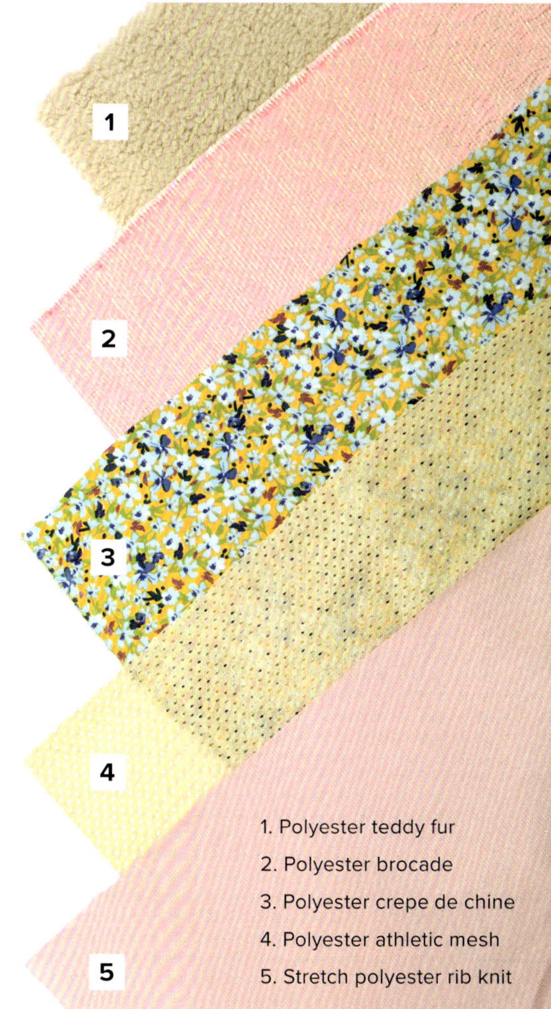

1. Polyester teddy fur
2. Polyester brocade
3. Polyester crepe de chine
4. Polyester athletic mesh
5. Stretch polyester rib knit

1. 95% polyester, 5% spandex velvet blend
2. 90% polyester, 10% spandex stretch velvet blend
3. 95% polyester, 5% spandex stretch French terry blend
4. 90% polyester, 10% spandex 1.5mm scuba blend

SPANDEX

Spandex, which you may see referred to as elastane or Lycra (spandex made by The Lycra Company), is almost always blended with another material to increase its stretchiness, recoverability, and wrinkle resistance. Common fabrics that include a percentage of spandex are stretch denim, dance and athletic gear, and jersey.

Spandex can be machine washed and dried, but care must be taken for the fabric it's blended with. Spandex can scorch; always start at low heat and use a press cloth when ironing.

1. EVA
2. PE
3. PU
4. PVC

Atypical Materials

This book includes many materials that are not traditional fibers but are commonly used for sewing and other crafts.

PVC (polyvinyl chloride), **PU** (polyurethane), **PE** (polyethylene), and **EVA** (ethylene-vinyl acetate) are all forms of plastic that can be manufactured into soft, flexible (sewable!) materials, foam, or both. These materials are all very sensitive to heat, which makes them difficult to press, but they offer some creative potential; some polyethylene plastics, for example, can be welded with just an iron! As a whole, they're not generally washable and should be spot cleaned and laid flat to dry.

Paper, **cork**, and **latex** are all natural materials that come from trees and other plants. **Leather** and **suede** come from animals, of course: They're skins! Generally, these particular materials won't fare well in the washer and dryer, but they can be spot cleaned or hand-washed with special techniques (detailed in their individual chapters).

1. Leather
2. Latex
3. Cork
4. Paper

Identifying Fabric

You may not know what your fabric is made of, which is tough when you need to care for or learn how to sew with it! Luckily, there are ways to get clues.

An easy way to begin identifying mystery material is with the "scrunch test." Tightly ball a piece of the fabric in your hand long enough to feel heat; that heat and pressure create wrinkles, which is what you want for the experiment! Natural materials, especially linen, hemp, and silk, will wrinkle, and those wrinkles won't fall out easily when you manipulate your fabric. Synthetics and synthetic blends, especially those with spandex added, will not wrinkle significantly, and wrinkles will easily fall out when you stretch and smooth the fabric.

Rayon undergoing scrunch test

You can also test the breathability of the fabric by using the scrunch test. Synthetic fabrics, which are not generally breathable, will begin feeling clammy within your hand. This is because as your hand heats the fabric, natural fibers will distribute the heat, while synthetics will reflect the heat and moisture of your skin.

The most reliable identifier of fiber, however, is a burn test: Different fibers burn very differently and give characteristic clues during and after being exposed to flame.

⚠ STAY SAFE!

Make sure you stay safe when burning anything, especially something that may contain plastic! Burn in a well-ventilated area and wear a respirator. Tie back your hair, do not wear baggy sleeves, and have water ready just in case. •

Silk undergoing the burn test

To begin, prewash your fabric. Finishing chemicals can affect burn test results (because they also burn!). Cut a swatch from your washed and dried fabric; then put it in your flame using tweezers. Observe how the fabric reacts to the flame, and inspect the ash left behind from the burn.

Generally, synthetic fibers melt, plant fibers burn and leave fine ash dust, and animal fibers burn and curl and leave a bead of ash.

Fiber	Condition During Burn	Ash
PLANT FIBERS		
Cotton	Steady yellow flame, scorches. Has a yellow-orange afterglow.	Gray or black ash, very fine
Linen	Steady yellow flame. Slower to ignite than cotton—compare it to a known cotton fabric in your stash.	Gray ash, feathery
Hemp	Burns quickly with a bright yellow-orange flame. Does not have an afterglow.	Black ash, feathery
Rayon/viscose	Burns very quickly with a bright yellow flame.	Small amount of feathery gray ash
Acetate	Burns quickly with a dark smoke; then melts after the flame has burned itself out. Will continue to melt when removed from the flame.	Hard beads that are difficult to crush
ANIMAL FIBERS		
Silk	Does not light easily; will curl away from the flame. Stops burning on its own when removed from the flame.	Soft, shiny beads of ash that crush easily
Wool	Ignites slowly and curls away from the flame. Burns orange and smoky. Stops burning on its own when removed from the flame.	Coarse, dark ash
SYNTHETIC FIBERS		
Acrylic/Polycrylic	Shrinks from the flame, catches quickly, and then burns and melts. Has a white and orange flame with black smoke.	Irregular beads that are difficult to crush
Nylon	Shrinks from the flame and melts before burning; burns slowly once it's lit. Stops burning when removed from the flame.	Gray beads that are difficult to crush
Polyester	Shrinks from the flame; then melts and burns slowly with an orange flame. Will struggle to burn when removed from the flame.	Black beads that do not crush
Spandex	Melts before burning; once removed from the flame, it will continue to melt.	Black, soft, sticky ash

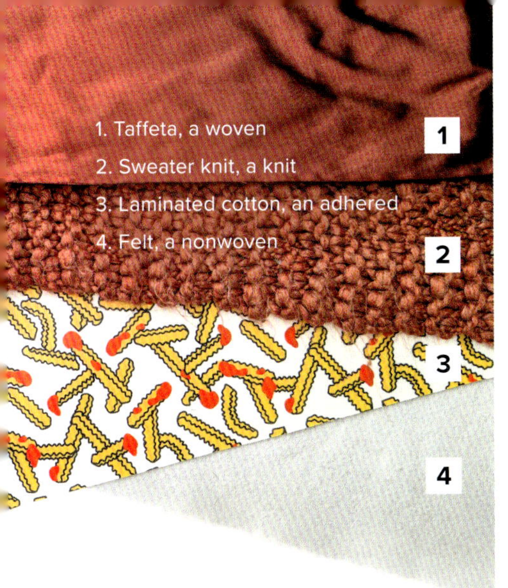

1. Taffeta, a woven
2. Sweater knit, a knit
3. Laminated cotton, an adhered
4. Felt, a nonwoven

Weaves

The **weave** of a material is the way the fibers are constructed to create a fabric. In many fabrics, this is an actual weave: In woven materials, vertical and horizontal yarns of a material are woven together to create distinct patterns of construction. In other materials, such as vinyl or quilt batting, the weave is actually a manufacturing process, often involving adhering a synthetic fiber to a woven backing.

CONFUSING TOPIC!

Yarn and thread mean very specific—and different—things when referring to fabrics and sewing. **Yarns** are the collection of fibers that make up a fabric. This is easy to remember if you think about fiber arts: When you knit a sweater, the yarn is what you loop together to make your fabric. **Thread** is also a long collection of fibers; it's what a sewist uses to join pieces of fabric. ●

Woven

Traditionally, **woven** fabrics are commonly made with one of three patterns: plain weave, satin weave, and twill weave.

In **plain weave**, also called linen weave or taffeta weave, yarns cross over and under each other at right angles to form a crisscross pattern. It is a very basic weave. Common fabrics in the plain weave are quilting cotton, chambray, and canvas.

Satin weave is recognizable by its finish: a shiny, smooth top and a dull back. Structurally, yarns crisscross much less often in satin weaves when compared to plain weaves; yarns "float" over their opposites. Both natural and synthetic materials can be satins, but in fabrics with short-staple fibers (such as cotton), the fabric formed from a satin weave is called a sateen. Common fabrics in the satin weave are charmeuse and damask. Other fabrics, like duchesse satins and crepe-backed satin, actually have the weave in their names.

The **twill weave** is distinguished by its offset thread-stepping, which creates a pattern of diagonal lines. Because the weave is asymmetrical, twill fabrics have different patterns on each side; usually the "front" of the fabric is the side with the more pronounced diagonal pattern. Common fabrics in the twill weave are denim and gabardine. Confusingly enough, twill is also a fabric in the twill weave category.

CONFUSING TOPIC!

Don't forget, *woven* is a type of weave. All fabrics have a weave, but not all fabrics are *woven!* ●

Knits

Knits are another major category of fabric construction. A **knit** is created by looping yarns together. Because of these interlocking loops, knits are always at least somewhat stretchy. This stretchiness means they're often intimidating for new sewists: They can be wiggly and require techniques specific to stretch projects. Conversely, that stretchiness also alleviates many common difficulties when patterning and fitting.

Knits, like weaves, can be further categorized: In this case, into warp knits and weft knits. Whether a knit is warp or weft determines its direction of stretch and the amount it unravels.

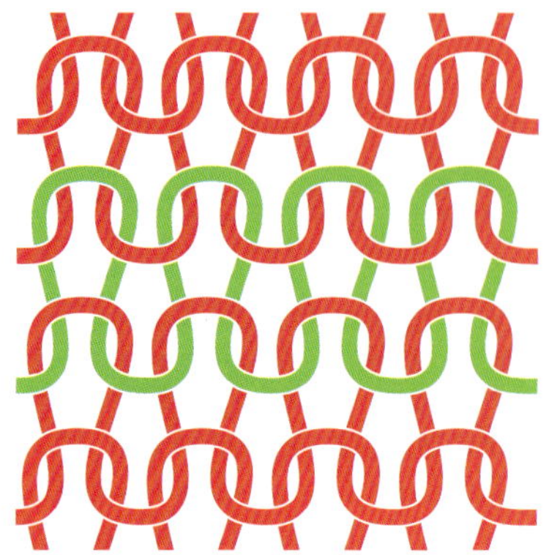

A **weft knit** is made with a single yarn, which is looped and knotted to create horizontal rows. Weft knits generally are very stretchy across their rows, and they may or may not stretch at all along the length of the fabric. Importantly, holes in weft knits tend to grow as the yarn becomes unraveled, meaning they are more delicate fabrics. Some examples of weft knits are jersey, ribbing, and interlock.

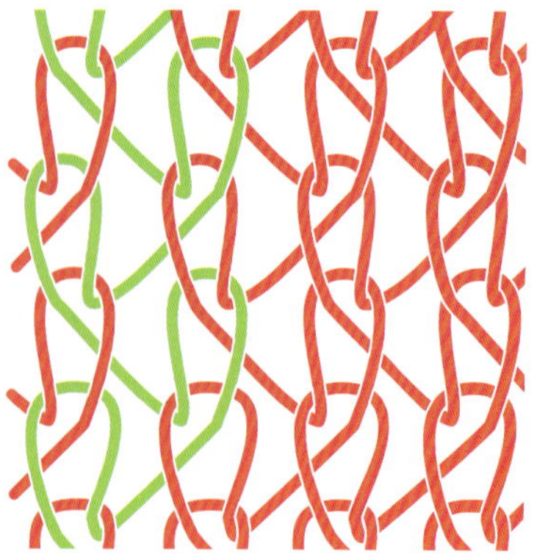

Warp knits are made with multiple yarns, which are looped and knotted vertically. They're generally much less stretchy and elastic than weft knits. Because warp knits are made from multiple yarns, a single broken yarn is much less likely to expand into a hole; warp knits are generally the more durable option of the two. Tricot, minky, and velour are common warp knits.

QUICK TIP!

Not sure if your fabric is a knit or a weave? Poke at an edge until it starts to come apart. If it frays, it's a weave. If it unravels, it's a knit. If it does neither, it's also probably a knit! Many knits do not unravel at all.

Layered on the top, a fraying woven; underneath is an unraveling knit

Nonwoven and Adhered

Finally, nonwovens are the "other" category of fabric construction. Any fabric that isn't constructed by weaving or knitting is a **nonwoven**. This category includes leather, felt, and even foam.

Adhered fabrics are some combination of the three varieties: Knits, wovens, and nonwoven materials can be adhered to another material to create all new textiles. Two examples are neoprene and cork: Neoprene is usually neoprene foam bonded to a knit fabric, and many thin cork fabrics include a fabric backing.

Parts of a Fabric

Fabric Direction

Many patterns and tutorials will refer you to a woven fabric's finished edge, which is called a **selvage**; this is the edge that was attached to the loom during manufacture. The yarns that run parallel to the selvage are called the **warp yarns**. Those that run perpendicular to the selvage are the **weft yarns**. If you imagine a 45″-wide fabric on a 20-yard bolt, the warp yarns are the ones running the whole 20 yards of the bolt, and the weft are those across the 45″ width.

Warp and weft yarns are important because they determine how the fabric behaves and can sometimes drastically affect how sewn projects are constructed. For that reason, we define three grains:

- **Straight grain** runs with the warp yarns (in a typical bolt of fabric, longways).
- **Cross grain** runs with the weft yarns (in a typical bolt of fabric, crossways).
- **Bias grain** runs exactly 45° diagonally across the fabric, intersecting both the warp and weft threads at 90° angles.

QUICK TIP!
Because the yarns are able to move and shift against each other more freely, woven fabrics have some natural mechanical stretch diagonally along the bias grain.

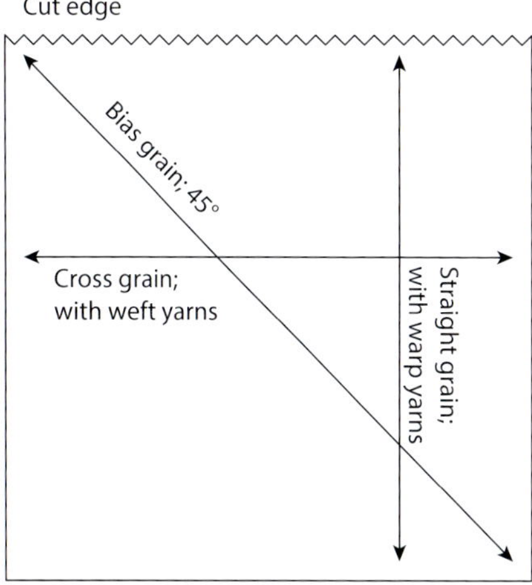

The straight grain (which runs with the warp yarns), the cross grain (which runs with the weft yarns), and the bias grain (which runs diagonally)

Sides of Fabric

Fabrics are generally one-sided. The front side is called the face or **right side**; the back is the **wrong side**. Often wrong sides are beautiful in their own right and work perfectly well as the display side of a project. Occasionally a fabric does not have a right and wrong side; these fabrics are called **double-faced**.

CONFUSING TOPIC!
Double cloth is a special category of fabric construction that's often confused with double-faced fabric.

To create double cloth, two fabrics are woven together during manufacturing to create a single textile. This can present interesting design and sewing decisions and can also make hemming much easier: At the edge you want to hem, snip the two fabrics apart, fold them in, and secure. Double cloth may be confused with double-faced fabrics, which are meant to be used with either side as the right side of the fabric. All double cloths are double-faced, but not all double-faced fabrics are double cloth; crepe-backed satin, for example, is beautiful on each side but is still only one layer of fabric.

The edge of a double cloth, snipped to prepare for a hem.

Sometimes, however, the right and wrong side of a fabric are *just* different enough that it's very important to mark which side is right and which is wrong. If you don't, you risk ending up with slightly different sheens on the two front panels of your garment, for example. This marking is easily done with washi tape or thread tacks (pg 40).

QUICK TIP!
Can't tell which side of the fabric is the right side? Look at the selvage: The holes left by the manufacturing process will be much more prominent on the right side. Make sure to mark it with chalk or tape so that you can tell even after your selvage is cut away!

The reverse of a pattern piece marked with washi tape

Stretch

Finally, fabrics are often described by their amount and direction of stretch.

Unless they have added spandex or other stretch fibers, woven fabrics have minimal stretch along their bias grain. Knit fabrics have more natural mechanical stretch, although even within the category there is vast variance in amount and direction of stretch.

Two-way stretch fabrics stretch just one way: across the width of the fabric. **Four-way** stretch fabrics stretch both across and along the fabric. These definitions are in addition to the stretch provided by the bias grain in wovens; a woven four-way stretch will actually stretch across, along, *and* on the diagonal of the fabric. A fabric's stretch can drastically affect both how it sews and how it performs; imagine creating a classic bikini swimsuit out of a fabric that doesn't stretch at all!

CONFUSING TOPIC!
Confusingly, sometimes two-way and four-way stretch fabrics are described as "one-way" and "two-way" stretch fabrics, respectively. When buying a two- or four-way stretch, make sure it's actually the one you expect by experimenting with its performance.

Choosing Fabric

When choosing fabric, there are many factors to consider.

How the fabric feels in the hand is called, suitably, the fabric's *hand:*

- **Weight:** Fabrics can range from extremely lightweight—almost floaty—to extremely heavy.
- **Drape:** The drape describes how a fabric hangs. It is affected not only by the weight, but also by the fabric's weave type and stretchiness.
- **Body:** The stiffness of a fabric's drape; a stiff fabric, such as organza, has a lot of body, even though it's lightweight.
- **Texture:** Fabrics may be soft, crinkled, smooth, ribbed, napped, piled, and many more.

QUICK TIP!

When describing fabric weight, retailers and manufacturers often use grams per square meter (GSM). Generally:

- **Very lightweight:** Under 100 GSM
- **Lightweight:** 100 to 200 GSM
- **Medium-weight:** 200 to 350 GSM
- **Heavyweight:** 350 to 475 GSM
- **Very heavyweight:** Over 475 GSM

CONFUSING TOPIC!

Many fabrics have a raised, fuzzy texture called a *pile* or *nap;* these words are sometimes used interchangeably, but piles and naps are constructed in different ways:

- A **pile** is an extra yarn that's looped and woven into the structure of the fabric and, therefore, sticks out from the base fabric. Those yarns may be cut short as part of the manufacturing process (velvet, corduroy), left long (faux fur), or even remain looped (towel terry).
- A **napped** fabric goes through the regular weaving process and is then brushed ("napped") to disturb the woven yarns and create a fuzzy texture. Flannel and fleece are classic napped fabrics.

Fleece (left) is napped and towel terry (right) has a pile.

Piled and napped fabrics need special consideration when working with them: Most notably, they can be delicate, and they often shift around during sewing. Additionally, many piles and naps are directional, the same way a cat's fur is! Even a short pile will look and feel dramatically different in each direction. For that reason, piled and napped fabrics should always be cut using a with-nap layout (pg 23).

Other characteristics apply to how the fabric looks:

- **Color and pattern:** Fabrics can be any color or pattern!
- **Sheen/finish:** Fabrics can be shiny to the point of reflectiveness or completely matte.
- **Opacity:** Fabrics can range from completely clear to completely opaque. Other fabrics are so loosely woven that you can see through the holes in the textile; this presents a different sort of opacity.

Finally, other characteristics relate to the fabric's performance:

- **Stretch:** Fabrics may be very stretchy, moderately stretchy, stretchy just along certain grains, not stretchy at all, and everything in between (pg 20).
- **Elasticity and stability:** Elasticity is the amount that a fabric bounces back after being stretched. The more elastic a fabric is, the better it will recover (and the less it will wrinkle!). Elastic fabrics may be described as stable, as will fabrics that do not distort with washing, hanging, or other uses. Some fabrics, such as low-elasticity stretchy fabrics or extremely loose weaves, will change shape over time. These fabrics are unstable.
- **Breathability, moisture resistance, and wicking:** Some fabrics are naturally breathable—moisture can pass through the fibers of the fabric. Others are naturally moisture resistant or moisture wicking—they pull moisture into themselves.

What about Upholstery Fabric?

The catch-all term *upholstery fabric* may refer to many different kinds of fabric, from medium-weight velour and corduroy to extremely heavyweight coated fabrics like polyurethane faux leather. Because of that wide range, upholstery fabric can be great not only for upholstery, but also for bag-making, costuming, and even garment-making. Plus, it is generally much wider on the bolt than typical fabric, which means it may be a more economical choice.

When buying upholstery fabrics, especially for projects other than upholstery, pay particular attention to fiber content and care instructions, because they may vary wildly. Upholstery fabrics may be coated with water and UV protections, which may make them drape, press, and wash in unexpected ways.

Cutting Layouts

Grain, texture, and stretch all contribute to how pattern pieces should be laid out on a piece of fabric. There are three main layouts: on the grain (and a more specific version of it, on the bias), puzzle-piece style, and with nap. You may need different layouts depending on both the fabric you're using and what you're making—using a layout that's inappropriate for your material or project could lead to issues both during and after construction.

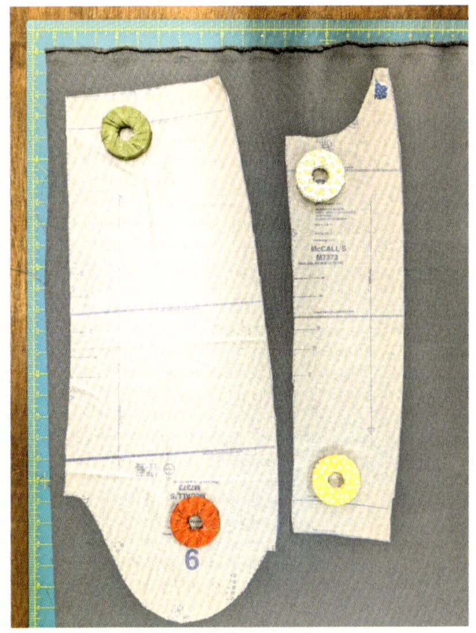

These pattern pieces are laid out **on the grain**; they all respect the same grain (usually, but not always, the warp), but do not need to respect the direction along that specific grain. Two bodice pieces, for example, may face different short/cut ends of the piece of fabric.

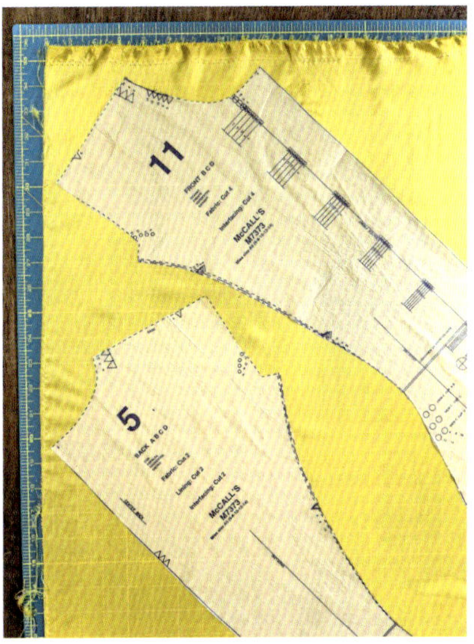

These pattern pieces are laid out **on the bias**; they will have increased stretchiness and an extra-dramatic drape. Generally, just certain pieces will need to be cut out on the bias—not the entire pattern.

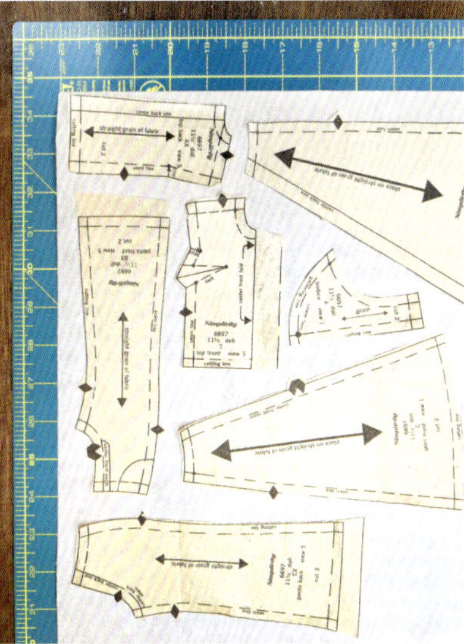

These pattern pieces are laid out **puzzle-piece style**; they don't need to respect direction at all. Fit those pieces as tightly as you can. It's your chance to be frugal with that super cool faux leather you found at the thrift store!

These pattern pieces are laid out **with nap**. All pieces are laid out not only parallel to the same grain (a with-nap layout is a specific kind of on-the-grain layout), but also all heading in the same direction on the fabric; all bodice pieces, for example, have their neckline edges arranged pointing toward the same end of the fabric.

Some fabrics don't have a nap but may need to be cut using a with-nap layout because of other factors, such as a pile, the structure of the weave, or a design of the material. Consult your pattern instructions and consider whether your fabric looks different from different angles; this will help you decide whether you need to cut with nap, just on the grain, or completely puzzle-piece style.

Supplies

This chapter covers many common and specialty tools and materials you may need when working with fabric. There are a lot, and you almost certainly don't have all of them!

Throughout this book, I assume nothing about your level of skill or access to tools. I provide options for sergers and conventional machines. I recommend specific needle types, stabilizer types, cutting tools, and marking strategies, but I encourage you to experiment with alternatives if you don't have exactly what the text recommends. Ultimately, understanding the *why* of tool usage can and will enable educated decision-making.

Don't forget: Sewing is a creative endeavor! We're here to be artsy fartsy and make cool stuff, and sometimes that requires thinking outside the box (or, in this case, the book).

Corset made of silk organza; skirt and bust drapes are hand-dyed silk fabric with dyed, embroidered, and felted detailing.

GARMENTS BY MAEVE FOLEY; MODELING BY FANTASTIGAL
Photo by Neil Bonabon

Machine Feet

The foot you put on your machine is generally determined by the seam, hem, or decorative element you're sewing, not the fabric you're using. There are a few exceptions, however, for techniques addressed in this book:

A **walking/even/dual-feed foot** ensures that the top and bottom layers of your fabric feed evenly through the machine, because machines usually only have *feed dogs*—the part of the machine that moves the fabric—on the bottom. Walking feet are great to use with stretchy, slinky, and sticky fabrics, which may get strangely manipulated by the feed dogs.

Other options for sticky fabrics are **nonstick/teflon feet**, which are made of or coated with nonstick materials, and **roller feet**, which have little wheels at the front and back of the feet to encourage fabric to move evenly underneath the foot.

A **straight-stitch foot** has a gap just large enough for the needle to pass through. This makes it ideal for delicate or slippery fabrics, which may otherwise get pulled beneath the needle plate.

Blind hem, edge stitching, overcast/overedge, felling, and **rolled-hem feet** are specifically made for specialty hem and seam treatments. These feet make those treatments easier to cleanly execute!

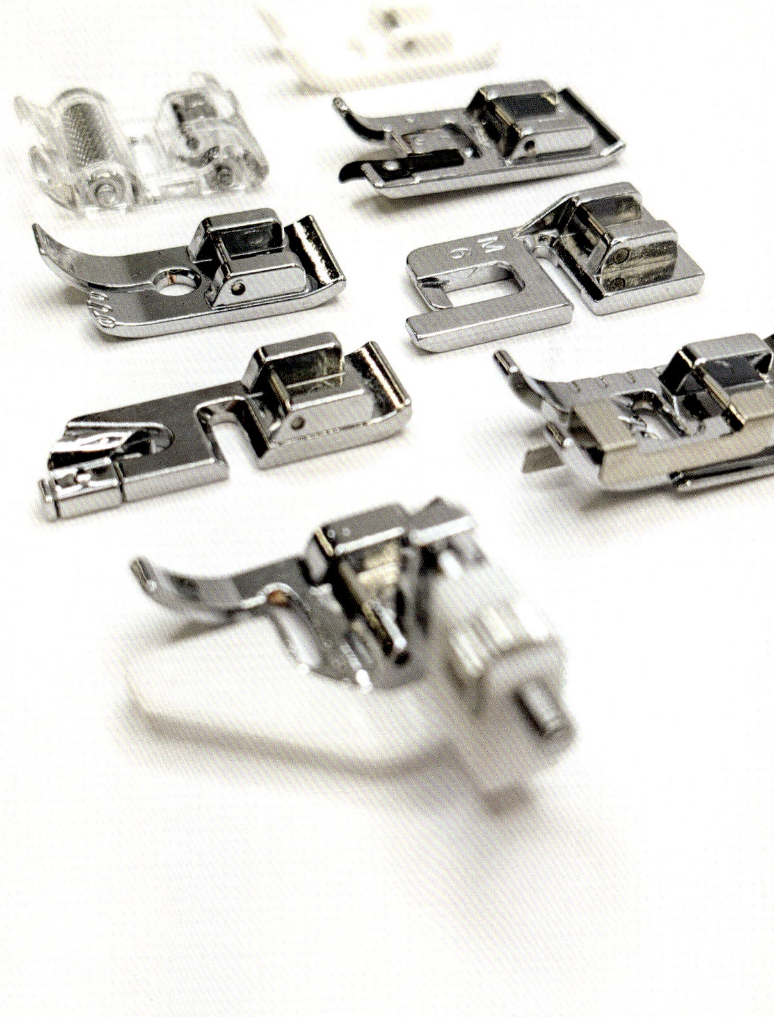

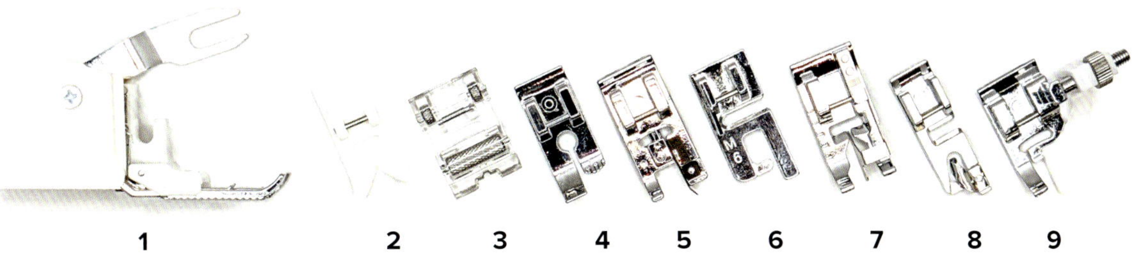

1. Walking foot
2. Nonstick foot
3. Roller foot
4. Straight-stitch foot
5. Overcast foot
6. Felling foot
7. Edge-stitch foot
8. Rolled-hem foot
9. Blind hem foot

Machine Needles

When choosing a machine needle, you'll generally have two choices to make: the *size* of the needle and the *type* of the needle. Needles are sized by their shaft diameter; a size 100 needle is 1mm across. A second number, such as the 16 in the size 100/16, refers to the American sizing system, which has been merged with the standard diameter measurement.

Generally, a smaller needle size is better for finer fabrics, and a thicker one is best for thicker fabrics. You want to have enough strength to push through the material, but the thinnest possible needle will create less of a hole.

As a general guideline, use:

- 60/8 for extremely fine fabrics like lace and chiffon
- 70/10 for fine fabrics like challis, voile, organza, lawn, tricot, and linen
- 80/12 for medium-weight fabrics like quilting cotton, muslin, linen, corduroy, and faux fur
- 90/14 for medium- to heavyweight fabrics like canvas and lightweight leather
- 100/16 for medium- to heavyweight fabrics like quilted fabric, neoprene, and duck canvas
- 110/18 for heavy fabrics like denim and heavyweight leather
- 120/20 for very heavy fabrics and unconventional materials like heavyweight denim and canvas

1 2 3 4 5 6 7 8 9 10

1. 70/10 universal
2. 100/16 denim
3. 60/8 microtex
4. 75/11 ballpoint
5. 90/14 stretch
6. 70/10 topstitch
7. 90/14 quilting
8. 90/14 leather
9. 80/12 metallic
10. Twin

Just as important as size, however, is needle type. Different needle types are designed for different kinds of fabrics and applications and, therefore, have different shapes and (especially) sharpnesses:

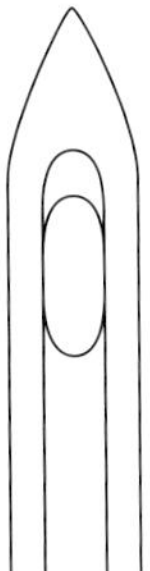

The **universal needle** is great for general sewing; keep a stock of them! It has a slightly rounded point and is especially suitable for medium-density woven fabrics.

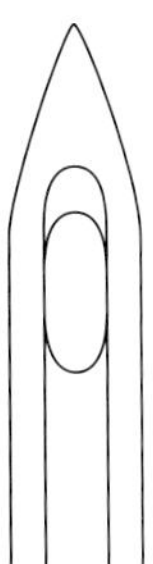

The **denim** or **jeans needle** is a strong, thick needle with a very sharp point. That sharp point is great for piercing through thick fabrics like denim, canvas, faux leather, and neoprene.

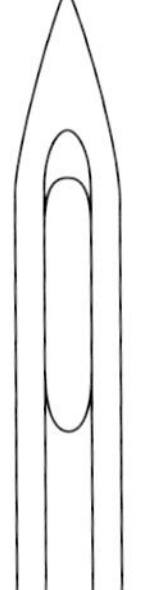

A **microtex needle** is very fine and has a sharp point for delicate or densely woven fabrics. This needle is also best for coated materials, because it can pierce through the coating.

Ballpoint and **jersey needles** have a rounded point, which is best for fabrics where you want the needle to go in between the yarns of the fabric instead of piercing and breaking them. These needles are especially suitable for medium-weight knits.

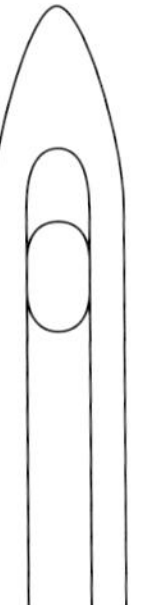

The **stretch needle** also has a ballpoint, but extra roundness above the eye of the needle and a smaller eye help prevent skipped stitches on stretchy fabrics. Stretch needles are perfect for stretch knits.

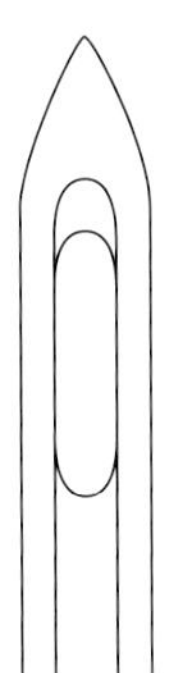

In the **topstitch needle**, a long opening provides less stress for topstitching, which results in fewer skipped stitches where they're particularly visible. It's great for buttonholes or when sewing with thicker thread, which won't fit comfortably in a conventional needle.

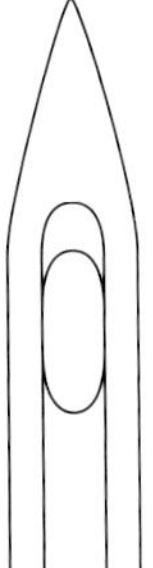

A **quilting needle** has a very long and sharp point—perfect for sewing through multiple layers! It's particularly useful for thick seams and multilayer projects.

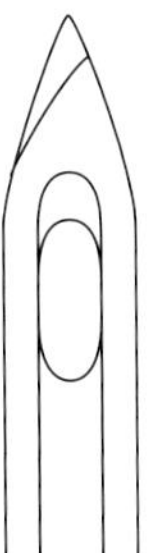

A **leather** or **wedge needle** has a blade point designed to cut through leather. It's also effective on other thick and sturdy materials, like suede and vinyl.

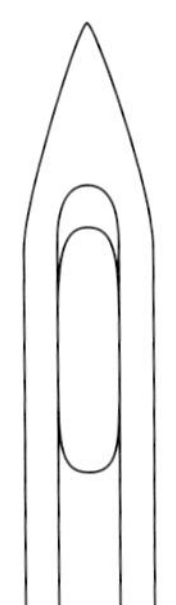

The **metallic needle** has a universal point, but its large opening provides less friction on fragile metallic thread.

Use a **twin needle** (also called a **double needle**) with a zigzag foot to create two lines of straight stitches on top of your fabric and a zigzag stitch on the bottom. This is especially great for stretchy knits, because the resulting stitch is both stretchy and strong.

Some needles are available in nonstick versions, which are great when sewing with sticky fabrics, stabilizers, or adhesives. Because they have a special coating, be particularly diligent to swatch test nonstick needles.

✸ QUICK TIP!

Jersey, ballpoint, and stretch needles are very similar ballpointed needles. If one is causing skipped stitches in your project, try one of the others on a swatch and see if it works better. ●

Stitch Plates

The **stitch plate**, or throat plate, is the shield of metal that your fabric slides along and needle punches into while you're sewing. The standard stitch plate, also called a zigzag stitch plate, is great for all-around sewing.

However, if you frequently sew slinky or lightweight fabrics or often fight with your fabric getting pulled into your feed dogs, you may want to consider a **straight stitch plate**. A straight stitch plate has only a small narrow hole (as opposed to a standard one, which has a wider oval hole to account for the width of a zigzag stitch). This small hole is great for sewing any fabrics that like to get sucked into the machine when sewing, like delicates, slipperies, and even piled fabrics. If you don't have a straight stitch plate but are in a situation where it would be helpful, you can emulate one by covering most of the hole in a standard stitch plate with tape.

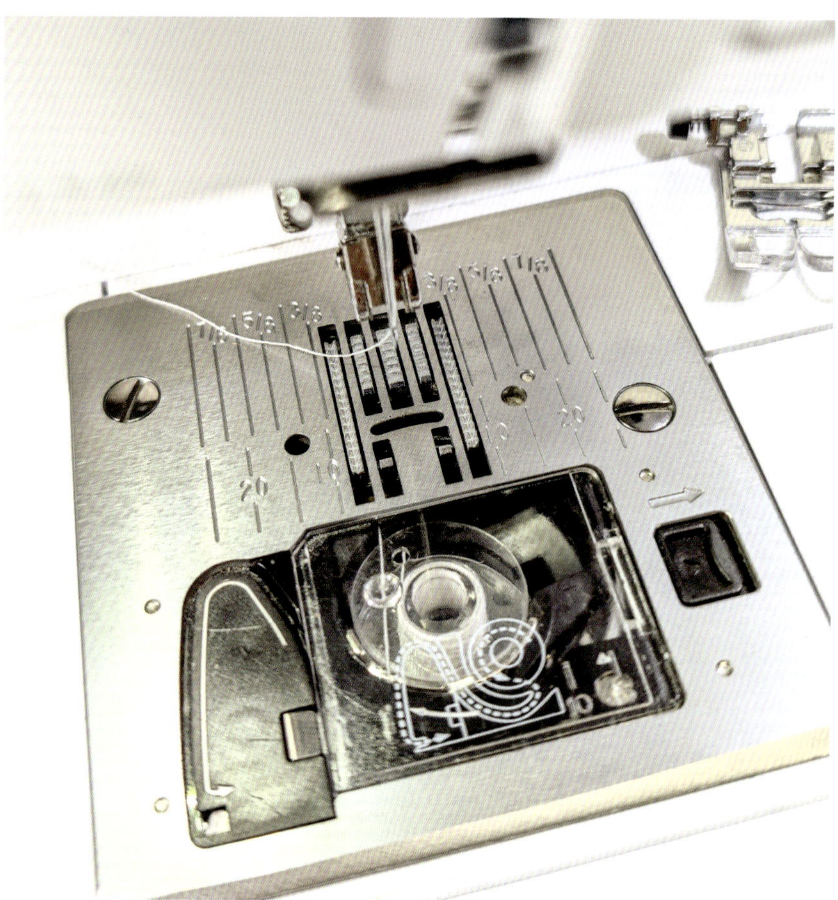

A standard/zigzag stitch plate

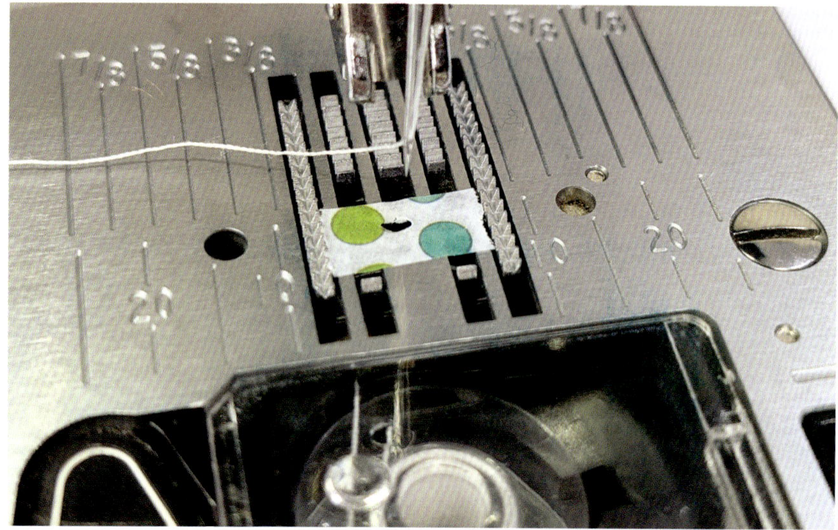

Tape on a standard stitch plate, emulating a straight stitch plate

Pins

When choosing pins for your fabric and project, there are several factors to consider:

- **Length of pin:** Longer pins are better for pinning many layers of fabric together, such as when quilting. Shorter pins are better when you need many pins close together lengthwise, such as when dealing with slippery fabrics.
- **Diameter of pin:** A thinner pin (0.5mm) will damage the fabric less, but a pin that's too thin may not be able to properly pierce a thicker fabric or multiple layers of fabric (or may bend as it goes through your material, making the pinning less accurate). To reduce the chance of damaging your project, use the thinnest effective pin.
- **Point:** As with machine needles, different point shapes are best for different fibers. Sharps are all-purpose, extra-sharps are equivalent to machine microtex needles, and ballpoints are rounded for knits.
- **Head style:** Head style is what many pin types are named after. It determines how secure the pin is in the fabric, whether the pins can be ironed over, and how easily the pin can be seen and grasped.

QUICK TIP!

Pins may come oiled. If you're using new pins on a delicate fabric, make sure to wipe them off first. ●

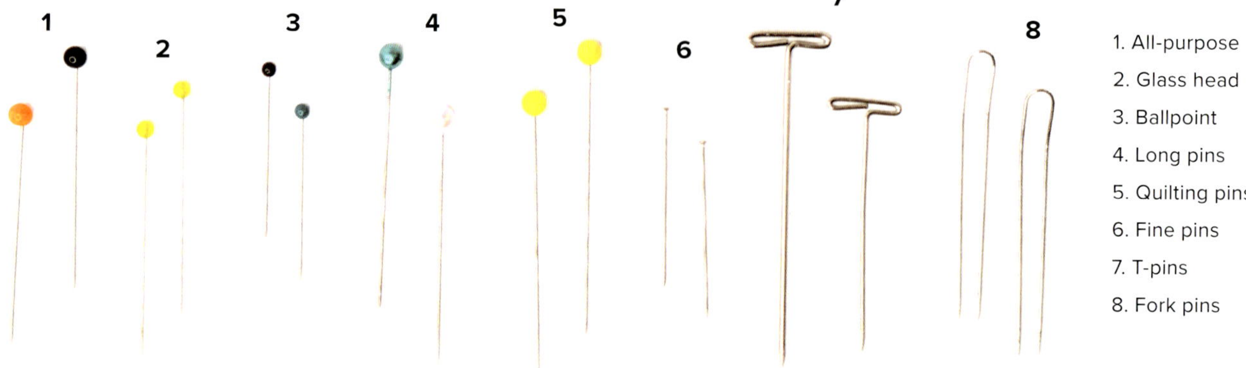

1. All-purpose
2. Glass head
3. Ballpoint
4. Long pins
5. Quilting pins
6. Fine pins
7. T-pins
8. Fork pins

The following pins are used for different applications; you may consider having an assortment on hand.

All-purpose pins, which are sharp and about 1½″ long, are great for general-purpose use. They often have plastic balls on the end for gripping and seeing, and may be called **ball head** or **round-head** pins ... but don't confuse them with ball*point* pins!

Glass-head pins are like all-purpose pins, but their ball heads are glass instead of plastic. Because of these special heads, they can be ironed over without the risk of melting.

Ballpoint pins are pins with rounded tips so they don't break the yarns in knit fabrics. They often also, confusingly, have a ball head.

Long pins and **quilting pins** are great for thick fabrics, where shorter ones may get lost or not properly secure the layers.

Silk/superfine/extra-fine/satin pins are sharp, fine pins for delicate fabrics. With these pins, you lower your chance of snagging the fabric or damaging a delicate weave. In the text of this book, I'll refer to them, as a group, as **fine pins**.

T-pins are particularly sturdy pins; they're great for thick fabrics. They won't easily bend or break when they're pushed through many layers of a very sturdy material.

Fork pins are good for slippery fabrics; because they pierce at two places, they are more secure than conventional pins and allow for much less shifting during the sewing process.

Safety pins are locking pins and, therefore, effective for fabrics where a regular straight pin will struggle to stay secured (for example, in a very open weave).

Sewing clips are not pins at all; they are small clips used on the edge of fabrics. Because they don't make holes, they're great for fabrics that can't "heal," like vinyl and leather. If left for too long, however, their teeth can leave permanent marks.

If your project is too bulky for sewing clips, you can also use **binder clips**.

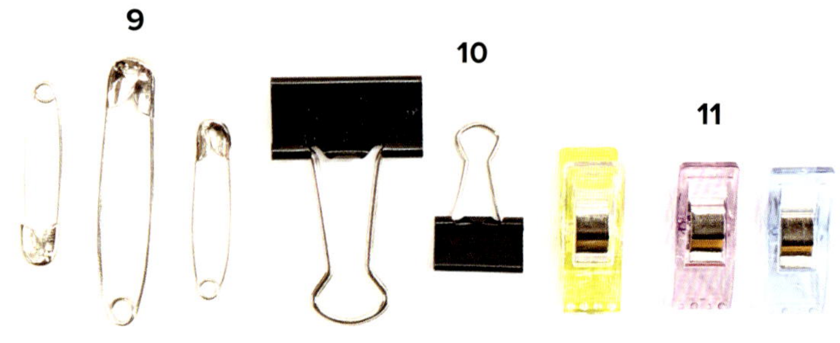

9. Safety pins
10. Binder clips
11. Sewing clips

Thread

Not all thread is created equal, and the thread you choose can affect both the durability and the look of your finished piece.

Threads generally come in four types:

- **Spun thread**, made of cotton or polyester, is made from short fibers spun into a single strand (like you would imagine being done on a spinning wheel).
- **Continuous-filament thread**, made of synthetic material or silk, is made of very long fibers twisted into a strand.
- **Core-spun thread** is made of two layers of material: a polyester core wrapped with cotton or polyester.
- **Monofilament thread**, also known as continuous-filament thread, is a single string of polyester; imagine an extremely fine fishing line. It is a strong thread and does not shed lint.

Like fabrics, threads are made from fibers, some of which may be natural:

- **Cotton threads** are matte and strong and tolerate heat. They produce lint. Cotton thread is not stretchy; it will break if subjected to extreme stretch. Cotton thread is great for sewing lightweight cotton and linen fabric.
- **Silk thread** is strong, shiny, and smooth and does not produce lint. It's also slightly stretchy. Silk works particularly well when sewing silk and wool fabrics, especially delicate versions.
- **Wool thread** is soft and durable but will get damaged if it gets too hot or wet.

Other threads are made from synthetic materials:

- **Rayon thread** is shiny and inexpensive, but not very durable or stretchy. It's best for decorative sewing, not for seams and hems.
- **Nylon thread** is inexpensive, smooth, and fairly elastic, but it does not tolerate heat well and comes in limited colors. It can become brittle.
- **Polyester thread** is strong, smooth, and inexpensive. It is slightly stretchy and can mimic cotton and silk thread.

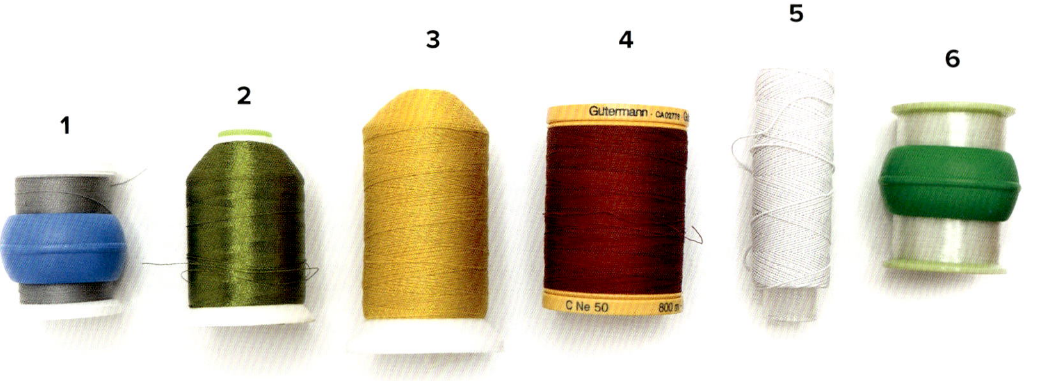

1. 35 wt. all-purpose polyester thread
2. 40 wt. metallic polyester embroidery thread
3. Tex 60 heavyweight cotton-wrapped polyester thread
4. Tex 20 lightweight cotton thread
5. Tex 100 elastic thread
6. Nylon monofilament invisible thread

Many threads, particularly core-spun varieties, are made from a combination of different kinds of fibers.

Finally, threads come in different weights, which are labeled using three main systems. On a specific spool of thread, these systems may be used in combination, or you may have to translate between them when comparing products.

A thread's **weight (wt)** is the number of kilograms per kilometer of thread. A 35 wt thread would weigh 1 kilogram if it were 35 kilometers long.

A thread's **denier (den)** is the number of grams a 9,000-meter length of that thread weighs; a 9,000-meter den 125 thread would weigh 125 grams. Often this style of measurement is styled with a slash; the number after the slash is how many thread strands are twisted to create the final product. So, a den 125/2 thread is two strands of den 125 thread twisted together.

Finally, a thread's **Tex** is how many grams 1,000 meters of the thread weighs. A Tex 25 thread would weigh 25 grams if it were 1,000 meters long.

All of these different construction techniques, fiber contents, and weights result in different kinds of thread.

All-purpose thread is generally cotton, polyester, or a cotton/polyester blend. Because it's medium-weight and comes in many colors, it is a great go-to thread.

Fine/lingerie thread, great for lightweight fabrics, and **heavy-duty/upholstery threads** generally share characteristics with all-purpose thread, just in lighter and heavier weights, respectively.

Elastic or **stretch thread** is great for the seams of stretch fabric and for gathering details like shirring and smocking. Because it's a thick thread, it cannot be threaded on the needle and must only be used on the bobbin.

Clear thread is a polyester monofilament thread that comes in clear and gray variations. Those varieties are used on light and dark fabrics, respectively, to create "invisible" stitching lines.

As with all elements of the sewing process, when in doubt, swatch your thread! Iron it aggressively with and without steam, and see if it holds up. Sew a seam and a hem on your fabric; then try to rip the connection. Is the thread too shiny for your project, or is it so fuzzy that it disappears into the fabric? These factors will help you determine whether the thread is right for your project.

Needles and Thread ... Working Together!

Although certain sizes of needles and thread are best for certain weights of fabric, it's actually most important that the needle and thread fit together. If the eye of a needle is too small for your thread, the thread will fray. A thread that's too small for a needle will move in the eye, causing poor stitches.

Your thread should sit comfortably in the groove of the eye of your needle without moving side to side while sewing. If you're experiencing skipped stitches during sewing, you may need to more closely match your needle and thread size. The easiest way to size your thread and needle is to thread the needle and then look at how much space the thread takes up in the eye of the needle; it should be 40 percent to 50 percent.

The following table is a starting point of how thread and needle size match up. If you're experiencing skipped stitches or frayed thread, consider switching to a different size thread or needle; thread sizing is confusing and inconsistent, and differences in materials and manufacturing techniques can change thread performance drastically. The most reliable indicator of thread and needle sizing matching up is its actual performance on your sewing project!

Descriptive Thread Size	Thread Size in wt	Thread Size in den	Thread Size in Tex	Needle Size
Monofilament, Lightweight	125 wt and thinner	den 72 and less	Tex 8 and less	60/8 and 70/10
Lightweight	62 to 50 wt	den 144 to 180	Tex 16 to 20	75/11 and 80/12
Medium-weight	40 to 33 wt	den 225 to 270	Tex 25	80/12 and 90/14
Heavyweight	25 wt and thicker	den 360 and greater	Tex 40 and greater	100/16 and 110/18

Pressing and Ironing

The words *ironing* and *pressing* are sometimes used interchangeably, but they are actually two different ways of using your iron. Ironing is what you do to completed pieces to remove wrinkles by using sweeping motions across swaths of fabric to smooth it out. Ironing may stretch the fabric out of shape, which could cause repercussions, especially when the material has not yet been cut and sewn. Pressing, conversely, is done completely with an up-and-down motion by pressing the iron onto the fabric, holding, and then removing. This technique is particularly great for in-progress work; it melds stitches into fabric and creates crisp hems and seams.

The Basics of Pressing

Heat and pressure are required for a good press, but both can damage fabrics! Pressing is a balancing act: How much heat and force can I use to give me a clean creation, without damaging my material?

Here are some general guidelines for effectively and safely pressing:

- Start with a cooler temperature and work up as needed.
- Always press on a soft material (like your ironing board's cover); use more padding and less pressure if your fabric is textured.
- When in doubt, use a press cloth.
- Always swatch test not only heat and pressure, but also steam.

Finger pressing provides a gentle alternative to conventional pressing. Use the tip of your finger for a very safe and delicate press, or use your nail for a sharper result.

Some specific tools lead to more effective and less damaging pressing.

An **iron** goes without saying, but a **steamer** is often a safer choice, especially for fabrics with piles and raised details. A **heat gun** is necessary for some speciality materials, like foam and vinyl.

A **cotton canvas cover** for your ironing board provides spectacular heat resistance, even heat distribution through the fabric, and a smooth surface with enough grip to provide some resistance for slippery fabrics. Plus, canvas is a durable fabric, so you'll extend the life of your cover by switching to canvas from a thinner cotton option.

A **silk organza press cloth**, made by simply pinking (pg 66) the edges of a piece of silk organza, is a worthwhile investment to your pressing arsenal. Silk organza tolerates heat fairly well and protects both your iron and your project material from damage. It's also see-through, allowing for more accurate pressing and fabric manipulation. If silk organza isn't in your budget yet, a piece of a cotton sheet, hemmed or pinked, is a great starter press cloth.

A **finger presser** allows you to press delicate fabrics without actually touching the fabric with your iron; it's great for fabrics sensitive to heat. You can press with just your finger, but a finger presser gives you just a bit more power in these situations.

Finger pressing can distort the fabric if not done carefully. A **seam roller**, on the other hand, allows you to quickly press a seam without distorting the fibers, because the tool rolls along the seam instead of pulling at it. This tool is great for projects where you want to finger press, but the fabric in question is a loose weave or otherwise easily pulled off grain.

1. Heavy-duty cotton ironing board cover
2. Silk organza press cloth
3. Mini iron with sharp tip
4. Full-size iron
5. Spray bottle with water
6. Seam roller
7. Finger presser

Using a Press Cloth

To use a press cloth, place it over the material you're pressing, so that you're pressing *through* the press cloth. Shown here is a silk organza press cloth; it's a great option because it tolerates heat well, but it is also easy to see through, so you can make sure your project fabric is behaving as intended. Other great press cloth options are bed sheets, baking and parchment paper, and towel terry (for textured materials).

✷ QUICK TIP!

Generally, certain fibers can tolerate certain amounts of heat. If you know the fiber content of your material, you know what temperature to set your iron to:

- **Low:** Synthetics
- **Medium:** Wool and silk
- **High:** Linen and cotton

When your fabric is a blend, use the heat setting for its lowest-heat-tolerable fiber; because spandex is a synthetic, you'd want to press a spandex/wool blend on low heat, for example.

When in doubt, start cooler and increase heat until you get an effective heat. There's no harm in taking more time and, therefore, avoiding damaging your fabric. ●

Cutting Tools

You can do a whole lot with just craft scissors and fabric shears, but specialty cutting tools will enable cleaner cuts with less hand and back strain!

⚠ STAY SAFE!

One aspect of successful sewing projects is getting clean cuts, which require very sharp blades. Always stay safe around your cutting tools. Do not use your rotary cutter toward yourself, especially toward your fingers. Do not cut materials that may fling bits into the air—like beading and sequins—without wearing eye protection. Store your cutting tools with blades retracted or otherwise sheathed.

Which Fabrics Are Okay for My Sewing Scissors?

We all know the oft-shared wisdom: *Never cut anything other than fabric with fabric scissors!* Paper very quickly dulls expensive shears, making them much less effective at cutting actual fabric projects. But the vast array of fabric and fabric accoutrements makes the rule a bit more complicated. Is it okay to use your fabric scissors on fusible interfacing? What about heavily coated vinyl fabrics? What about acrylic felt? What about trims, sequins, and glitter fabric?

Ultimately, the choice is up to you how you use your tools. You may decide to sharpen your scissors more frequently, so you don't need to be as precious with what you cut. Or you may decide to buy a second set of fabric shears; one pair can be your delicate and medium-weight scissors, and the other will cut heavyweight, coated, and embroidered fabrics. You may decide based on your own crafting habits that cutting felt and interfacing is okay for fabric shears, but sequins and vinyls call for the cheapie craft scissors.

If you do intend to pursue frequent sharpenings (or, in general, intend to keep your shears for a long time), make sure to get a pair with separating blades. This separation will make sharpening and repair much easier and more effective, whether you're doing it yourself or paying a professional.

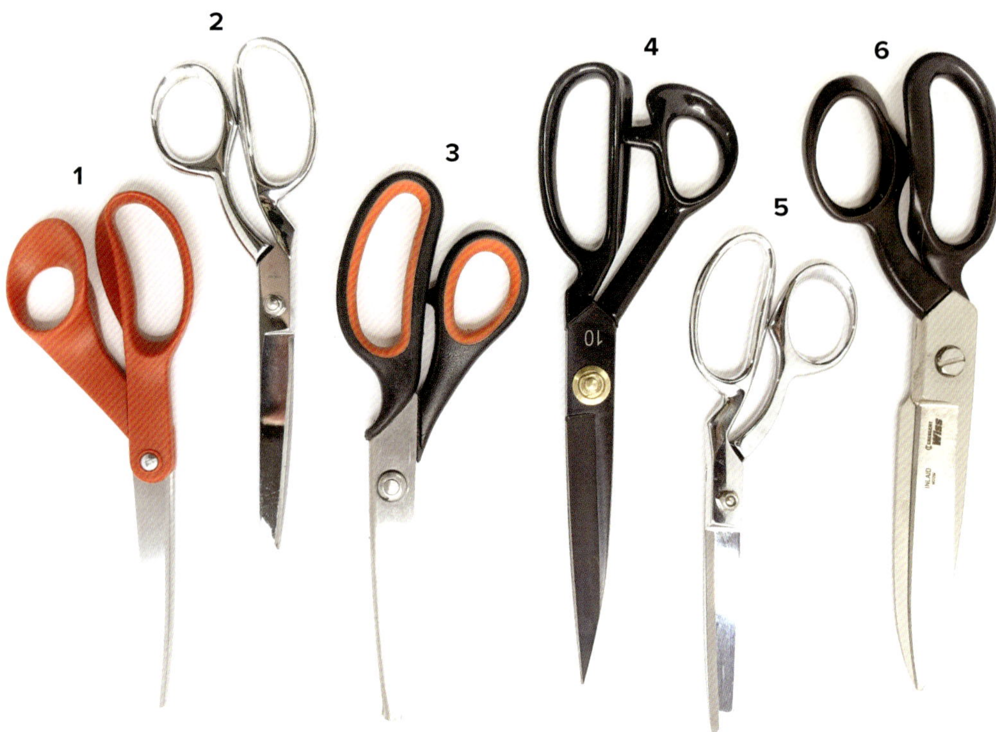

1. Craft scissors
2. 8″ sewing shears
3. Pinking shears
4. 10″ sewing shears
5. Serrated-edge shears
6. Heavy-duty shears

All-around scissors/craft scissors are your general-purpose scissors. Because they're used for non-fabric materials, they almost certainly won't be as sharp as your fabric shears. Keep this in mind when cutting fabrics that require a very sharp blade. Notice also the tips of your scissors—many have one sharp and one blunt tip. A blunt tip results in less accurate and delicate cuts.

Sewing shears are sharp, precise, and often very long scissors. They should be restricted to use on fabric in order to extend their time before needing to be sharpened.

Sewing shears may or may not be **bent-handled shears**. The bent handle makes these shears lay flat on your work surface; the fabric, therefore, isn't disturbed as much by the process of cutting.

Heavy-duty shears have thick blades and substantial handles; they're great for cutting thick or tough materials. They also may be bent-handled.

1. Blade sharpener
2. Thread snippers
3. Serrated-edge industrial-strength scissors
4. Box cutter
5. Rotary cutter

A pair of **thread** or **embroidery snips**, which are very delicate and have two pointed ends, are great for extremely small cuts that require immense accuracy. They're often spring-action, meaning less strain on hands and fingers.

You may consider **serrated-edge shears** if you're often working with slinky and slippery fabrics. The serrations on the blade grab onto the yarns of fabrics, causing the fabric to shift around less during cutting.

A **rotary cutter** has a round blade that you roll across a surface to cut—like a pizza cutter for fabric! Because it doesn't need to get below the fabric, it can result in more accurate cuts with less fabric shifting.

Craft knives are light, thin, and very sharp. They're great for delicate work.

Retractable-blade knives, also known as **box cutters** (pg 200), are much more substantial cutting tools that can be used for heavy-duty materials. Both have replaceable blades, making them economical choices for materials that dull blades quickly.

Rotary cutters, craft knives, and retractable-blade knives should all be used on **self-healing mats**, which protect your blade and your work surface.

Pinking shears have dramatic jagged edges on their blades. In fabrics prone to fraying, these help reduce fraying until a more permanent seam finish can be implemented. In fabrics that fray very little, pinking (pg 66) is sufficient as the seam finish itself.

A cutting mat, box cutter, and rotary cutter

Left-Handed Cutting Tools

My cutting tools, pictured, are set up left-handed. If you're a lefty, buying left-handed tools or modifying them for left-handed use (as in the case for a rotary cutter) will increase your cutting visibility and accuracy. "Ambidextrous" scissors are usable by lefties but are set up right-handed.

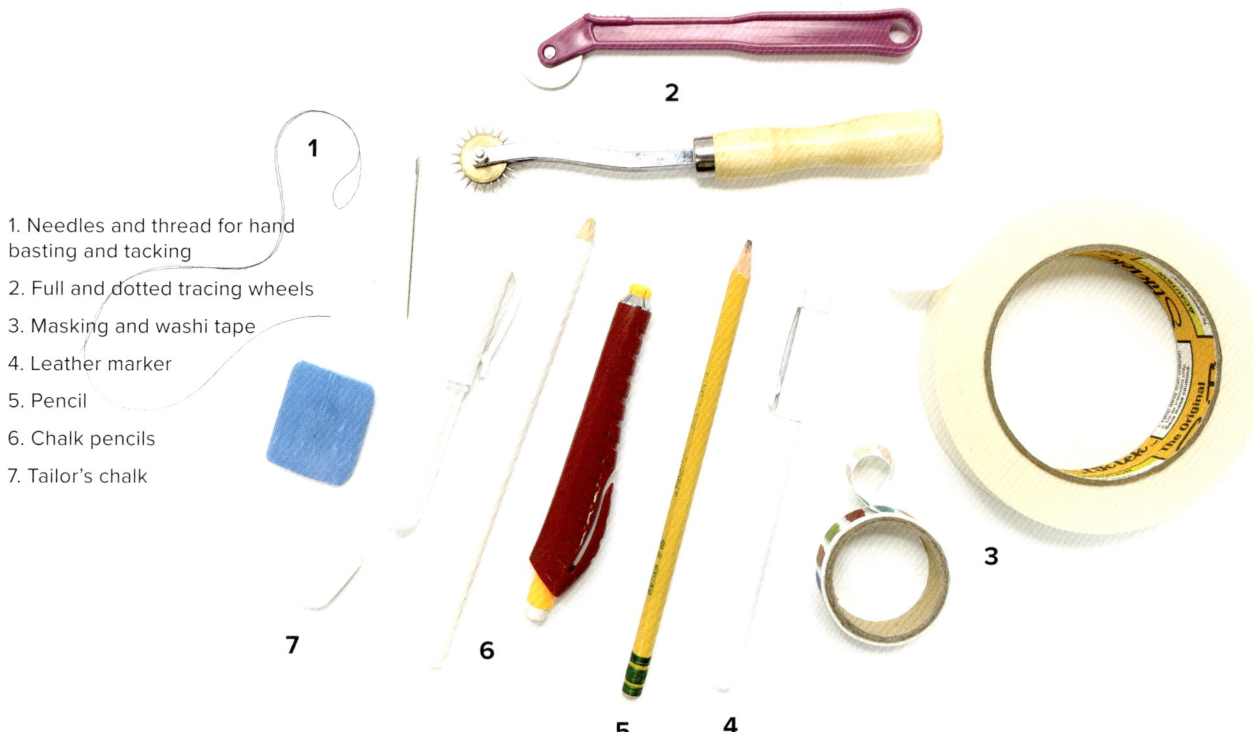

1. Needles and thread for hand basting and tacking
2. Full and dotted tracing wheels
3. Masking and washi tape
4. Leather marker
5. Pencil
6. Chalk pencils
7. Tailor's chalk

Marking Tools

Choosing a mark-making tool can be tricky: Marks need to be visible and removable, but not *so* removable that they disappear before you're done using them. Like all sewing tools, different materials work best with different marking tools.

Markers, pencils, and **pens** are a simple starting point. Regular marking tools, especially washable ones like kids' markers, can work very well for marking within seam allowances and on specialty materials such as vinyl and EVA foam.

Tailor's chalk and **chalk pencils** are white or colored chalk in block or pen form. They can almost always be brushed or washed away, but they may also be brushed away accidentally. Don't lose your marks before you use them!

For especially delicate or finicky fabrics, lines or knots of thread are fairly riskless marking techniques and are visible from both sides of the fabric. These marking techniques are called **thread tracing** and **tailor's tacks**, respectively.

Heat and **water disappearing pens, pencils**, and **markers** have disappearing ink that's activated by heat (including friction) or water. Be careful when using these on heat- or water-sensitive fabrics.

With other tools, like **disappearing markers**, the ink disappears on its own over time (usually about 48 hours) without the need for heat or water.

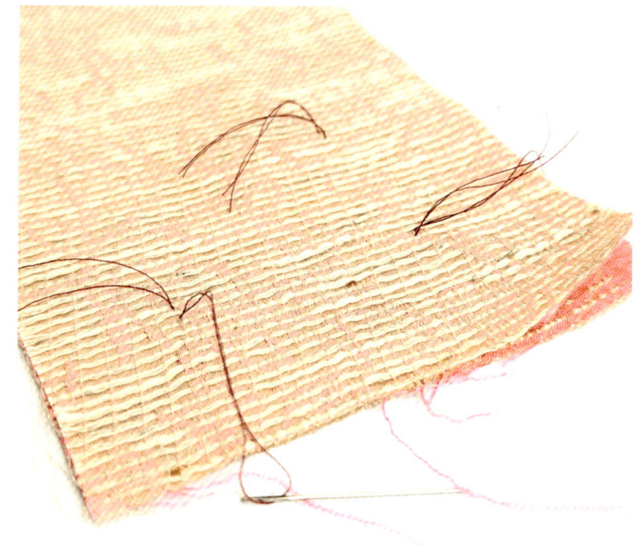

Tailor's tacks

1. Disappearing-ink pens
2. Water-soluble wax pencils
3. Markers
4. Pen
5. Fabric markers

Tracing paper is a kind of paper that has transferable coating that gets pushed onto the fabric by a tracing wheel, pencil, or other blunt tool.

A **tracing wheel** (pg 110) looks like a tiny pizza cutter but isn't intended for cutting! It may come in dotted or full-line varieties; the dotted version has dull spikes instead of a round blade, and the full-line variety is duller and flatter than a pizza cutter. Tracing wheels can be used with tracing paper to transfer lines, or through just pattern pieces to make gentle marks in the fabric, which can then be traced over with another mark-making tool or with thread tracing. Because they're metal and being pressed into the fabric, tracing wheels should be used carefully with thin or delicate fabrics.

Transparent tape, masking tape, washi tape, and other low-adhesive tapes, as long as they are removed from the fabric before the adhesive begins to break down, are particularly great for marking areas of fabric that will be visible in the final piece (such as topstitching).

A **leather marking tool** leaves a white or silver mark on leather, which can be rubbed off when the mark is no longer needed.

Safety pins can be used similarly to tailor's tacks to mark positions in a project. They are especially useful on netting and other holey materials that may not show typical marking tools easily.

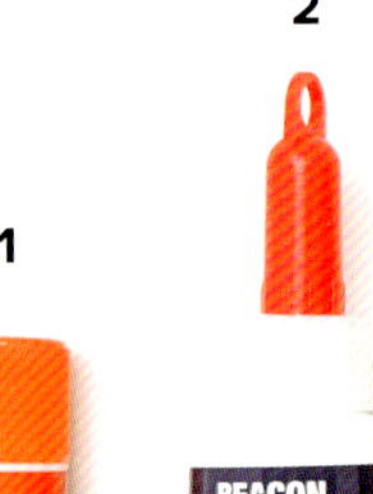

1. PVA glue stick
2. Basting glue
3. Tacky glue
4. Spray adhesive
5. Spray basting glue

Adhesives

Glue is sometimes the best option when creating a "sewn" creation! Of course, not all glues are appropriate for all applications.

Tacky glue and other **fabric glues** are great permanent adhesives for many embellishments, or for when sewing isn't right for your situation and you're using a medium-weight fabric.

Basting tape (often referred to by its brand name, Wonder Tape [Dritz]) and **basting glue** are temporary adhesives; they can be removed when basting is no longer needed.

Alternatively, a **PVA glue stick** is a cheap, accessible, and nontoxic option for basting glue. Definitely have one handy in your sewing supply stash!

Fusible adhesive adheres layers of fabric when activated by heat and pressure from your iron. This option comes in sheet, tape, thread, and sprayable forms.

Spray adhesive may be temporary, permanent, or repositionable. Temporary spray adhesives are great for basting, especially for large sections of fabrics (like quilts). The repositionable option works well for placing appliqués and other detailing, and the permanent version is an alternative to sewing.

Hot glue is great for many fabric projects; the thermoplastic sinks into many fabrics, creating a very strong hold. Felt and faux fur are bonded particularly well with it.

Many medium- to heavyweight fabrics work well with **contact cement** (pg 204), especially foam-based products like scuba and EVA foam. Contact cement is also perfect for latex and leatherworking.

1. Glue gun and hot glue
2. Silicone pad
3. Water-soluble sewable basting tape
4. Contact cement
5. Fabric glue pen
6. Fusible hem tape
7. Fusible sheet

⚠ STAY SAFE!

Stay safe with adhesives. Always read and follow all manufacturer safety instructions. Protect your eyes, lungs, and skin when using dangerous aerosolized adhesives (like spray adhesives) or adhesives that gas off (like contact cement). Take care to not burn yourself with hot glue or while activating heat-activated adhesives. •

Interfacing

Interfacing can be used for many different reasons, the most common of which are:

- To add stiffness/and or body to a fabric that lacks it (like a silk challis) or a piece of a creation that needs it (like a collar or cuff).
- To stabilize fabric in a section of a piece that will need extra security, such as around buttonholes.
- To prevent or reduce stretch, such as in the shoulder seams of jersey garments.

Commercial Interfacing

Just as with fabric, commercial interfacing comes in different varieties. It comes in many different weights, from featherweight to heavyweight. It's sold as prepackaged sheets, by the yard, and in precut strips of stabilizer, which are perfect for hems and seams. It comes in different colors—most commonly, black and white. It also comes in different structural forms:

Woven interfacing, just like woven fabric, is made of yarns intersecting at right angles and, therefore, has a grain. It's a great option when you want to maintain the natural drape of woven fabrics.

Knit interfacing has inherent crosswise stretch and is, therefore, best for pieces where you want to maintain some stretch.

Nonwoven interfacing is the easiest version to find at big-box stores. Because it's made of fused synthetic fibers, it doesn't have a grain and won't fray. This makes it easy to use: It doesn't have to be aligned with the grain of the fabric. With the fusible version, you can even piece together smaller pieces on a larger piece of fabric to save on materials.

Structurally, you generally want to use the interfacing that matches the type of fabric it will be complementing: Use knit interfacing with knits, woven interfacing with wovens, and nonwoven interfacing with nonwovens. Nonwoven interfacing is also the best option when you want to dramatically affect your fabric's hand, because it is neither knit nor woven.

In terms of weight, use a weight at or slightly heavier than the fabric you're using, so that your interfacing supports but doesn't overwhelm your main material. Increase in weight if you want dramatic effects; decrease if you want less support.

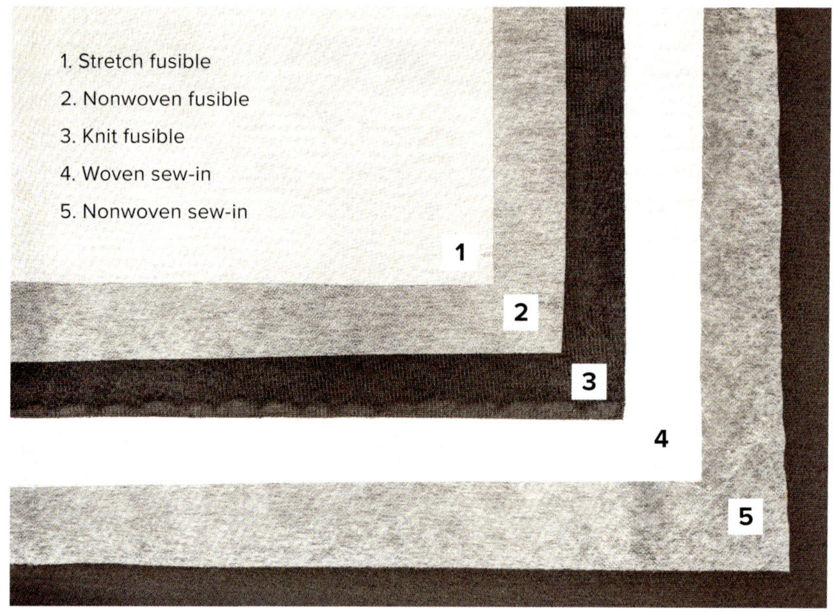

Importantly, many forms of interfacing come in **sew-in** and **fusible** versions. Fusible interfacings are covered in many dots of adhesive, which are activated by heat to adhere to fabric. Fusible interfacing is great because it can substantially change the structure of your fabric (if so desired) because, once fused, the interfacing and your fabric become a single layer. However it can also be risky—especially with delicate fabrics, which may be marred by the heat of the iron or by the adhesive itself.

QUICK TIP!
The adhesive on fusible interfacing is activated by heat. For that reason, when using the material make sure to let it and your fabric completely cool before moving on with your sewing process. Working with your project when the glue hasn't fully set may cause shifting or bubbles. •

QUICK TIP!
Because it does not fray, nonwoven fusible interfacing can also be used to prevent fabric's edges from fraying, in the case where edges can't be cleanly finished or an unhemmed look is desired (pg 120). Just adhere your interfacing right up to the point where you want your fabric's clean edge to begin, or apply interfacing into the "hem allowance" and then trim up to the hem to get a perfect match. •

Alternative Interfacings

Commercial interfacings aren't the only options for stiffening or supporting fabrics. Some interfacings are much thicker and more substantial than classic sew-in or fusible interfacing, and they are intended to provide a piece with substantial structure, thickness, or both. These options include fleece and batting interfacing, fusible foam (which is a foam fused with fabric), and thermoplastics such as Kobracast (by Worbla) and FOSSHAPE (by Wonderflex World). Learn more about these structural materials in Utility Materials (pg 205).

Lining fabric and self-fabric are often great options for interfacing, especially when you're working with a delicate, lightweight, or sheer outer fabric. These options can be sewn in just like sew-in interfacings, or you can use a double-sided fusible sheet such as HeatnBond (by Therm O Web) to turn them into fusible interfacings.

CONFUSING TOPIC!
Self-fabric is a common interfacing option, especially for lightweight and sheer fabrics. This simply means using the exact same fabric for both the outer fabric and the interfacing of your project! Self-fabric as interfacing is often a great option because it adds structure to your creation without the potential for an extra material showing through or drastically changing the behavior of the fabric you've chosen for your project. Just don't forget to buy extra material! •

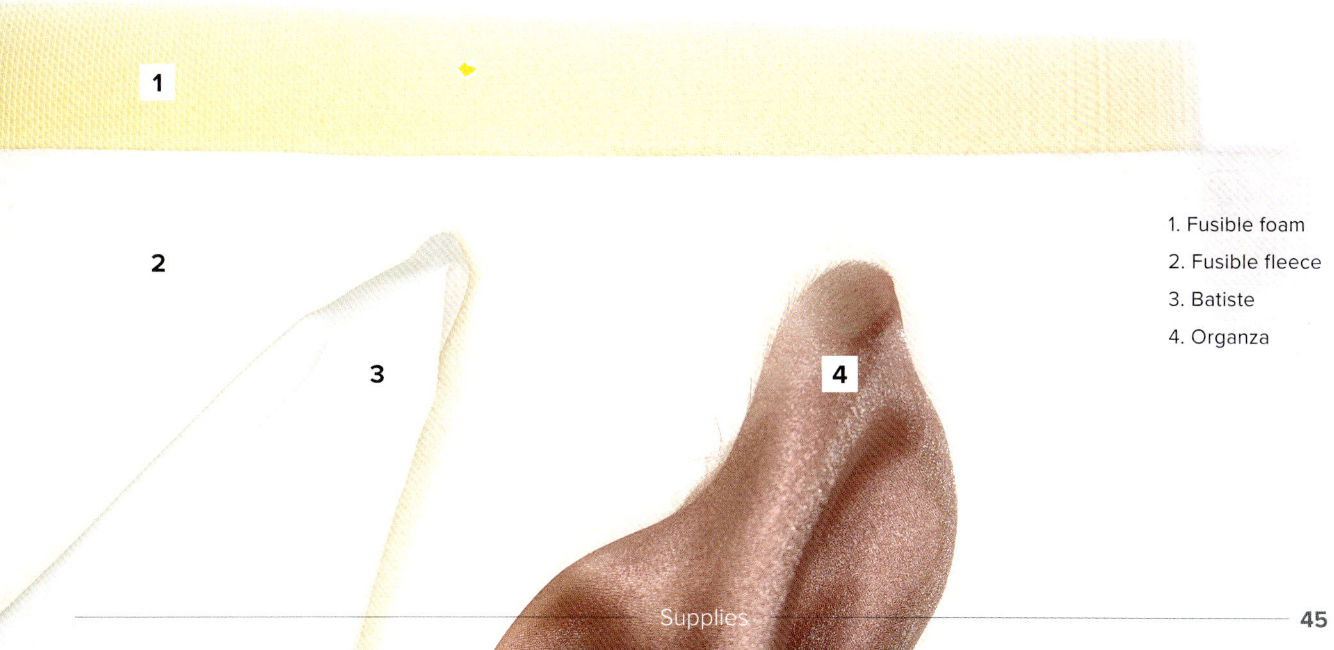

1. Fusible foam
2. Fusible fleece
3. Batiste
4. Organza

Other fabrics that work particularly well for interfacing are batiste and organza. Batiste is lightweight and sheer, so it provides stability without adding a lot of weight or stiffness. Organza is much stiffer but still lightweight and airy; it's great for adding structure to lightweight materials.

✸ QUICK TIP!

If you will be washing or otherwise shrinking your base fabric, the interfacing will also need to be prewashed. Otherwise, the interfacing may shrink and create unsightly pulls on your outer fabric.

- To preshrink woven or knit fusible, soak the material in hot water for ten minutes. Roll it in a towel to soak up extra water, then let it sit to air dry.
- To preshrink nonwoven fusible interfacing, steam it from 2″ above the interfacing, and then let it sit to air dry.
- Woven and nonwoven sew-in interfacings are machine washable and should be prepared according to their manufacturer's instructions, which will differ by fabric type.

Don't forget to also prewash and shrink any lining or self-fabrics you may be using as interfacing. ●

Stabilizer

Like interfacing, stabilizer attaches to an outer fabric to increase its stability. Stabilizers serve a different purpose, however: to prevent the fabric from moving, wrinkling, or stretching during sewing so that you get a good result. They may also prevent some fabrics from getting sucked beneath a sewing machine's plate, from getting stuck in the feed dogs, or from sticking to the presser foot.

Tissue paper is commonly used as a stabilizer because it's easy to find and inexpensive—but, because it's paper, it dulls needles. Tearaway stabilizer is very similar, but it is made of nonwoven fabric and, therefore, will not excessively dull needles. Either can be torn away from the fabric once sewing is done. Either can be secured with basting stitches (pg 99) or spray adhesive, pinned or clipped to the seam, or simply fed through the machine with your fabric without securing it beforehand.

Some stabilizers come with adhesive built in which are activated with the heat of an iron. Iron-on stabilizer can also be torn away after sewing is complete.

Finally, stabilizers can be heat- or water-soluble. Instead of tearing away when you're done with them, you remove these stabilizers with either heat or water. These are great options in very translucent fabrics, where bits of tearaway stabilizer may be visible even after tearing the main body of the stabilizer away.

Water-soluble (top) and tearaway (bottom) stabilizers

Starch

If a permanent interfacing or a wash-away or tearaway stabilizer isn't the kind of stiffening you need for your material, you may consider starching instead. Starching products—which may or may not contain actual cornstarch—will stiffen your material and then easily wash out with water and gentle soap. It's the perfect solution when you need a fabric to be stiffer to make sewing easier but want to be able to recapture the material's original drape after construction.

Starch comes in three common varieties:

- Prepackaged, which may be sold as a liquid or as a powder.
- Homemade, using water and cornstarch (2 teaspoons of cornstarch in 1 cup of warm water).
- Homemade, using gelatin (1 teaspoon of gelatin in 2 cups of water).

To starch a material, either spray it (using a spray bottle or aerosol can) or submerge it (a washing machine, sink, or bucket all work for this purpose). Follow the manufacturer's directions, and always swatch your starch strategy before committing to your entire piece.

1. Prepackaged stiffener
2. Water for mixing your own stabilizer
3. Cornstarch
4. Gelatin

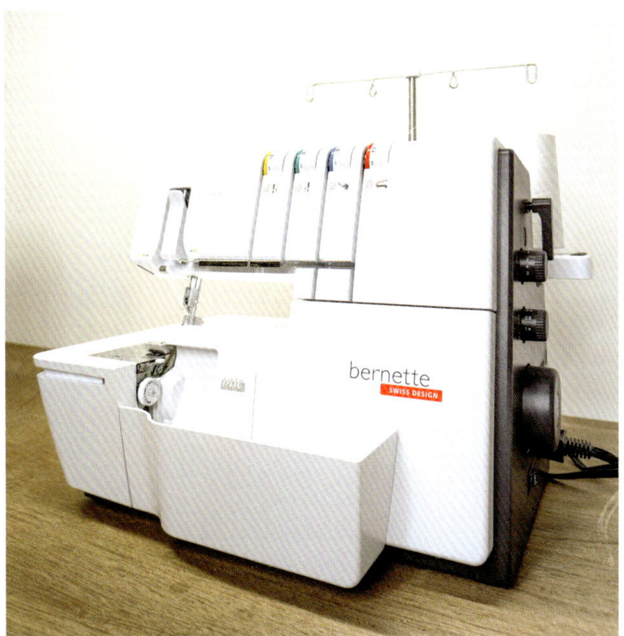

The Serger

If you have a serger, a lot of new techniques open up for you. A **serger**, also called an **overlock machine**, is a specialty sewing machine that has multiple needles and a set of blades. This combination of hardware allows it to create complex stitches while simultaneously cutting the fabric. Most notably because it both cuts and stitches, a serger can create very clean overcast stitches; the threads wrap around the raw edge of the material, protecting it from fraying.

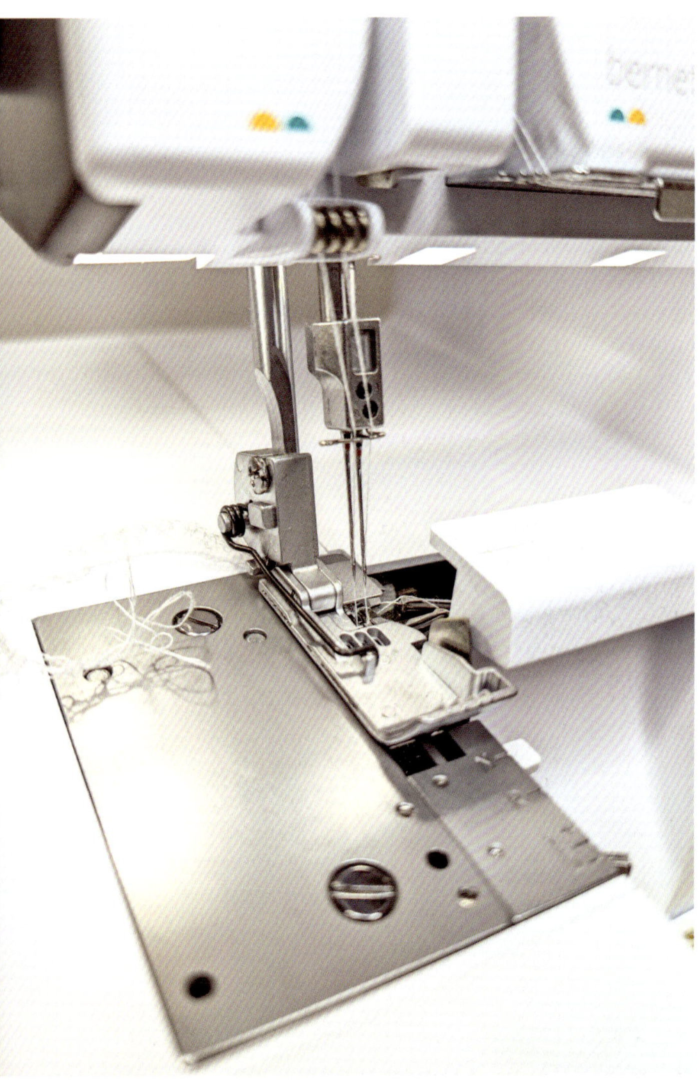

A serger's double needles and blade

Many norms of using a conventional machine apply to serger sewing. For example, use shorter (2–2.5mm) and narrower (3.5–5mm) stitches for lightweight fabrics, and longer (4–5mm) and wider (5–7.5mm) stitches for heavy-duty fabrics. Generally, longer stitches allow seams to pucker and weaken the seams. But in some fabrics, making many holes close together (with a short stitch length) weakens the fabric. Similarly, wide stitch widths on delicate fabrics may pucker and weaken the seams, but narrow widths on heavy fabrics made it difficult to press the seam flat or to topstitch.

STAY SAFE!

Never sew over pins with a serger. Not only will you damage your machine, but your blade may fling broken pin pieces toward your body. •

Modern sergers almost always come with a differential feed feature. A differential feed controls the relative speed between the upper and lower feed dogs, which in turn controls the speed at which fabric moves through the machine. When adjusting, test with swatches of your fabric until you get a successful seam with no puckers or extra tension. A differential feed is particularly useful when sewing sheer, sleek, and stretchy fabrics, which tend to either stretch or shift during sewing, causing bubbles and ripples in your seam.

QUICK TIP!

When utilizing the cutting feature on your serger, don't forget to transfer any markings or notches that are in the seam allowance before cutting them away! •

When sewing with a serger, change the needle just as you would for your conventional machine—for example, use a ballpoint needle for knits. Take care to replace your needles diligently; sergers sew very rapidly, so needles dull more quickly than when used in a conventional machine. If you're sewing with synthetic materials, your knives will also dull! If your raw edges aren't clean—or if your blades are pulling at your material instead of cutting it—your blades may need to be replaced.

Hems, Seams, and Techniques

There are many hems, seams, and other techniques discussed in this book that you may or may not be familiar with. If you come across one that you don't recognize, come here to refresh your memory or to find the page number for its detailed explanation.

Yuumi (*League of Legends*) made with luxury teddy fur with a medium (1″) pile and a nonstretch knit back

COSTUME AND MODELING BY JAZZBERRYJAM
Photo by Vampiria Photography

Stitches

There are a few types of conventional machine stitches referenced in this book.

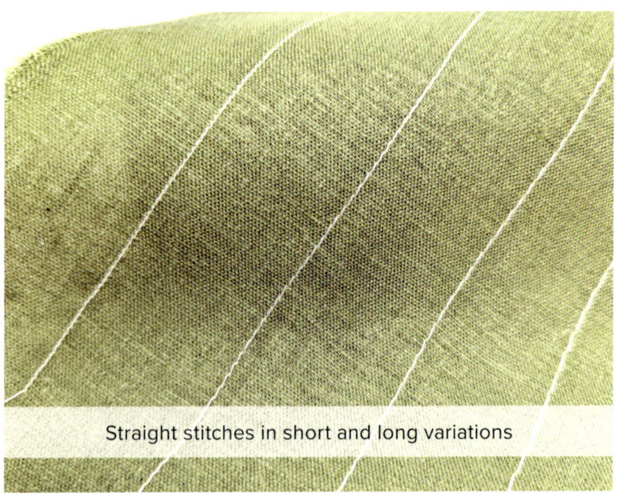

Straight stitches in short and long variations

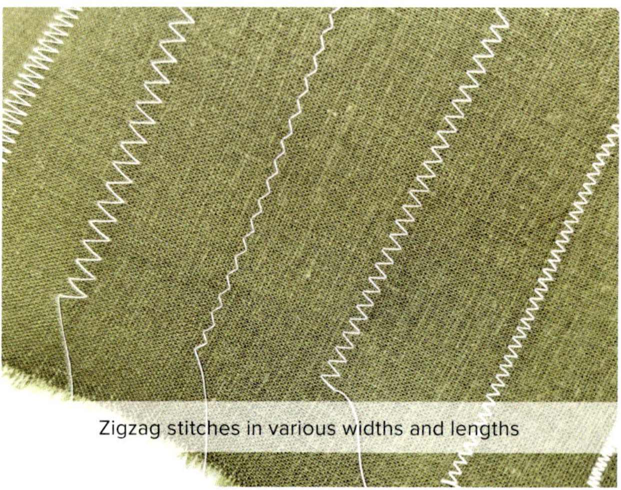

Zigzag stitches in various widths and lengths

A **straight stitch** is strong, blends into fabrics, and does not use much thread. Generally, lengthening the stitch is best for thicker fabrics or for materials where holes introduce weakness.

A **zigzag stitch** is naturally stretchy, making it perfect for stretchy fabrics! A wider zigzag stitch will stretch more but will also use more thread, require a larger seam allowance, and be very visible.

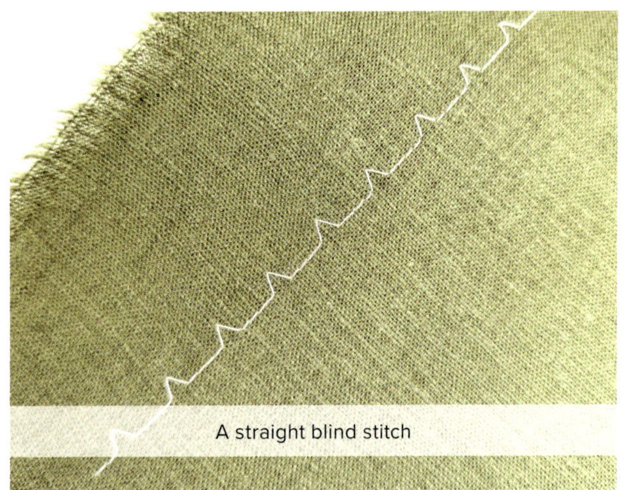

A straight blind stitch

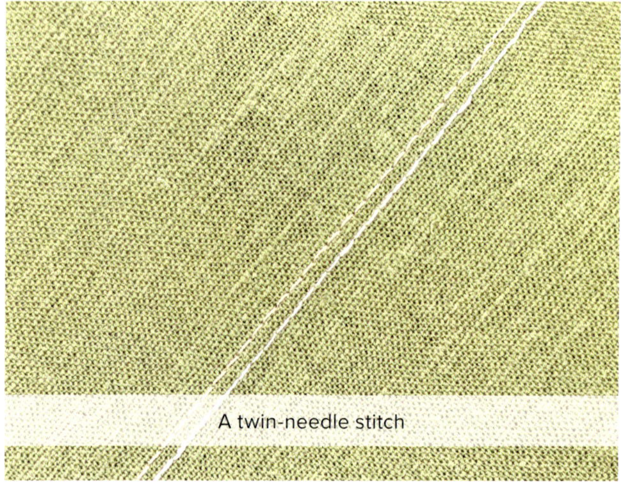

A twin-needle stitch

A **blind stitch**, which can be either straight or zigzag (for non-stretch and stretch fabrics, respectively), is used to create a blind hem (pg 84).

A **twin-needle stitch** uses a special needle—a twin needle—to create two parallel rows of straight stitching on one side with a zigzag stitch on the reverse. This stitch is stretchy, making it perfect for knits, but it can also be used to create two perfect rows of topstitching.

If you have a serger, the list of relevant stitches expands significantly.

A two-thread overlock stitch in wide and narrow variations

The **two-thread overlock stitch** works for lightweight seaming but is not particularly strong.

A three-thread overlock stitch and a three-thread stretch overlock stitch

Three-thread overlock stitches are perfect for both seaming and raw edge finishing light- to medium-weight fabrics, especially stretchy ones. It is stretchier, but not as strong, as the four-thread overlock. Some machines offer a **three-thread stretch overlock stitch**, which has even more stretch than a basic three-thread overlock.

A four-thread overlock with integrated safety stitch

The **four-thread overlock stitch** is a very strong and stretchy stitch that's great on almost all fabrics, including heavyweight materials. Your four-thread overlock stitch may or may not have a safety stitch integrated; a four-thread safety stitch (in wide or narrow variations) increases the strength and fray-protection of the basic four-thread overlock stitch but does not stretch like a basic four-thread overlock stitch does.

Two- and three-thread flatlock stitches

The **two-thread flatlock stitch** seams fabrics together into a visible line of stitching; the **three-thread flatlock stitch** is a stronger version. The top and bottom of the stitch are vastly different; either can be used for the visible side of a piece.

A two- and three-thread rolled-hem stitches

The **two-** and **three-thread rolled-hem stitches** create rolled hems, which can also be used as raw-edge protection for a seam.

A two-thread wrapped overlock in wide and narrow variations

A **two-** and **three-thread wrapped overlock stitch** finishes a raw edge by wrapping around the fabric.

Seams

The following seams are referenced in this book.

A plain seam

A **plain seam** (pg 66) is your conventional seam: With fabric right sides together, a single line of stitches connects the materials. A plain seam is fast and low-bulk but does not protect raw edges.

Reinforced seams

A **reinforced seam** (pg 100), sometimes referred to as a **double-stitched seam**, is a plain seam with an extra row of stitches. This extra row makes the seam stronger and somewhat protects the raw edge from fraying into the seamline.

A four-thread overedge stitch seam

A serger can make seams with just **overedge stitches** (pg 70). These seams are naturally stretchy and come with built-in raw edge protection.

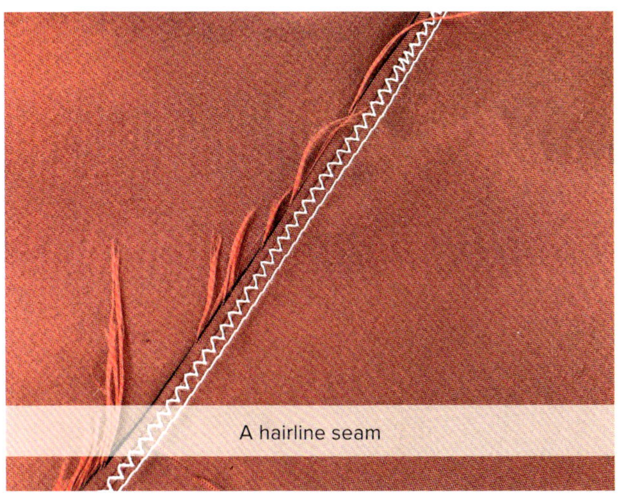
A hairline seam

A **hairline seam** (pg 122) uses edge stitching (pg 105)—you may see it referred to as an **edge-stitched seam**—to create a very scant seam allowance with a row of stitches. Because it's so narrow, it looks nice from the front if you're working with a translucent material, but materials that are very prone to fraying will still be at risk.

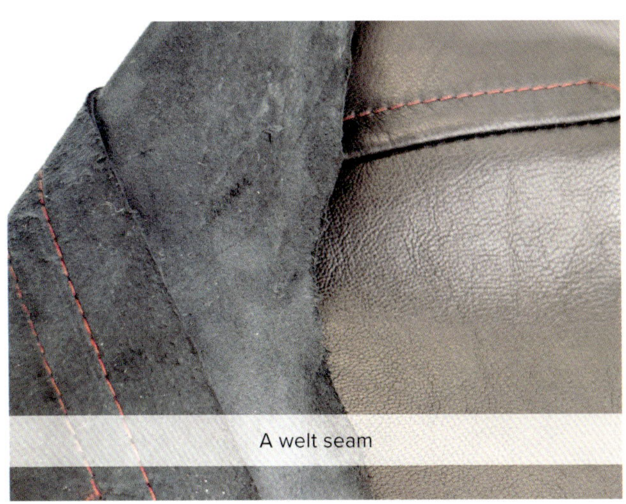
A welt seam

A **welt seam** (pg 165) strengthens a seam with additional stitching but does not protect raw edges. It's great for strengthening bulky materials that will not fray or that already have some other kind of seam finishing.

A flat-fell seam and mock flat-fell seam

A **flat-fell** seam (pg 81) encases raw edges, protecting them from fraying away. Flat-fell seams are strong and are, therefore, often used for pants. A **mock flat-fell seam**, which has overedged (pg 138) raw edges, has a similar look and strength but has less bulk.

✱ QUICK TIP!

If you're going to use a specialty seam or seam finish, plan ahead! Some techniques require larger seam allowances; others need the seam allowances to be trimmed closely before sewing. ●

A French and a mock French seam

A **French seam** (pg 114) also completely encloses raw edges; it's perfect for very lightweight and translucent materials, because the reverse of the seam is as beautiful as the right side. A **mock French seam** (pg 114) also encloses raw edges but is easier to apply in some situations (such as when the main seam has already been sewn).

A rolled-edge seam

A **rolled-edge seam** (pg 132) combines two layers of rolled hem, rolling them into one tiny seam. A rolled-edge seam is one of the most discreet seams possible (and is, therefore, great for sheers), but it can be very difficult to implement.

A lapped seam and a reversible lapped seam

A **lapped seam** (pg 160), also known as an **overlapped seam**, simply overlaps two materials! It's a low-bulk technique, and great for materials that do not fray. An alternate version, a **reversible lapped seam** (pg 88), finishes raw edges before seaming, which keeps down bulk while protecting from fraying.

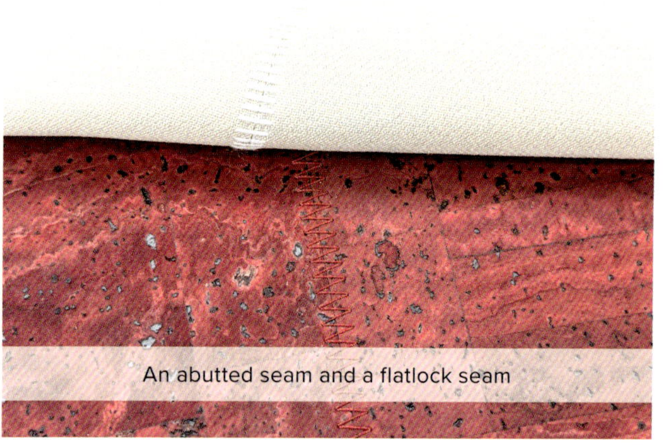

An abutted seam and a flatlock seam

Both **abutted** (pg 171) (also known as **butted**) and **flatlock seams** (pg 147) connect materials edge to edge. Because these seams don't allow for raw edge protection, they're only used for materials that don't fray. They're perfect for extremely thick materials, like EVA foam, because there is zero overlap between the connecting pieces. Flatlock seams can be modified to allow for raw edge protection.

Seam Finishes

The following seam finishes are referenced in this book.

Pinked raw edges

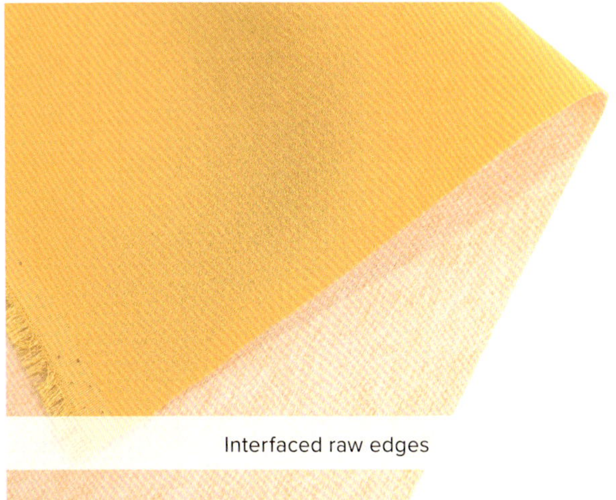
Interfaced raw edges

Perhaps the simplest way to finish raw edges is by **pinking** them with pinking shears (pg 66). This works well for fabrics that fray very little, or for when you don't want a harsh line to show through to the front of your piece.

If you fuse **interfacing** all the way to the edge of your piece (pg 120), the interfacing itself will prevent the fabric from fraying. It will also add structure, depending on the weight of the interfacing.

Fray Check (by Dritz) and tacky glue used as seam sealant

Seared raw edges

Seam sealants (pg 56) add an actual product to the raw edges, which helps prevent fraying but also may wash out or cause a scratchy texture.

If your material is synthetic, you can **sear** (pg 121)—lightly melt—the fibers at the raw edge to prevent fraying.

Raw edges topstitched and glued

Topstitching (pg 177) or gluing down raw edges somewhat protects raw edges from fraying. They also flatten the front of the seam, creating a clean look.

Raw edges overlocked together and separately

Overedging (pg 138) protects raw edges with loops of stitching. The three versions mentioned in this book are accomplished with overlock and wrapped stitches (using a serger) and zigzag stitches (using a conventional machine).

Ribbon-bound, Hong Kong, self-bound, and complete bias-bound finishes

Bound seam finishes (pg 73) use another material (or, in the case of self-bound, excess seam allowance) to completely enclose the raw edges. This is a protective seam finish, but with contrasting materials it can be decorative as well.

Seam Sealant

Seam sealant is not specifically called out in the text of this book, but if you want a raw-edge look with no fraying, it's always an option. Two common seam sealants are Fray Check (by Dritz) and similar products and regular PVA glue, such as tacky glue. Either can be carefully applied to light- and medium-weight fabrics to seal their edges, which reduces fraying and raveling. Thicker materials are better sealed with PVA glue.

Always swatch test before using seam sealant on your final piece. Some fabrics are stained by seam sealants; others fray so dramatically that seam sealant won't adequately protect your raw edges.

Hems

The following hems are referenced in this book.

Raw edge finishes

Single- and double-fold hems in conventional widths, narrow and wide

If your fabric allows for it, you can leave your edge unhemmed. **Raw** edges take no time and create no bulk but do not protect the fabric at all. Instead of leaving hems entirely raw, you may also want to consider some of the raw edge finishes: bound (pg 73), pinked (pg 66), seam sealed (pg 56), seared (pg 121), interfaced (pg 120), or overedged (pg 138).

A **single-fold hem** (pg 85) is the most basic hem: The edge of the fabric is folded up once and then secured. A **double-fold hem** (pg 85) encloses the raw edge by folding it twice. Either one can be made **narrow** or **wide**.

✱ NARROW OR WIDE?

A narrow hem is great for lightweight fabrics, because it doesn't add bulk. A wide hem is perfect for preserving material, such as in pants legs that may need to be let out at a later time. ●

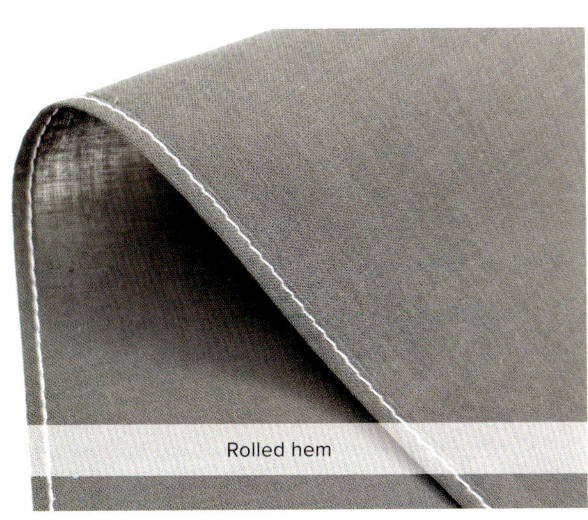

Rolled hem

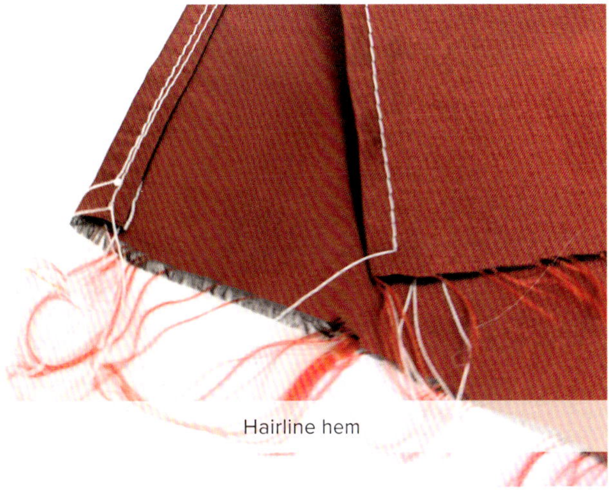

Hairline hem

A **rolled hem** (pg 132) is extremely narrow; because it adds protection but not bulk, it's great for lightweight and sheer fabrics. On a conventional machine, a rolled hem can be difficult to execute, even with a rolled-hem presser foot; on a serger, it's super easy.

A **hairline hem** (pg 122), which you may know as an **edge-stitched hem**, is an extremely thin hem, great for lightweight materials. Because it's completed with multiple lines of stitching, it can be much easier to cleanly complete than a rolled hem.

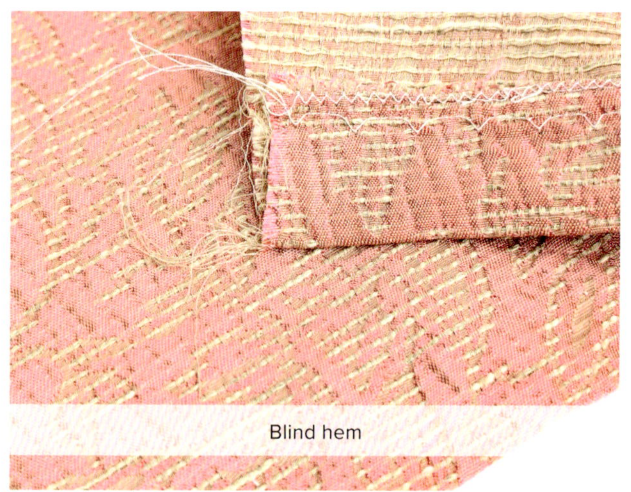

Blind hem

A **blind hem** (pg 84) combines a particular kind of folding, a blind hem foot, and a special stitch—a blind stitch—to create a hem that's almost invisible on the right side of your project.

Mock cover hem

A twin needle can create a **mock cover hem** (pg 104); the real version is impossible without a coverstitch machine or a high-end five-thread serger. A mock cover hem is stretchy and professional-looking; it's great for tees and other knit projects.

Facing and horsehair-braid hems

Facing and **horsehair-braid hems** (pg 124) add another layer entirely to your creation, which is a great option if you want to add some structure while also finishing the edge, or if your material is difficult to hem on its own.

Bevels

Some materials, like EVA foam, are not traditionally hemmed. Instead, a **bevel** (pg 198) on the raw edge adds a level of polish.

Other Techniques

Basting stitches and PVA glue

Using a tracing wheel

A **basting stitch** (pg 99), added either by machine or by hand, temporarily joins fabrics to make them easier to sew. Glue or tape can also be used to baste; it will then be removed or washed out.

Using a **tracing wheel** (pg 110), with or without **transfer paper**, allows you to transfer interior markings to your fabric, or to transfer patterns without cutting into your pattern paper.

A pattern weighted throughout the fabric

Pinning and clipping densely

Weighting or **pinning into cardboard** (pg 111) will greatly reduce shifting during the marking and cutting process, because the pattern and fabric will be connected to your cutting surface. This technique is great for slinky, slippery, and very lightweight fabrics.

When sewing with slinky and delicate fabrics, it's often advantageous to **pin** (or clip) **densely** (pg 134) so that the fabric has less opportunity to contort when you're sending it through your machine.

Cutting with a box cutter

Fashion fabric which has been flatlined to a lining material

Cutting cleanly and accurately with a **box cutter** (pg 200) can take some practice, but it's worth it for the great results you'll get when working with unconventional materials.

Flatlining (pg 141) is an alternative to conventional lining, which connects the materials before construction. It's a great option when either material is difficult to work with on its own or for when you don't want construction details to show through to the front of your piece.

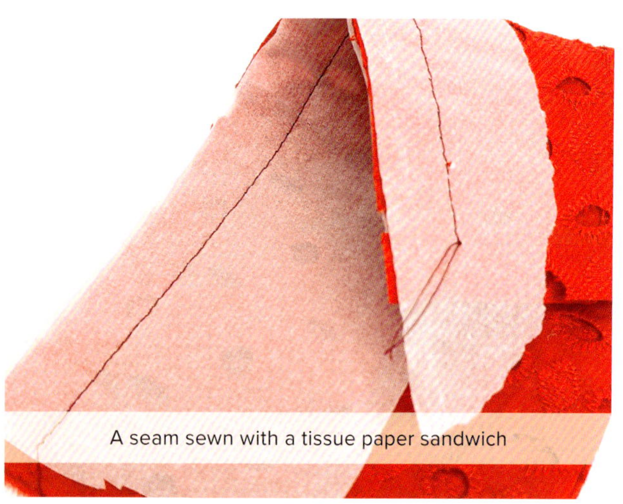
A seam sewn with a tissue paper sandwich

A seam that's been edgestitched

Sewing with a **parchment** or **tissue paper sandwich** (pg 155) allows your machine to more easily sew very delicate, holey, or sticky materials.

An **edge stitch** (pg 105) is a type of topstitch that's very close to the seam. It strengthens the seam but can be more subtle than a typical topstitch.

Stretch sewing

One way to sew a stretchy seam is by slightly **stretching the fabric as you sew** (pg 100).

Taut sewing

When **taut sewing** (pg 113), which is best with fabrics that are *not* stretchy, you send the fabric through the machine with it gripped taut between each hand.

Easing fabric into the sewing machine

Easing fabric (pg 101), in the context of machine sewing, is somewhat the opposite of taut and stretch sewing; you allow the feed dogs to do all of the feeding, which leads to a complete lack of stretch in the seam.

A manufactured and homemade seam jumper

You can use a **seam jumper** (pg 77)—either a manufactured one or one you make out of paper—to help your sewing machine get over large humps in your creations (where multiple seams of a thick fabric intersect, for example).

Using contact cement

Contact cement (pg 204) is an extremely strong glue commonly used in crafting projects with materials like foam and vinyl, but it does take some practice and timing.

Graded raw edges

Grading (pg 94) is cutting seam allowances to different heights. This may be to facilitate a special seam finish, decrease bulk, or decrease raw edge visibility from the front of your creation.

Protecting the front of creation from dents

When pressing seams open on lightweight or sensitive materials, it's usually necessary to **protect the front of the creation** (pg 72) so that it doesn't acquire pressed dents from the seam allowance.

Abutted seams reinforced with hot glue, fabric, tape, and fusible interfacing

Abutted seams, because they're connected without overlapping, can be quite weak. They're easily strengthened with a **reinforcing material** (pg 171)—glue, fabric, tape, or the like—on the reverse of the material.

Lightweight and Medium-weight Wovens

Lightweight and medium-weight wovens are the basic fabrics of the sewing world. They're not *all* beginner fabrics, but many of them are; even fabrics outside of the easy sewing category of this chapter can be great places to begin a sewing journey. These materials are great for apparel, accessories, and home decor.

Quilt made of quilting cotton, a classic easy-sew fabric

QUILT BY PATTY MURPHY, FROM *ZERO WASTE QUILTING* (C&T PUBLISHING)

Easy Sewing

Quilting cotton, muslin/calico, and linen wovens are among the easiest fabrics to sew with. They're also inexpensive, making them the perfect beginner fabrics. All three are plain weaves.

Quilting cotton, because it's made specifically for quilters, has a huge amount of pattern and style diversity. It does not have a great drape compared to other medium-weight wovens, but it will soften with repeated washes.

✸ QUICK TIP!

Quilting cotton requires special consideration when purchasing: if you will be using it for a garment or other creation where the fabric's pattern layout will matter, make sure the fabric's print is aligned on the grain. Some quilting fabric manufacturers' pattern tolerances are less strict than in fabrics made specifically for garments; they may be printed askew! Imagine cutting out a dress pattern only to realize your perfect vertical stripes are *very slightly* diagonal. •

Linen wovens is an umbrella term that could mean any number of woven linen materials, but what I'm referring to in this section (and what you'll most commonly see in the sewing world) are linen and linen-blend medium-weight woven fabrics—think bedsheets! Linen wovens are durable, cool, and prone to wrinkling and fraying. Medium-weight **hemp fabric** should be sewn just like linen wovens.

In the United States, **muslin** is the name for a form of unprocessed and undyed cotton; elsewhere this fabric is referred to as **calico**. Muslin/calico is densely woven, stiff, and coarse.

Dog accessories made from patterned cotton fabrics

ACCESSORIES BY BLUETIEDESIGNS
Photo by bluetiedesigns

?? CONFUSING TOPIC!

In the United States, a muslin also refers to a mock-up of a garment—which though often made of (American) muslin fabric, may be made of something else entirely. Extra confusingly, you may hear this garment referred to as a **toile**, which *also* refers to a type of fabric; a delicate, semi-sheer fabric often printed with delicate repeating patterns. For the sake of clarity, in this book I will use the word **mock-up** to refer to a practice or fitting piece.

Outside of the United States, muslin is the name of *another* cotton plain weave. This muslin fabric ranges from sheer to medium-weight and is a much looser weave than calico/muslin. Gauze—the fabric, not the medical bandaging—is a type of muslin. •

?? CONFUSING TOPIC!

In the United States, calico is also a pattern of small, repetitive flowers. Cotton fabric featuring this kind of calico is suitable for quilting and garments. American calico sews just like quilting cotton. •

1

2

3

1. Linen woven
2. Quilting cotton
3. Muslin

Fabric Preparation and Care

Quilting cotton, muslin, gauze, and linen wovens will all shrink dramatically. They should be prewashed twice if they will be washed after construction. Even steam will shrink them.

Because linen and muslin fray, consider overedging (pg 138) the edges of your fabric before prewashing it.

✸ QUICK TIP!
If you're only using muslin to make a mock-up, you don't necessarily need to prewash it. If you intend to use steam as you sew, though, you should prewash so that you don't spoil your mock-up by shrinking with steam. •

When washing these fabrics after construction, care must be taken to prevent further shrinking—especially if you didn't prewash or steam during construction. Always machine wash on a gentle cycle with cool or warm water, not hot. Quilting cotton can be tumble dried on low heat, but woven linens and muslin should hang to dry. Linen pieces, especially, benefit from hang drying; that prevents them from succumbing to the dramatic wrinkling they're prone to.

Pressing

All three easy-sew fabrics can be pressed on hot, but remember that steam may cause them to further shrink. Linen acquires a wrinkly texture that may be desired. If it is, do not overpress; you don't want to "correct" this crinkly texture!

Pattern Transfer/Marking

Easy-sew fabrics are also easy to mark. Chalk, disappearing ink, and tailor's tacks are all great options.

Cutting

Regular fabric shears or a rotary cutter are all that's necessary to cut easy-sew fabrics. You can cut multiple layers at once. Lay out patterns on the grain, unless a printed pattern requires a with-nap layout.

Pinning and Alternatives

All-purpose pins and clips work perfectly fine for easy-sew fabrics.

Interfacing

Self-fabric, sew-in, or fusible woven interfacing, and sew-in or fusible nonwoven interfacing all work well for easy-sew fabrics. Be sure to take into account the shrinking factor of both your base fabric and your interfacing, especially when using fusible interfacing. If either your fabric or fusible interface shrink after they've been adhered, it can create bubbling on the front of your creation or cause the two materials to become unadhered. If you'll be washing or steaming your finished piece, it's important to preshrink your interfacing (pg 46).

Sewing

An 80/12 universal sewing machine needle works well for all the easy-sew fabrics. Linen may benefit from a 70/10; it can be a lighter weight than the others. Start with a 2.5mm straight stitch sewn with all-purpose polyester thread and a standard machine foot.

Because these fabrics fray, edges should be protected (finished). Great seam options are three- or four-thread overlocked or three-thread wrapped (pg 70), French seamed (pg 114), flat-felled (pg 81), or bound (pg 73). Hems can be three- or four-thread overlocked (pg 138), double folded (pg 85), or bound (pg 73).

Quilting cotton frays considerably less than the other two easy-sew fabrics; if an exposed raw edge will not be particularly hard-wearing, you can consider just pinking (pg 66). A plain seam (pg 66) and a single-fold hem (pg 85) or mock cover hem (pg 104) are safe and easy options.

Tutorial Time: Pinking

Pinking—using a special pair of scissors to cut notches in a fabric edge—provides some amount of fray protection. It also creates a less harsh line, when a seam allowance may show through to the front of a piece.

Press your seams first—this will make it easier to get a clean cut. Then cut along each of your raw edges with your pinking shears.

When pinking a hem, you may find it easier to pink the raw edge *before* folding and pressing.

Tutorial Time: Plain Seams

A plain seam is the simplest seam. It is appropriate for many different materials.

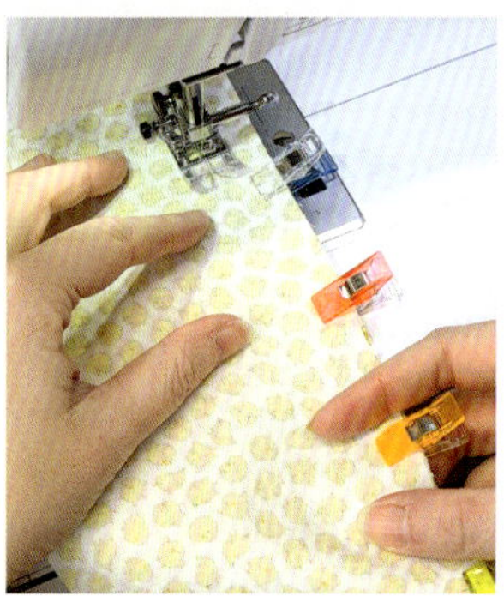

1. With right sides together, sew a line of stitching along your seamline.

2. Press your seam open, and then finish or leave your seam allowance edges raw, but remember: A plain seam with a straight stitch by itself will not prevent your fabric from fraying.

You can achieve the same seam with a line of overlock stitches, which *will* protect the raw edges.

An Unconventional Easy-Sew Fabric

Utility nonwovens, which are technically spunbond nonwoven fabric made from polypropylene, are the material reusable shopping bags and many medical gowns and masks are made of. Utility nonwovens are very easy to sew with because they're durable, do not fray, and are easy to machine wash and sew.

The only complication with utility nonwovens is that holes are permanent. For that reason, use fabric clips instead of pins. Otherwise, follow the guidelines outlined in the rest of this chapter!

Note that you may see utility nonwovens referred to as cambric, which is an entirely different fabric (pg 107). Today, utility nonwoven materials often serve the purpose that cambric has historically: that of a lightweight, densely woven, and sturdy utility material.

Suiting and Shirting

Suiting and shirting fabrics are medium- to heavyweight fabrics commonly and historically used for menswear; in modern fashion they are also used for structured dresses, outerwear, and even lining for those garments. All of these fabrics were historically made from cotton, wool, silk, or a natural blend, which gave them durability and warmth. Now, they may be 100 percent synthetic or synthetic blends.

Suit is a cotton twill coat with custom-printed polyester crepe lining, cotton twill trousers, and a cotton poplin shirt.

SUIT AND MODELING BY MAEVE FOLEY
Photo by hailthenaninator

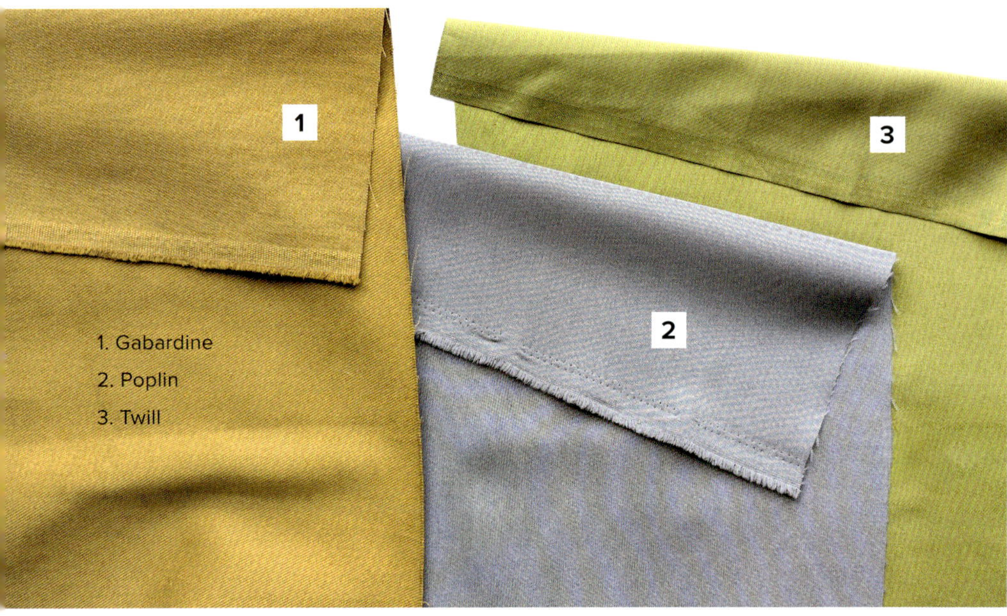

1. Gabardine
2. Poplin
3. Twill

Several twill weave fabrics, with their characteristic diagonal ribs, are included in this suiting section.

Gabardine is firmly woven and often smooth and shiny. It is dense and durable, but the ribs can be damaged when sewing and pressing.

Twill is (confusingly) also the name of a *specific fabric* in the twill weave family. It is durable and has a nice drape. **Chino** is a similar fabric that is a lighter weight and usually 100 percent cotton.

1. Twill
2. Poplin
3. Broadcloth

Two common plain weaves are also shirting/suiting fabrics.

Broadcloth is tightly woven and the most lightweight of the suiting fabrics; it is most commonly used for shirts. It is soft and smooth.

The weight of **poplin** can vary quite significantly; it can be lightweight and airy or heavy enough for a suit jacket. Poplin has very fine ribbing running across the weft. Poplin is very densely woven and, therefore, strong and crisp. It has a slight sheen.

?? CONFUSING TOPIC!

Confusingly, in modern parlance, *poplin* can also refer to any strong plain weave fabric; if you want poplin with ribbing, make sure to confirm before you order!

You may also see poplin referred to as **tabinet**. ●

?? CONFUSING TOPIC!

Broadcloth may also refer to a feltlike fabric made from densely woven wool. The two are very easy to differentiate; shirting broadcloth is lightweight and drapey, while the other is heavy, textured, and more suitable for a coat or upholstery. ●

Fabric Preparation and Care

Broadcloth will shrink; if it will be washed or steamed in its final form, it should be machine washed cold and delicate and then tumble dried before it's sewn.

Otherwise, suiting fabric should be prewashed carefully and according to its fiber content. Generally, gabardine and poplin can be hand washed or machine washed on a cold gentle cycle, then tumble dried or hung to dry. Twill can be machine washed cold or warm and then hung to dry. As always, consider the fiber content of your fabric before washing or drying.

✸ QUICK TIP!
Remember, you can swatch the prewash and care for your fabrics! Especially for fabrics like gabardine that may be made of cotton, wool, synthetics, or blends of the three, sometimes the safest route is to send a square through the machine and see how it comes out. •

Pressing

In general, press according to your fabric's fiber content. Cotton suiting and shirting fabrics can be pressed on high and steamed. For synthetic and synthetic blends of these fabrics, start at a low temperature and increase until the pressing is effective.

Take care to not damage your suiting's ribs when pressing. Instead of pressing one extended time with pressure, press lightly several times. Similarly, when pressing seams, the seam allowance can leave indents on the front of your piece. Press with a piece of cardboard between the seam allowance and the main portion of the piece (pg 72) to prevent this issue.

If your suiting is wool or a wool blend, overpressing will cause shiny patches. Start with a low heat and increase until you get an effective press. Do not linger in one spot for too long and always use a press cloth.

Pattern Transfer/Marking

Suitings are durable and easy to mark; chalk, disappearing ink, and tailor's tacks are common and easy options.

Cutting

All of the suiting fabrics can be cut with a normal rotary cutter or fabric shears and in multiple layers.

Broadcloth has a subtle wrong side and right side; mark the wrong side as you cut your pieces so you don't end up with subtle pattern and finish differences in your final creation.

Twills have a direction! Gabardine and twill should both be cut using a with-nap layout to prevent alternating ribs on your final creation. Other suiting and shirting fabrics can be cut on the grain.

Pinning and Alternatives

All-purpose pins and sewing clips work well on suiting fabrics.

Interfacing

Sew-in or fusible woven or nonwoven interfacing work well for broadcloth and poplin, but remember: If you prewashed your fabric, you'll also need to shrink your interfacing (pg 46).

Because of their ribs, fusible interfacing struggles to adhere to gabardine and twill. Plus, their ribs can be damaged by the fusing process. For that reason, a sew-in woven or nonwoven interfacing is better for those suiting fabrics.

Sewing

Broadcloth and poplin are best sewn with an 80/12 universal sewing machine needle. For gabardine, use a 90/14 universal, which will also probably work well for twill, but you may discover that you need to upgrade to a denim needle when sewing through multiple layers of that fabric.

All the suiting and shirting materials work well with a 2.5mm straight stitch using a standard presser foot and all-purpose polyester thread, although twill may benefit from heavy-duty thread in high-stress applications (like shoulder and crotch seams).

Broadcloth and twill are both prone to fraying and, therefore, need their raw edges protected. For seams, overedge (three- or four-thread overlock or three-thread wrapped overlock (below), flat-fell (pg 81), or bind (pg 73). For hems, double fold (pg 85), bind (pg 73), or overedge (pg 138).

Tutorial Time: Seaming with Overedge Stitches

Almost any seam can include overedge stitches (pg 138). The easiest is a modified plain seam (pg 66), which sews and protects at the same time.

On the serger, set your machine to your desired overedge stitch, and then align your seamline with your serger's leftmost needle. Sew the seam; the serger will cut off excess seam allowance and then wrap the raw edge.

On the conventional sewing machine, set your stitch to a zigzag, then sew so that the zigzag stitch hits or very slightly passes the edge of your fabric.

Gabardine and poplin fray less dramatically; if they won't be heavily used, their raw edges do not need to be enclosed. An overedge (four-thread overlock, pg 138) or plain seam (pg 66) (with or without pinking, pg 66) is easy to implement. Hems can be a single fold (pg 85) or mock cover hem (pg 104).

Because suiting fabrics can be substantial, you may want to topstitch (pg 177) seam allowances down to get a cleaner look on the right side of your piece.

Lightweight Wovens

Lightweight wovens are delicate and floaty, but not nearly as tricky to work with as the sheers and silky fabrics covered in Sheers (pg 107) and Shinies and Sleeks (pg 116). They can be a great intermediate step for a sewist who wants to move from easily sewn medium-weight wovens to tricky, slinky fabrics like slippery wovens and stretchy knits. Lightweight wovens work especially well for apparel.

Included in the lightweight wovens category are crepe de chine, challis, chambray, and gauze. All four are plain weaves and can be found in synthetic versions, but historically they were quite different.

Crepe de chine was historically made from either silk or a silk and wool blend. It can be light- to medium-weight, but it is delicate regardless of its weight. It can be matte or have a light sheen. Like most crepe fabrics, crepe de chine frays dramatically.

Challis, which is sometimes referred to as challie or chally, was historically a silk and wool blend. It has a smooth flowy drape and is much less crisp than crepe de chine. It can be textured (often with a crinkle), but it is more often smooth and printed with floral patterns.

Chambray consists almost entirely of cotton and combines white and (often) light blue yarns to create a denim-like appearance, though it is significantly thinner and softer.

Gauze—the fabric, not the medical material—was historically made from silk and now is made from polyester, cotton, and miscellaneous synthetic materials. Within the gauze category, there's a vast array of both weight and weave density; some gauzes are thin enough to be veils, while others are typical shirting fabric. If your gauze is more like a net, use the Nets chapter (pg 128) as guidance; that's also where medical gauze is covered.

Original design Lavender Town Witch (inspired by *Pokémon*) made with a variety of lightweight linens and cottons, among other materials

COSTUME AND MODELING BY LIZARD LEIGH
Photo by Molly Doyle

1. Fabric gauze
2. Crepe de chine
3. Challis
4. Chambray

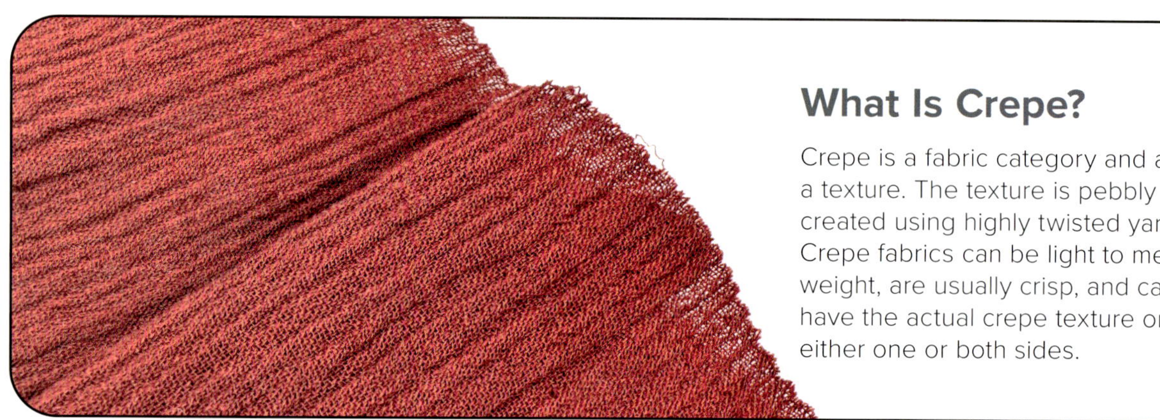

What Is Crepe?

Crepe is a fabric category and also a texture. The texture is pebbly and created using highly twisted yarns. Crepe fabrics can be light to medium weight, are usually crisp, and can have the actual crepe texture on either one or both sides.

Fabric Preparation and Care

Prewash lightweight woven fabrics as they will be cared for after construction. Because they are cotton, chambray and cotton gauze will shrink; particular care should be taken to pretreat them.

All four fabrics should be machine washed cold on the delicate cycle and hung to dry. Be sure to wash and dry a swatch before committing to a machine wash; these lightweight fabrics may be better hand washed or dry-cleaned, especially if they're made of silk.

Pressing

Crepe de chine, challis, and gauze should be pressed according to their fiber content: Use a silk/wool/medium setting if the fabric is silk or wool, or a synthetic/low setting (increasing the heat until effective) if it's synthetic. Chambray, alternatively, is best pressed with high heat. Steam may shrink cotton chambray more than a prewash, so if you intend to steam your finished piece, be sure to steam your base fabric before construction.

Because they're so thin, lightweight wovens may acquire creases on the front of pieces after pressing seams. To prevent this, press seams open with a piece of cardboard between the seam allowance and the main body of the fabric.

Consider pressing all four fabrics with a press cloth, due to their semi-delicate natures.

Tutorial Time: Protecting When Pressing

Cut pieces of thin cardboard wider than your seam allowance; then place them between your seam allowances and the body of your piece. Press without letting the iron overlap the edges of the cardboard; doing so may cause a dent, and that's what we're trying to avoid!

Pattern Transfer/Marking

Chalk, disappearing ink, and tailor's tacks all work well on lightweight wovens.

Cutting

Because they can be quite floaty, lightweight wovens may slip during the cutting process. For that reason, cutting with a rotary cutter in one layer is best. Conventional or serrated sewing shears are also great choices. You may also want to weight or vertically pin (pg 111) during the pattern transfer process to prevent shifting.

All three fabrics fray, but crepe de chine frays dramatically; consider cutting it with pinking shears (pg 66) or interfacing it immediately after cutting to prevent the fabric from losing much material.

Pinning and Alternatives

Clips or fine pins are best for lightweight wovens. Pin or clip densely (pg 134) to prevent shifting; lightweight wovens aren't as slippery as shinies, but their lightweight nature causes them to move around during the sewing process. Cut lightweight wovens on the grain, unless a specific printed pattern requires a with-nap layout.

Interfacing

Lightweight wovens work well interfaced with self-fabric, sew-in, or nonwoven interfacing. Fusible interfacing can be used safely with chambray, but only with caution on challis, crepe de chine, and gauze. The semi-delicate fabrics may show adhesive through to the front of the fabric and may not be able to tolerate the heat and pressure necessary to adhere fusible products.

Sewing

Use a 70/10 universal machine needle with crepe de chine, challis, and gauze, and an 80/12 universal machine needle with chambray. A 2.5mm straight stitch, a standard foot, and fine polyester, cotton, or silk thread is a good go-to sewing setup.

Because they fray, seam and hem options must enclose raw edges. Serging works well on all lightweight wovens; use a two- or three-thread overlock or wrapped overlock (pg 70) for seaming. Flat-fell seams (pg 81), French seams (pg 114), and binding seam allowance (pg 73) are great options. For hems, consider a double-fold hem (pg 85); binding (pg 73); or a conventional machine, two-thread, or three-thread rolled hem (pg 132).

Tutorial Time: Binding

Binding can be used on all raw edges. When used on seam allowance, it completely protects the raw edges but adds bulk; when used as a hem, it is a decorative finish that can add structure.

1. To install bias tape, begin by opening up the bias tape and then pinning your binding to your fabric, right side to right side, matching raw edges.

2. Sew along the first fold in the binding from the raw edge.

3. Fold the binding over so that it encloses the raw edge. The middle fold of the binding should not squish the fashion fabric's raw edge; if it does, trim down the fabric.

4. Make sure your third fold is tucked to the inside—there should not be any edges of either the fashion fabric or the binding left raw. Carefully stitch from the front of the piece along the first seamline or as an edge stitch (pg 105). This will catch the back side of the binding, securing all layers.

A **Hong Kong finish** (left) encloses seam allowances separately, protecting them both. Conventionally, this method leaves the underside of the binding's raw edge unfolded. Installing with a protected lower edge fold is fine, too; it trades some bulk for extra fray protection. A **complete bias bound** seam (right) encloses both raw edges of the seam allowance together.

A **ribbon bound** edge is installed similarly, but because ribbon does not have raw edges, it only requires one fold!

1. Press your ribbon lengthwise so that one half is slightly wider than the other. Press carefully: Many ribbons are made of heat-sensitive synthetic materials.

2. Pin or otherwise secure the ribbon with the shorter side on the right side of your fabric. When pinning, make sure to catch both halves of the ribbon.

3. Edgestitch (pg 105) the ribbon from the right side of your fabric. Because the ribbon on the wrong side is slightly longer, it will be caught in the stitches.

In a **self-bound seam**, an extra-large seam allowance is folded over to protect itself. Make sure to cut accordingly if you'll be using this method; you may need to increase the size of your seam allowances in order to have enough material to fold over.

1. Sew your seam as usual; then cut one of the seam allowances to half its original width.

2. Press the wider seam allowance toward the shorter one, meeting their raw edges.

3. Press the same piece again, but meet at the seamline. Your longer seam allowance should now be folded twice, enclosing both its and the shorter side's raw edges. Pin, clip, or baste (pg 99).

4. Edgestitch (pg 105), securing the wider seam allowance, but avoid sewing onto the body of your piece.

Heavyweight Wovens

Heavyweight wovens vary wildly in their use and fiber contents, but they all benefit from techniques to reduce bulk in seams and hems. Their thick and tough makeup can make sewing tricky.

If you're making a piece with multiple layers, you may encounter a problem sewing over thick bumps in your piece or even starting your line of sewing because of the thickness of the fabric. A seam jumper (pg 77) is a great tool in this situation. You can either buy a premade product or create your own using folded cardboard.

Similarly, you may find that your machine (whether conventional sewing or serger) struggles to feed thick fabrics under the presser foot, especially as seams build up. In these cases, consider reducing the pressure on the foot to allow more space for the fabric. You may also consider a walking foot if the fabric doesn't move freely through the machine.

Although many of the fabrics in this section call for thick but all-purpose sewing machine needles, you may find that you need the same size needle but in denim. Denim needles are stronger, thicker, and sharper than standard sewing machine needles, so they won't bend or break as easily when sewing multiple layers of thick fabric.

Replica dress of a Rus woman during the late Iron Age made in part with heavyweight wool fabrics

GARMENTS AND MODELING BY KRISTA
Photo by Quinn Kollig

Tutorial Time: Using a Seam Jumper

A seam jumper helps a conventional sewing machine "jump" over large humps of fabric, preventing skipped stitches and broken needles.

1. Stop sewing when you notice your presser foot raising in the front as it approaches a bulky seam.

2. Lower the needle, raise the presser foot, and place the seam jumper underneath the presser foot. If you made your own, you may need to add or subtract material so that it matches the height of the bulky seam. If you're using a manufactured seam jumper, choose the height that's closest to your material's.

3. Lower your presser foot and sew. Let the presser foot glide off the seam jumper.

What about Ripstop?

Ripstop is not included in this book because it is not a specific kind of fabric; it's a technique for making fabric stronger and less prone to tearing without adding weight. Thicker and stronger yarns, often nylon, are woven in with regular yarns, creating a checkerboard pattern in the textile. Ripstop comes in many weights and is great for outdoor gear, flags, kites, and heavy-duty bags.

When sewing with ripstop, use an 80/12 microtex needle and a slightly longer stitch length (about 3mm). Pin, clip, or baste (pg 99) your seams before sewing and consider using a walking foot. Raw edges can be finished with a four-thread overlock (pg 138), or they can be seared (pg 121) to prevent the nylon from fraying during use.

If you're having trouble with ripstop slipping around during the sewing process, use the techniques covered in Shinies and Sleeks (pg 116).

Canvas and Denim

Plain canvas is a durable plain weave usually made of cotton, linen, or a synthetic. **Duck canvas** is tighter woven than its plain sibling and, therefore, even more stiff and durable. Both types of canvas are commonly treated for waterproofing, which makes them great choices for work clothes, tents, bags, and shoes. Canvas is usually very heavyweight; lighter versions are often used for suiting and other structured apparel.

Denim is the twill-weave version of duck canvas. It is strong and durable, but it frays. Denim is traditionally woven with dark warp yarns and white weft yarns, creating its distinctive color and pattern. Denim is almost always cotton and, therefore, has little stretch, but it can be blended with spandex to create stretch denim.

What about Drill and Ticking?

Drill is a durable, easy-care twill fabric that's often used to make khaki pants. **Ticking**, historically used to cover mattresses, is strong and fine and, nowadays, most often used for interior design. Both materials are similar to denim and canvas but less common. If you're sewing with them, follow the techniques in this section.

Working with Stretch Denim

Nowadays, many denim fabrics and garments come with a small amount of spandex included to improve their comfort, but some denim has so much stretch fiber added that it significantly changes the behavior of the fabric. If you're having issues sewing with stretch denim, consider experimenting with the strategies covered in Stretch Knits (pg 95), which very lightweight and stretchy denim can resemble.

Apron made with printed canvas

APRON BY STEVE AND ANNYE DRISCOLL
Photo by Annye Driscoll

Fabric Preparation and Care

Denim will shrink. Both denim and stretch denim should be machine washed cold or warm and then either laid flat to dry or tumble dried, according to how the fabric will be cared for after construction. After construction, consider washing rarely in order to preserve the integrity of both the cotton and the dye.

Both duck and plain canvas will soften in the wash and may shrink. If you intend to wash them after construction, make sure to machine prewash cold and lay flat to dry. Be careful of what products you use with treated versions of the fabrics; regular laundry detergents may strip the waterproofing.

Pressing

Denim, duck, and plain canvas should all be ironed at high heat with steam. However, any amount of spandex in denim adds an element of risk: You must be careful not to scorch its synthetic content when pressing! Start at low heat and increase until you get an effective press. You may even consider finger- or roller-pressing particularly high-spandex stretch denims.

If your fabrics are waterproofed, ironing can damage the waterproof coating. Decrease the heat to medium and use a press cloth. Iron the inside of your piece or the wrong side of the fabric (if the waterproofing is only on the right side) whenever possible to protect the coating.

Pattern Transfer/Marking

Chalk and disappearing ink work well on canvas and denim.

Cutting

Use a rotary cutter or fabric shears to cut canvas and denim. However, if you commonly sew with delicate fabrics, you may want to have a separate pair of sewing shears for heavyweight fabrics; cutting through substantial canvas and denim fabrics will dull scissors faster than if you only work with light- or medium-weight materials. Cut in just one layer; heavyweight wovens may be too thick to accurately cut in more.

Cut canvas on the grain. Because of the twill weave, denim technically has a direction and, therefore, is best cut using a with-nap layout. However, the difference is often not noticeable. Sew two scrap pieces of your denim together disrespecting the nap and inspect the piece in different lighting conditions and from different angles. Can you tell a difference between the two pieces? If not, you're good to cut respecting just the grain. If so, use a with-nap layout.

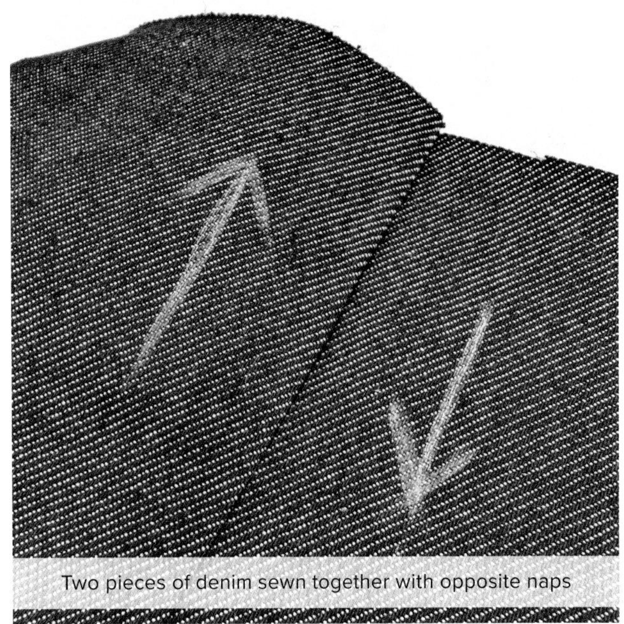

Two pieces of denim sewn together with opposite naps

Pinning and Alternatives

Lightweight denim can be pinned with all-purpose pins. Otherwise, heavyweight wovens will work best with clips or T-pins; all-purpose pins may bend when pushed through multiple layers.

Interfacing

Denim and canvas work best with sew-in or fusible woven or nonwoven interfacing. If your canvas is waterproofed, consider using a sew-in option so that the fusing process doesn't damage the coating.

Sewing

Heavyweight wovens work great with denim machine needles. Use a size 90/14 or 100/16 with duck and plain canvas, but with denim you'll need to choose based on the weight of the fabric. A typical heavyweight denim will require a thick needle like 100/18, but a lightweight denim may do best with a 90/14.

Use a 3mm straight stitch with heavy-duty cotton or polyester thread and the standard machine foot. If you're encountering skipped stitches on these thicker fabrics, consider reducing the presser foot pressure. Consider trying a topstitching needle: The larger eye will accommodate thick thread.

For a stretchier, lighter-weight denim, change to a 2.5mm straight or zigzag stitch (according to its amount of stretch) and all-purpose cotton or polyester thread.

Canvas and denim fray and their heavyweight seam allowances cause bulk, both of which require special consideration in the sewing process. An overlock (wide three-thread overlock or four-thread overlock) secures raw edges and trims seam allowance at the same time, solving both issues. Flat felling (pg 81) is the traditional seam type for denim jeans; it encloses raw edges, moves the seam allowance to one side, and has a topstitch to create a clean finish. A welt seam (pg 165) is a modified flat-fell and is also a great option for versions of these fabrics; because a welt seam has exposed raw edges, it's best for seams that won't be under heavy use.

Alternatively, consider overedging the edges of your canvas or denim pattern pieces before construction (pg 138). Protecting the fabric in this way allows you to use low-bulk options, like plain seams (pg 66), without worrying about your material fraying into the seamline.

Tutorial Time: Flat-Fell and Mock Flat-Fell Seams

Flat-fell and mock flat-fell seams protect raw edges. They feature two lines of topstitching—a classic look for many garments.

1. With right sides together, straight stitch along the seamline. Press.

2. Decide which direction your seam will face; traditionally, when flat felling on garments, the seam allowances face away from the front of the body. Trim the side of the seam allowance on that side to half its original width.

3. Fold the wider seam allowance in half, enclosing the shorter one inside. Press.

As an alternative to cutting and folding the seam allowances, you can use an overlock, zigzag, or wrapped stitch for a similar effect. This creates a mock flat-fell seam.

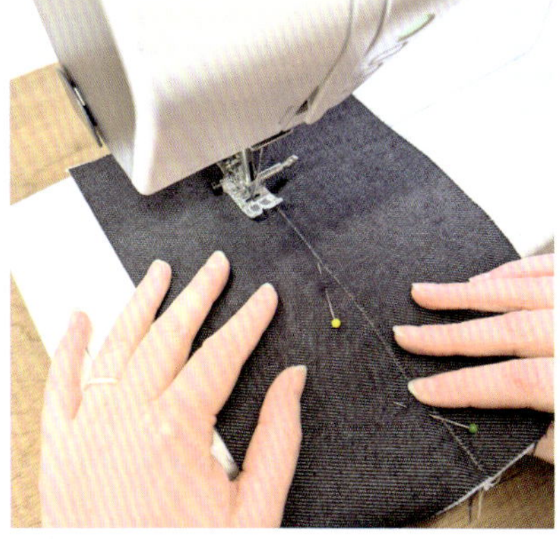

Edgestitch (pg 105) then topstitch (pg 177) the seam allowance down, creating two rows of stitching detail on the right side of the fabric.

If the thickness of the fabric allows for it, a wide double-fold hem (pg 85) works well with heavyweight wovens (and allows for sleeves and pant legs to be lengthened as needed!). Raw hems and seam edges can also be overedged (pg 138), which will contain fraying.

Because canvas and denim are often working fabrics, consider reinforcing (pg 100) any seams that will be under great stress. A second line of stitches just inside the sewn line, in either a straight stitch or a zigzag, accomplishes this task easily.

1. Brocade 2. Brocade 3. Damask

Jacquards

A jacquard is a kind of loom used to make fabrics with complex patterns. These patterns have the look and feel of embroidery but are actually woven into the weft of the fabrics.

There are two common types of jacquard fabric:

Brocade, which is sometimes referred to as just **jacquard**, is heavy and luxurious. It has both a sheen and a nap. Often more than one color of yarn is used in the patterning process, which creates a tapestry-like appearance. Brocade can be any weight, but it is most commonly heavy and used for upholstery and curtains.

Damasks have a denser weave than brocade, which makes them stronger and more durable and less prone to fraying. Damasks have a distinctive texture and sheen. They are usually made with just two colors of yarn, making them reversible.

Brocades and damasks can be made of a vast array of fibers: silk, cotton, rayon, linen, polyester, and blends of all kinds. When buying these fabrics, pay particular attention to their labels and take note of care instructions.

Brocade fabrics fray like wild; many of their sewing and care techniques must take that aspect of the materials into account.

Fabric Preparation and Care

Brocades and damasks should be prewashed as they'll be washed after construction. Because they can be made of so many varying fibers, how you do so will vary wildly. If the fabric is not silk, start with a gentle cycle with cold or warm water and then dry on low heat. Silks should be dry-cleaned only. Remember: You can always send a small piece through the wash/dry cycle to see how it reacts!

Because jacquards fray ridiculously, you may want to secure the edges of your fabric with overedge stitching (pg 138) before prewashing.

Fine art piece, *The Comfy Chair*, made from jacquard upholstery fabric, and embellished with denim, knitted blankets, waffle and jersey knits, and flannel

PIECE BY LAURA ANN SCHROEDER
Photo by Laura Ann Schroeder

Pressing

When pressing damasks and brocades, you will need to tailor your pressing temperature according to the fiber content of the fabric, but medium heat with steam and a press cloth will work for most varieties. Always press on a padded surface (like a thick terry cloth) to protect the raised motifs.

Some jacquard fabrics include metallic threads; be particularly careful when pressing these fabrics, as metals are sensitive to heat. Use a press cloth and start at a low heat, increasing only as much as needed to be effective. Instead of long, high-pressure pressing (which can scorch the metallic fibers), press multiple times in one spot with gentle, quick motions.

Pattern Transfer/Marking

Chalks, tacks, and disappearing ink will generally be good options for marking jacquards. However, more complex designs may cause the markings to disappear into the pattern; in this case, consider thread tracing your cutline with highly contrasting thread.

Because they fray so dramatically, notches cut *into* jacquard's seam allowances may fray all the way to the seamline. When your pattern calls for a notch, either cut the notch *away* from the seam allowance or mark with a tailor's tack.

Cutting

Brocades and damasks cut well with rotary cutters and fabric shears, but consider using pinking shears (pg 66) due to their intense fraying. You can also sew around your pattern piece (using an overedge (pg 138), straight stitch, or zigzag stitch) or attach interfacing immediately after cutting to prevent the fabric from fraying all the way to the seamline.

Cutting notches *out* to protect the seamline

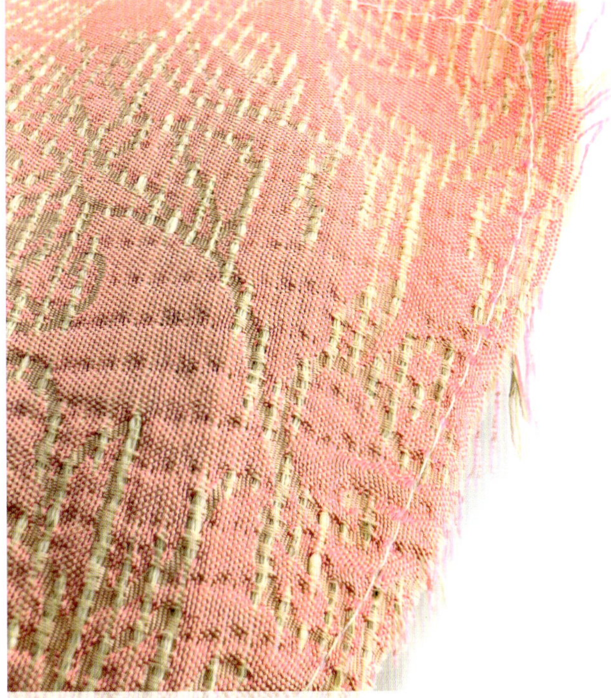

Even just a straight stitch sewn around the edge of a pattern piece immediately after cutting will help prevent fraying.

Pinning and Alternatives

T-pins and sewing clips work best for jacquards due to their heavy weight. If you're working with multiple layers, consider longer pins.

Interfacing

Sew-in or fusible nonwoven interfacings work well with jacquard fabrics. Just make sure to protect metallic threads and raised motifs during the fusing process!

Batiste and organza, used as sew-in interfacings, also work well in this case. These two fabrics are lightweight and sheer but relatively stiff. Therefore, they provide structure without adding significant bulk to a seam or finished piece.

Sewing

Sew jacquards using a 2.5–3.5mm straight stitch, an 80/12 universal needle, a standard or walking foot, and all-purpose cotton or polyester thread.

Raw edges must be protected; even a pinked seam allowance in a finished piece may fray into the seamline. Overedging (zigzagging or three- or four-thread overlock, pg 138) pattern pieces before sewing will do the trick; you can also overedge after construction if you don't fear your fabric fraying away as you sew. Flat felling (pg 81) and binding (pg 73) are clean, protective options. In addition to protected plain seams (pg 66), consider reversible lapped seams (pg 88), which reduce bulk while protecting raw edges.

For hems, facings (with self-fabric, a lining, or batiste or organza, pg 124) and blind hems (pg 84) work well and keep down bulk. Otherwise, a single fold (pg 85) with an overedged (zigzag, three-thread wrapped, or three- or four-thread overlock, pg 138) raw edge or a wide double-fold (pg 85) are easy to implement.

Tutorial Time: Blind Hems

Blind hems combine a special fold and either a blind stitch (on a conventional machine) or a flatlock stitch (on a serger) to create a hem that's almost invisible on the right side of the fabric. The raw edge of a blind hem will not be enclosed. If necessary, finish it before beginning the hem.

1. Press the hem to the inside along the hemline. Then, with the fabric facing wrong side up, flip the folded hem under the body of the piece, tucking until the hem's edge extends past where the body fabric flips.

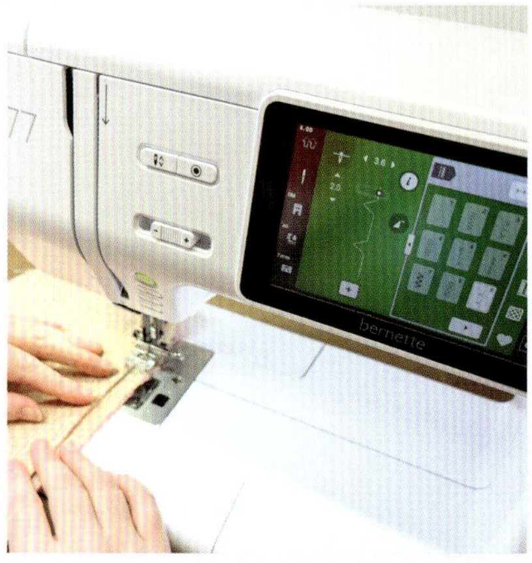

2. On a conventional machine, install a standard foot or blind hem foot and set the stitch to the blind stitch. On a serger, set the machine to the flatlock stitch. Sew along the edge of the hem, just *barely* catching threads of the body fabric with the intermittent wide stitches.

Tutorial Time: Single and Double-Fold Hems

Single and double-fold hems are a very basic form of hemming that are great for many different materials. They can be executed with or without first protecting the raw edge and have both wide and narrow variations.

1. To sew a single-fold hem, press your fabric at the hemline; then sew. This will result in a line of stitching on the right side of your piece.

2. To create a double-fold hem, first press your fabric halfway to the hemline. You may feel comfortable proceeding to the second fold without securing this one, or you may want to baste it for security (pg 99).

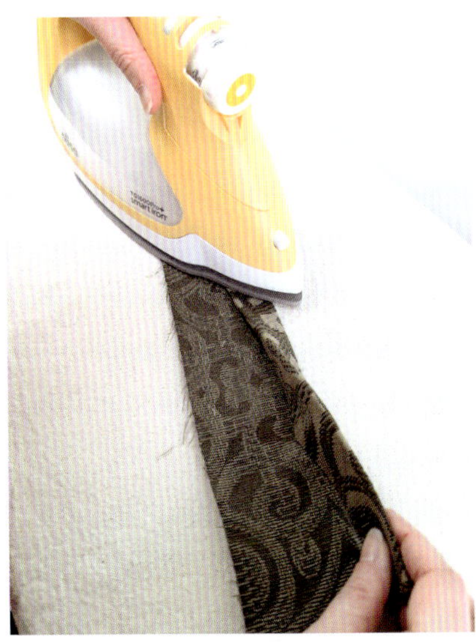

3. Fold the fabric at the hemline, creating your second fold. Press.

4. Sew.

Lengthen or shorten your folds to make your single and double folds either wide or narrow.

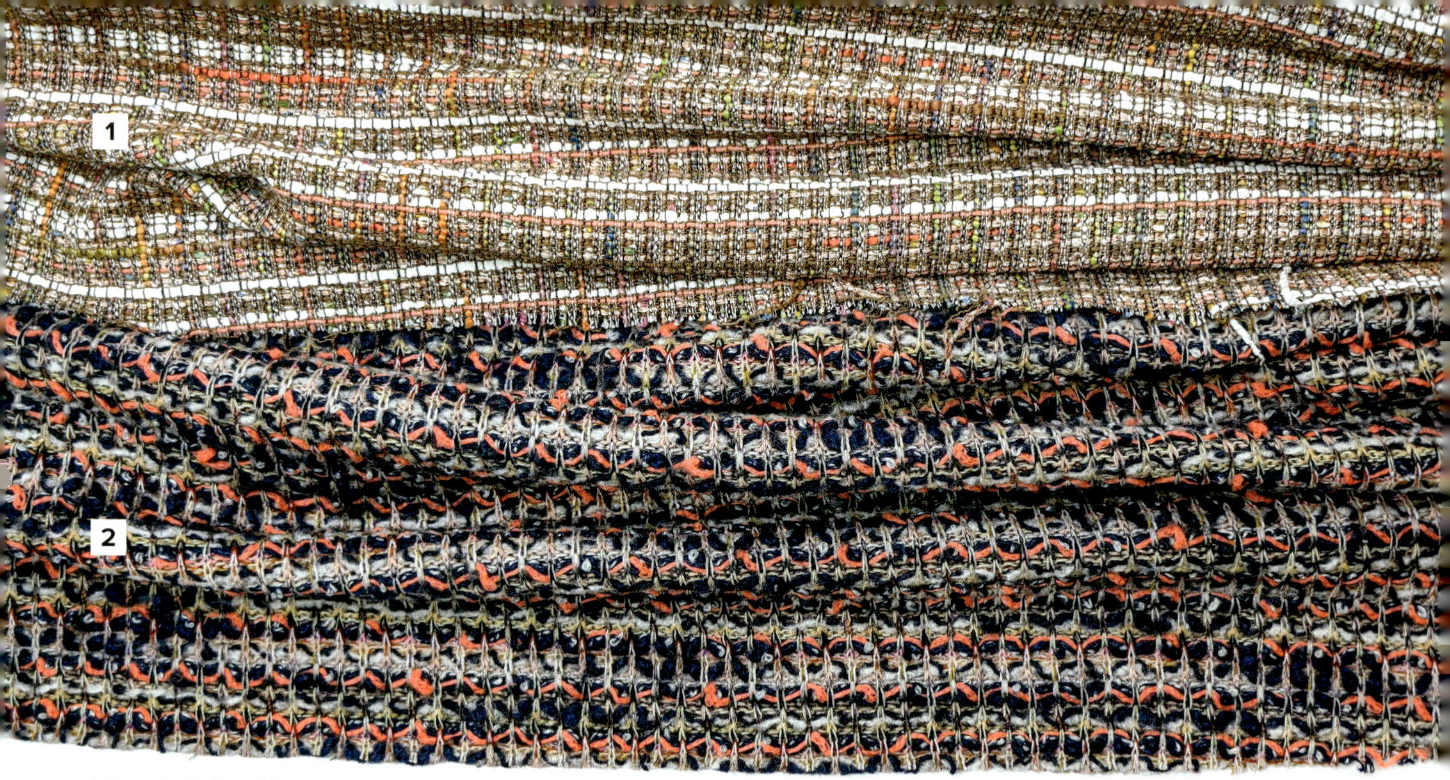

1. Tweed 2. Bouclé

Textured Heavyweights

Textured heavyweights offer additional complication in the sewing process because they have raised fibers. These fabrics are often used for outerwear, accessories, and upholstery.

Bouclé is easily recognizable; it's a plain weave fabric made with looped curling and textured yarns that create its distinctive texture. It's warm, but it can be scratchy against the skin. It's a loose weave and, therefore, frays like crazy.

Tweed is a category term for heavyweight, rough, and durable woolens. Because the wool fibers that make the fabric are fairly unprocessed, tweed is textured, scratchy, and nubby. Nowadays, tweed fabrics can also be made from polyester and other synthetic fibers. You may recognize two popular tweed fabrics—herringbone and houndstooth.

Kitchen witch's skirt made from a wool blend tweed

DOLL AND MODELING BY SHARON STAHL (BAUBLE & HAG)
Photo by Sharon Stahl (Bauble & Hag)

Nubby? Slubby?!

Often *nubby* and *slubby* are used interchangeably to describe a deliberately and finely textured fabric—but they're actually not the same!

The yarns that create fabrics sometimes have variations in their diameter, called *slubs*. A *nub* is a loop or knot in the yarn. After being woven into fabric, both nubs and slubs are visible in the resulting textile as raised textures—they're delicate details.

Linen, wool, and silk can be naturally slubby, or synthetic yarns can be intentionally created with a slubbed texture. Bouclé and chenille are examples of nubby fabrics.

Dupioni (left) is slubby. Bouclé (right) is nubby.

Fabric Preparation and Care

Prewashing bouclé and tweed isn't necessary unless your final piece will be washed. If it will be, wash it according to its fiber type. Wool should be hand washed gently and laid flat to dry. Synthetic bouclé and tweed may be able to be gently machine washed, but even polyester versions of these fabrics can be delicate; bouclé's yarn loops can be easily damaged while washing. Consider dry-cleaning or spot cleaning with gentle detergent, or carefully steam if you wish to preshrink. If you do machine wash bouclé, always wash it in a delicates bag. Remember: Your textured heavyweight may be composed of multiple fibers! Make sure your washing and drying strategies respect the entire composition of the fabric.

Pressing

Bouclé's texture presents difficulties when it comes to pressing. Consider steaming instead, or press from the back of the fabric while cushioning the front to protect the looped texture. Start with low heat and increase until effective, especially if the fabric includes synthetic or metallic fibers. Consider finger-pressing seams during the sewing process.

Tweed is much simpler: Press with high heat if it's wool, but use a low/synthetic heat if it is synthetic or a blend. Use a press cloth. Don't forget that wool will develop shiny patches if it's overpressed.

Pattern Transfer/Marking

Bouclé is most easily marked with chalk or disappearing ink on the reverse of the fabric. Tailor's tacks work well, too, as long as they are in a very contrasting color that won't get lost in the texture of the fabric.

To mark tweed, use chalk or disappearing ink. Highly contrasting tailor's tacks may be necessary if your tweed's pattern is very bright or busy.

Cutting

Bouclé and tweed can both be cut with a regular rotary cutter or pair of sewing shears, but their heavy weight may make it difficult to cut more than one layer at a time.

Both bouclé and tweed may have a directional pattern, and a twill-weave tweed may appear different depending on direction. For those reasons, consider using a with-nap layout for these textured heavyweights.

Pinning and Alternatives

Clips and T-pins work perfectly well for bouclé and tweed fabrics, but you may want longer pins (such as quilting pins) to make sure they don't get lost in bouclé's textured pile.

Interfacing

Sew-in woven or nonwoven interfacing, batiste, and organza all work well as interfacing for bouclé and tweed. Fusible woven or nonwoven is also appropriate for tweed; it should not be used with bouclé because pressing that fabric risks damaging the pile.

Sewing

A 3mm straight stitch using a walking foot, an 80/12 universal machine needle, and all-purpose cotton or polyester thread works well with bouclé. With tweed, use a 3mm straight stitch, a 90/14 universal or denim machine needle, a standard machine foot, and all-purpose or heavy-duty polyester thread.

Both of these fabrics fray, so raw edges must be protected. Bouclé's thick raw edges are best overedged (with a three- or four-thread overlock stitch, pg 138) or bound (pg 73) with a plain (pg 66) or reinforced (pg 100) seam; tweed can be sewn with those options or with a flat-felled (pg 81) or welt (pg 165) seam. For both, a reversible lapped seam (below) is a great option; that seam works particularly well for loosely woven heavyweights, which need their raw edges protected while keeping down bulk.

Tutorial Time: Reversible Lapped Seams

Reversible lapped seams combine the raw-edge protection of an overedge stitch with the minimal bulk of a lapped seam (pg 160).

1. Decide how much overlap you want in your seam; this will determine how much seam allowance you need. After trimming to your desired length, overedge stitch (pg 138) the raw edges on both your pieces of material.

2. Overlap your pieces, aligning at the seamline. Straight stitch on the seamline.

Hems should be faced (pg 124), bound (pg 73), or single folded (pg 85) with a finished raw edge.

For particularly loose-weave bouclé and tweed, you may need to incorporate techniques from Meshes (pg 126) or Nets (pg 128). In particular, you may need to stabilize or use parchment paper when sewing so that your machine has something to grab onto instead of the particularly holey fabrics.

Classic Knits

Knit fabric has more natural stretch than woven fabric. Even among knits, however, there exists large stretch variation. Knits can, therefore, be categorized based on their stretchiness: Sturdy knits have relatively little stretch (up to 25 percent) and are able to hold their shape; stretch knits are much stretchier and have more elasticity, and they can be quite wiggly to work with when compared to their sturdy cousins.

Some generalizations can be made for all knits. The three-thread overlock stitch is a great raw-edge finish for all types of knits and can be used for the actual seam for lightweight and open-weave knits. In medium- and heavyweight knits, the four-thread overlock stitch is great for seaming.

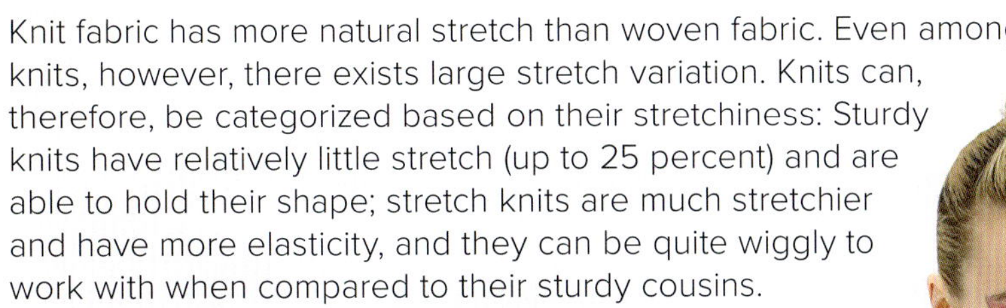

Ice skating garment made from power mesh and spandex performance fabric

GARMENT AND MODELING BY SONJA HILMER
Photo by Robin Ritoss Photography

When to Use a Straight Stitch

Generally, a zigzag stitch—which is naturally stretchy—is best for classic knits and other stretchy fabrics. However, you may opt for a straight stitch when:

- Stitches will be visible, and a zigzag is not desired (as when topstitching).
- Stretch is not desired in a stretchy fabric, such as when sewing a shoulder seam.

If you want a stretchy straight stitch, you can stretch sew (pg 100).

Because of their stretchiness and natural elasticity, knits resist wrinkling much more than woven fabrics do ... but that stretchiness must also be considered during almost every step of the sewing process. Most notably, stretch fabrics work best with different seams, hems, and finishes when compared to woven fabrics, and stretch will affect pattern layout and fit.

✸ QUICK TIP!
Though it may not be obvious, technically, all knits have a direction and both a right and wrong side; the knitting process is not symmetrical! That means that a with-nap pattern layout is appropriate for all knits and care must be taken to label the front and back of pattern pieces. Often, however, the difference in sides and directions is impossible to see, and an on-the-grain layout works fine. Before cutting your knit fabric, take just a moment to inspect your fabric in different lighting conditions. ●

Tutorial Time: Using a Stretch Gauge

When choosing your stretch fabric and its pattern, you'll need to consider both the direction of the stretch and the amount of stretch. Use a stretch gauge to measure the amount of stretch. If your pattern calls for multidirectional stretch, make sure to check all relevant directions on your stretch gauge.

1. Fold your fabric over so that you're stretching with 2 layers of fabric, and place a pin at each end of the interval called for on your stretch gauge; in the pattern pictured, the first pin (black) is at the beginning of the interval and the second (white) is 4″ further along the fold. Hold your fabric and your gauge securely in your left hand.

2. With your right hand, stretch the fabric. If it reaches the "to here" marking, it has enough stretch for your chosen pattern.

Other stretch gauges have percentage stretch markings instead. Stretch your fabric as much as it will allow without distortion or damage; the percentage it reaches is its amount of stretch.

Sturdy Knits

Generally, sturdy knits are less stretchy and elastic than stretch knits. They also usually have more body than those fabrics. Sturdy knits are often used for garments and, especially in tricot's case, to stabilize stretchier knits.

Tricot is densely knitted and doesn't have much natural stretch. It's soft but sturdy. It can have a sheen or a matte finish and can be sheer (but is not always). It works particularly great as interfacing, flatlining, or lining for other, stretchier kinds of knits. Tricot stabilizing tape is perfect for stabilizing seams under stress, like shoulder seams.

Double knit is a two-layer knit that is, therefore, heavier, less stretchy, and generally easier to work with than the slinkier lightweight single knits. **Ponte**, which is often referred to as just double knit, is structured, sturdy, and easy to work with.

Another double knit is **interlock**, which is actually two layers of jersey knit (pg 95) knitted together; for that reason it's sometimes referred to as **double jersey**. It is light- to medium-weight and soft with moderate stretch. It has fine ribs on both the right and wrong sides. Unlike single-knit jersey, interlock does not curl at the edges.

Bishamon *(Noragami)* suit coat made from ponte and lined with gabardine

COSPLAY AND MODELING BY KAITLYN PELTZER-MAGSINO (EOWINTH COSPLAY)
Photo by H.E-X Studios

1. Ponte
2. Interlock
3. Interlock
4. Tricot

Scuba knit is a thick knit that's extremely warm, with a full drape and a slight sheen. It is often confused with neoprene due to their shared sponginess, but scuba knit does not include the foam that defines neoprene and is, therefore, much lighter weight. Scuba knit needs special consideration due to its bulk.

Some scuba knits, pontes, and tricots have spandex added and are consequently much more difficult to sew with. If you're having trouble with your sturdy knits due to added stretch, refer to Stretch Knits (pg 95).

Fabric Preparation and Care

Make sure you prewash your sturdy knit according to its fiber content. Some knits that have been stretched during manufacture or on the bolt may shrink or return to their original shape during a prewash. It also sets you up for success by removing all finishing chemicals that may interfere with your needle and thread.

Pressing

Press sturdy knits with care; their synthetic contents are sensitive to heat. Begin at low heat and increase until an effective press is reached, and use a press cloth to prevent scorching synthetic content. If they have stretch, press instead of iron; the sweeping motions of ironing may distort the knit.

You may find that your scuba knit has been treated with a waterproofing coating. In that case, particular care must be taken to protect the coating. Press on the wrong side of the fabric at as low a temperature as possible, or just finger press. Always use a press cloth.

Pattern Transfer/Marking

Low-stretch knits are easy to mark. Disappearing ink and chalk are great options.

Cutting

Knits can crease permanently. Before cutting into your fabric, inspect it for creases. If a crease doesn't steam out, it's permanent, and pattern pieces should be laid out around the crease.

Even sturdy knits have some mechanical stretch. When laying out and cutting your pattern pieces, take a moment to consider what direction you want your stretch, and then make sure your pattern layout respects that decision. Usually that will mean cutting on the grain along the direction of less stress.

A rotary cutter is best for cutting sturdy knits; if you decide to leave your edges raw, a rotary cutter will result in a very clean edge. Otherwise, fabric shears work well.

Pinning and Alternatives

Interlock, ponte, and tricot are best either clipped or pinned with ballpoint pins. Tricot and lighter versions of these fabrics can be slippery when sewn; pin or clip densely (pg 134) to prevent shifting during sewing.

Because of its very dense structure, scuba knit can be damaged by pins. Clips are a much better option.

In general, be very careful when pinning knits. On knits that ravel, one broken thread will cause a hole that will gradually grow over time. When you can, only pin in the seam allowance and with ballpoint pins.

Interfacing

Fusible interfacing often works well with low-stretch knits, but it must be used with caution; many of these fabrics are damaged by high heat and steam because of their high synthetic fiber content.

Sew-in interfacings are simpler choices. Use stretch or knit interfacing with interlock, ponte, and tricot, and use knit or nonwoven interfacing with scuba knit. Tricot itself is a classic interfacing option, great for providing support to both sturdy and stretch knits.

Sewing

For sturdy knits, use a *new* 70/10 ballpoint machine needle. These fabrics will quickly dull needles; using a new needle with each project will make your sewing much more successful—and less frustrating!

Use a standard machine foot with interlock and ponte. For tricot and scuba knit, a walking foot will help feed the finicky fabrics through the machine. Because of scuba knit's bulk, you may need to reduce the pressure on your machine foot.

A 2.5mm straight or narrow zigzag stitch works great for tricot, interlock, and point, while scuba knit does best with a 3mm straight stitch. If your material has added spandex, err toward a zigzag stitch.

All-purpose—or in the case of scuba knit, heavy-duty—polyester thread will work well with sturdy knits. However, you may consider putting wooly nylon thread in the bobbin to sew them. This thread has some natural stretch, which reduces the chance of breakage. It cannot be put in the needle of a machine.

Tricot resists raveling and interlock and ponte don't ravel at all, so those three sturdy knits can be sewn with very simple seams. Use a plain seam (pg 66), leaving the raw edges free. On a serger, a narrow three-thread overlock or flatlock seam (pg 147) is easy to implement on these fabrics.

Because they're so ravel resistant, hems aren't even necessary! If you do want to finish your edges, mock cover (pg 104), single-fold (pg 85), and double-fold hems (pg 85) are all accessible and acceptable options.

Because of its bulk, scuba should be treated a bit differently. A three-thread flatlock seam (pg 147) or a reinforced seam (pg 100) will create a beautiful result. Avoid seam and hem options that will increase bulk; because scuba knit does not ravel, these options aren't necessary and will only create unsightly bumps. On tight-fitting garments, grade (below) and/or pink (pg 66) the raw edges to reduce the visibility of inner seamlines. For hems, leave raw, bind (pg 73), or implement a mock cover hem (pg 104).

Grading Seam Allowances

Generally, seam allowances are either left at their original width or trimmed down as one to a matching length. However, this will increase the visibility of the raw edges on tight-fitting garments because the two layers create a doubled-up ridge on the right side of the piece. Grading is the solution to that issue! Simply trim each material in the seam allowance to a different width so that the bump feathers out, creating a more subtle imperfection on the front of your piece.

This strategy can be used in any seam, but it is particularly useful not only for tight-fitting garments where the seam allowance will be pressed against the body, but also for enclosed raw edges (such as French and felled) and enclosed seam allowances (such as in collars and lapels).

Vaggie *(Hazbin Hotel)* socks and glovelettes made from printed spandex

DOLL CUSTOMIZATION BY ENCHANTERIUM
Photo by Enchanterium

Stretch Knits

Jersey ranges quite wildly in both weight and stretch, but it most commonly is lightweight with medium stretch. Because it is a weft knit, the right side has V-shaped stitches, and the wrong side shows the loops of the knit. Jersey often includes spandex to increase stretch and elasticity. You may see jersey fabrics referred to as **single jersey** to differentiate them from double jersey fabrics (such as interlock).

Common types of jersey you may see while fabric shopping are:

- **Fine jersey**, the basic lightweight version of jersey.
- **Silk jersey**, a slinky and shiny kind of jersey that is often made from silk.
- **Wool jersey**, which is soft and drapey.

Various weights and fiber contents of jersey

1. Ribbing
2. Swimsuit fabric
3. Ribbing

Extremely stretchy knits are often referred to as spandex or Lycra after the fiber that gives them that trait. I'll call them **swimsuit fabrics**, but they may also be used for bodysuits, skintight dresses and pants, and other athletic gear. It is an extremely stretchy fabric both across and down, and it's great for all body-hugging applications.

Ribbing is named after the obvious ribs on both sides of the fabric. It is a double knit and extremely stretchy. You can buy ribbing specifically made to finish necklines and sleeve openings, although it is also sold as a regular-width fabric.

Fabric Preparation and Care

Like sturdy knits, stretch knits should be prewashed to remove chemicals from the manufacturing process and to return them to their natural shape because they may distort during the manufacturing and retail process. Stretch knits can be machine washed cold. Jersey can be tumble dried, but swimsuit fabric and ribbing should be laid flat to dry. Do not hang knits to dry or even to store them; hanging will distort the knit, leaving stretched-out bubbles in your fabric.

If your stretch knit is a sensitive natural fiber like silk or wool, take care to swatch test washing, drying, and pressing. If you intend to dry-clean your piece, it will need to be steamed (either by you or by a professional) before you construct your piece.

If your knit is cotton, one prewash may not be enough to keep it from shrinking in future launders. Consider washing and drying it three times instead.

If your knit can ravel, overedge (pg 138) the edges before prewashing.

Pressing

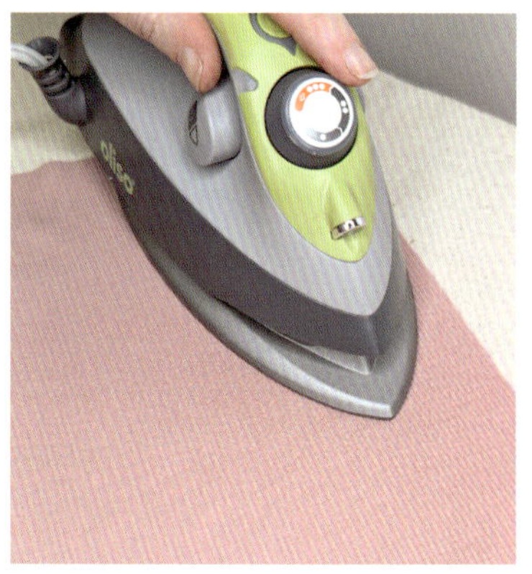

Stretch knits are tricky to press. They have high synthetic content, they can be distorted by aggressive ironing, and those with ribs can be flattened. Luckily, stretch knits should not need as much pressing as wovens; the recoverability provided by their synthetic fibers means they won't wrinkle and crease as easily as those with no stretch.

When you do need to press ribbed knits, press *lengthwise* along the rib; pressing across the ribs may distort them. Ribbing in particular, with its prominent texture, should be treated carefully; consider using a finger presser or seam roller with steam instead of using your actual iron.

Spandex and other synthetic materials—often most, if not all, of the content in stretch knits—are sensitive to heat. Always use a press cloth to prevent scorching. Start at a low heat, and only increase the heat of the iron until pressing is effective.

When pressing seams, begin by pressing the seam while closed. Be careful not to distort the seam or fabric—press, don't iron! While the fabric is still warm, open the seam, steam it, and apply pressure with a clapper, a seam roller, a finger presser, or your own hands. Allow the fabric to cool before working with it again so that the weave doesn't get pulled out of place.

In general, it's best to minimize ironing and pressing these fabrics.

Pattern Transfer/Marking

Knits can both fade and crease permanently. Before cutting fabric, ensure that your laid-out pattern pieces do not cross an undesirable portion of the fabric. If there is a crease from manufacturing or its time in retail, try to steam out the crease. If it doesn't steam out, it's permanent.

Otherwise, marking and pattern placement for stretch knits are fairly simple. Disappearing ink and chalk both mark easily. In very prominent ribbing, tailor's tacks in a contrasting color may be much easier to see than typical marking tools.

Cutting

When placing pattern pieces, consider the stretch of the fabric. Ribbing and jersey are stretchiest across the knit; if you're making a garment, you want the fabric to go around your body in this direction for the best fit and mobility.

Because many knits do not require edge finishing, you may want to leave hems raw. In that case, a rotary cutter will get you the cleanest, nicest-looking cut for the finished piece. Conventional fabric shears are a fine choice as well. Be careful to not let knits hang off your cutting surface as you work on them; gravity will pull the portion of the fabric on the table out of shape and distort your pattern pieces.

If you're creating a bodysuit, swimsuit, undergarment, or something else that will need to stretch around your body, consider marking pattern symbols with a marker or clipping *away* from the seamline instead of clipping in. These seams will be under stress, and clipping in weakens them.

Consider cutting one layer at a time, especially for wiggly slinkies like swimsuit fabric. Use weights or pins pushed through the knit and into cardboard (pg 111). Weighting over the entire piece of fabric, including inside the seam allowances, will greatly reduce the fabric shifting without marring the fabric. If you're still struggling with out-of-control wiggliness, you can apply interfacing or washable starch before cutting to make these fabrics easier to handle.

✷ QUICK TIP!

Don't forget! Knits have right side and wrong side and (sometimes very subtle) directional loops.

To make sure you construct your piece correctly, mark the wrong sides with chalk or a piece of washi tape. When in doubt, stretch your fabric; when stretched, knits will curl toward the right side of the fabric.

Before cutting, inspect your fabric in different lighting conditions; if the directions look different, patterns should be arranged in a with-nap orientation. Otherwise, lay out the pieces to follow your desired direction of stretch. ●

Pinning and Alternatives

Be very careful with pins, especially outside of the seam allowance of your project. Always use ballpoint pins. If you break a thread in the fabric, a hole will be formed that will gradually unravel and will not heal itself as one in a woven textile would. Instead, consider weights (pg 111) when cutting and clips when sewing.

Despite that danger, you do want to pin (or, better yet, clip) densely (pg 134) to reduce shifting during sewing. Basting (pg 99) will achieve this goal even better: You can baste with tape, a glue stick, or contrasting thread to great effect.

Interfacing

Generally, you should default to sew-in interfacing options when creating with stretch knits. The adhesive on fusibles may pull away as your fabric stretches, causing bubbles and reducing the effectiveness of your interfacing. Tricot is almost always a safe option—tricot itself is a knit, so it's adding a similar fabric to provide body and support.

Lightweight knit and nonwoven interfacings can be used when you want part of a knit piece to have little or no stretch (as with buttonholes). Nonwoven interfacing has some all-way stretch and is, therefore, great for facings, which must move with the garment. Knit interfacings only stretch across, so they're better for situations where more sturdiness is needed.

Seams that will be under pressure, like shoulder and crotch seams, may need to be permanently stabilized. You may want to add elastic or interfacing for this task. Edgestitching (pg 105) with a regular stitch length and without stretching as you sew also provides structure; the act of sewing the seam allowance to the body of the piece provides some stabilization. If you do decide to install interfacing, tricot is once again a great choice; in fact, it often comes precut for this purpose.

As always, preshrink interfacings. If you do not, interfacings will shrink and the fabric will not, causing bubbling and rippling in the fabric.

QUICK TIP!
When stitching details—such as decorative topstitching—consider using tearaway stabilizer. This will prevent warped and stretched fibers underneath your stitches. •

Sewing

Sewing with stretch knits is tricky; set yourself up for success! If your machine needs it, clean and lubricate it. Consider having it serviced, if it's about that time in the schedule. Synthetic fibers leave lint; frequently clean the bobbin case and plate to prevent issues. Shears, rotary cutters, needles, and pins should also be wiped clean when using knits; lint buildup can affect their performance, too.

Start with a 70/10 ballpoint needle for jersey, a 75/11 stretch needle for swimsuit fabric, and an 80/12 ballpoint needle for ribbing. That's just where to begin, though; stretch knits are finicky when it comes to needles, and experimentation may be necessary. If you're getting skipped stitches, change to a universal, stretch, or ballpoint needle. The size of the needle can also make a big difference—consider moving up or down one size and trying again. Don't forget that synthetic fibers dull needles and an old needle could be the culprit!

Use all-purpose polyester thread for stretch knits; a regular weight for medium- and heavyweight fabrics, and a fine thread for lightweight knits (such as slinky jerseys and swimsuit fabrics). Higher-end thread may also grant better results; nicer thread behaves better with synthetic fibers and stretchy fabrics.

Use a 1.5mm zigzag stitch with jersey and swimsuit fabrics and a 2.5mm zigzag stitch with ribbing.

Roller feet, walking feet, and reducing foot pressure will all help with fabric shifting, which is a common frustration when sewing with stretch knits. If your seams ripple during sewing, reduce the presser foot pressure.

Consider basting (pg 99) your seams before you sew to reduce stretch during sewing. A glue stick or basting tape works well for this purpose. You can also sandwich your fabric between layers of tissue paper (pg 155) or use tearaway stabilizer.

Tutorial Time: Basting

Basting serves several purposes. It can reduce stretch during sewing, making for a cleaner seam. It can prevent shifting on slippery and delicate fabrics. It enables fitting before construction—very handy for materials on which needle holes are permanent.

Unless they're being used for fitting, basting stitches should generally be within the seam allowance to avoid damaging the body of the piece.

To machine baste, set your conventional machine to a very long stitch length and sew. Similarly, a line of very long hand stitches secures the material for much easier handling.

You can also use a glue stick, basting spray, or basting tape to baste. These products come with the advantage that they work right up to the seamline, making it easier to fit without removing stitches. They can be washed out after construction is complete.

Similarly, you may find that your fabric curls and rolls as you work with it, making it difficult to get even stitching lines. If you run into this issue, use spray starch before sewing; then wash it out when construction is complete. Basting with a glue stick (above) will also work to reduce curling.

And that's not the last reason to consider basting when working with stretch knits! Many stretch stitch methods have multiple threads and may even cut the fabric, making mistakes costly to repair. Plus, pieces made with these fabrics are often very closely fitted. For those reasons, consider basting your piece to confirm fitting before committing to a final stretchy stitch. Basting for this reason can be done on a conventional machine with a long stretch stitch.

Because many stretch knits don't ravel, choosing your type of seam doesn't need to be complicated; a plain seam (pg 66) is perfectly acceptable. Of course, if you want to have a stretchy seam, you need to use a stretchy stitch. A short and narrow zigzag stitch is inherently stretchy. You can also use a stretched straight stitch: Sew a regular stitch, but stretch the fabric as you sew (pg 100).

Tutorial Time: Stretch Sewing

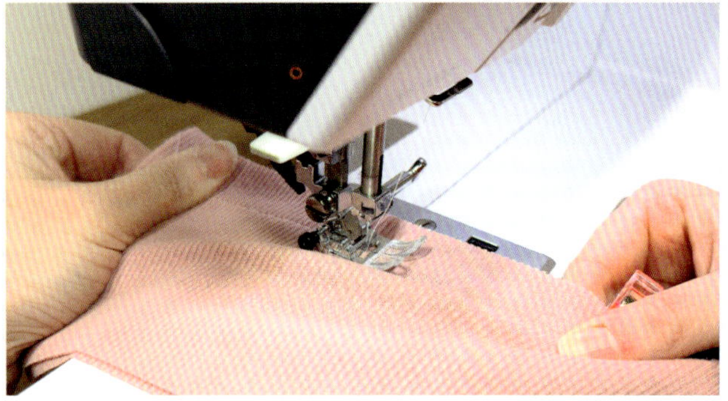

When stretch sewing, stretch the fabric with both hands as it feeds through your machine. Importantly, do not *pull* the fabric through; you want the feed dogs to control the fabric's movement while you control its amount of stretch. This technique creates a naturally stretchy seam, even when sewing with a straight stitch (which does not usually have built-in stretch). Stretch sewing can result in ripply seams; make sure to practice on a scrap piece of your material, and consider only using the technique when a zigzag stitch won't work (such as when topstitching).

Because it is both stretchy and reinforced, a twin-needle stitch (ballpoint and at least 2mm apart) is a great option for both hems (creating a mock cover hem, pg 104) and seams. You can also create a reinforced seam (below) with one needle: Just sew two lines of stitching. Alternatively, use a conventional sewing machine to sew your seam and then protect raw edges by sewing them together with a zigzag or three-thread overlock on your serger. With all these methods, you'll get both stretch and security.

Tutorial Time: Reinforced Seams

Reinforced seams are very easy to implement, and they not only protect the seamline but also reduce fraying.

Sew a plain seam (pg 66), and then sew a second line of stitches in your seam allowance.

This can be any combination of stitches; you can even combine a serger and a conventional machine to create a reinforced seam with protected raw edges. Just make sure to use stitches that work well for your fabric and project—two rows of narrow zigzag stitches will work well for a cotton jersey, for example.

Overlock machines are great for sewing knits. Use a three- or four-thread overlock stitch; these options work for seams, edge finishes, and hems. Increase the width of the stitch with the weight of the fabric. Utilize the differential feed feature (pg 48) or ease the fabric through the serger (below).

Tutorial Time: Easing Fabric through the Machine

When easing fabric through the machine, you want to allow the feed dogs to do 100 percent of the work. This means maintaining a looseness in front of the machine. This technique prevents you from unintentionally stretching the fabric as you sew.

A flatlock seam (pg 147) is a bit of an unconventional choice, because it results in a visible row of stitches. But it's a flat and stretchy seam, making it perfect for athletic wear in particular.

Many stretch knits, including jerseys, don't ravel and, therefore, usually don't need to be hemmed. However, you may want the look of a hem or to protect the fabric or the skin. The simplest solution, other than leaving an edge raw, is a hairline hem (pg 122). Blind hems (pg 84) also work wonderfully on knits. Single and double folds (pg 85) are classic decorative finishes for knit hems, and they have the added benefit of adding some structure to the edge.

Binding (pg 73), especially with the same fabric as the main body of your creation, is a common technique for hemming stretch knits. If your bound hem will be under stress or will need to stretch, make sure to cut the binding in the direction with the most stretch and use a zigzag stitch.

Prevent rippled hems and seams by reducing the presser foot pressure. You may also get rippled hems if you stretch while you sew; unlike seams, you should not stretch-sew hems.

QUICK TIP!

If you're struggling to get a seam started without wiggly lightweight fabric bunching or getting pulled into the machine, pull slightly on the thread tails, do not backstitch, and then knot or sew in the tails after the seam is complete. Alternatively, begin sewing a few inches into the seamline so that the cut edge of the fabric is not under the presser foot. You can come back to that section once the bulk of the seamline is complete and, therefore, much less wiggly.

Sweater Knits

Sweater knit fabrics are like a home-knit sweater! They can be medium- to heavyweight, are napped, and ravel considerably and immediately. Because sweater knits are both stretchy and loosely woven, they need particularly careful consideration when sewing. If you're having trouble with the stretchiness of your sweater knit, consider the advice in Stretch Knits (pg 95); sweater knits feature all the difficulties of stretch knits, with the addition of (sometimes very prominent) holes!

The *Rogue Sweater,* named for its white fiber flecks among the brown yarn inspired by its crafter's favourite X-Men character of the same name, is made from 100 percent recycled polyester fiber yarn.

GARMENT AND MODELING BY EMILY
Photo by Emily

1. Loose weave
2. Tight weave
3. Loose weave

Fabric Preparation and Care

Sweater knits should be hand washed and then laid flat to dry; even more so than other knits, sweater knits should never be hung to dry. Generally, a gentle wash will be enough to remove any wrinkles. If your fabric has become particularly distorted (or if your finished piece needs shaping), you also may want to block (or, in the case of synthetic sweater knit, "kill") your sweater knit fabric in order to return it to its original shape ... or to encourage it to take a specific new one.

Tutorial Time: Blocking and Killing

There are various methods for blocking; some are more suitable for different materials or projects. The one described here is most suited for flat projects—like unsewn fabric.

1. Let your fabric soak in warm water until it is saturated. Remove your material from the water; then lay it flat on a towel. Roll it up to remove all excess water.

2. On a flat piece of foam or corrugated cardboard, pin your material in the shape you want it to remember. If you're an experienced fiber artist, you may have a dedicated blocking mat and blocking pins for this step. Leave it to dry completely.

To kill a synthetic sweater knit, you need to use heat; moisture alone won't do the job as it does for wool, cotton, and other natural fibers. Lay flat and pin your material *first;* then carefully steam. Don't melt the fibers entirely! You want to heat them just enough so that they become pliable and, therefore, remember the shape they're pinned into.

Pressing

Sweater knits should be pressed as little as possible on the lowest heat possible. The blocking process should eliminate any wrinkles.

Pattern Transfer/Marking

You may be able to mark tighter-weave sweater knits with conventional marking tools—chalk works particularly well. Mark chunky, holey sweater knits with contrasting tailor's tacks, thread tracing, or safety pins.

Cutting

Because chunky sweater knits tend to shift, distort, and ravel during sewing, consider adding a large seam allowance to your pattern pieces. Always cut in one layer to get a more accurate result. As with other stretch knits, never let your sweater knits hang off of your cutting surface; gravity will pull the fabric, ruining your cutting. Cut using a with-nap layout.

Pinning and Alternatives

Tightly woven sweater knits can be pinned with conventional long pins, but most sweater knits will be better pinned with sewing clips or safety pins. Conventional pins may be lost in thick yarns or may not be able to secure the fabric due to the size of the holes in the knit. Secure densely (pg 134) to help mitigate shifting during sewing.

Be very careful to not break any threads while pinning or otherwise securing sweater knits. One broken thread will ravel into an ever-growing hole. Pin in the seam allowance and only with ballpoint pins.

Interfacing

Sew-in knit or stretch interfacing is best for denser sweater knits. However, interfacing will be visible through the holes of very loosely woven chunky knits; these fabrics are better supported with an underlayer of batiste or organza.

Sewing

Sew sweater knits with a 90/14 ballpoint needle, a 2.5mm narrow zigzag stitch, and all-purpose polyester thread. A walking or roller foot helps feed the layers of thick fabric through your machine. Consider reducing the pressure on the foot so that there's more room for fabric to feed through.

For seams, a plain seam (pg 66) using a four- or three-thread overlock stitch (pg 70) or a wide zigzag will keep the knit from raveling.

For hems, consider a mock cover hem (below) or double-fold hem (pg 85). A twin-needle stitch or a faux twin-needle stitch—two lines of zigzag stitching that together create a reinforced stitched seam—provides both strength and a decorative element to your hems.

Tutorial Time: Mock Cover Hems

Mock cover hems and stitches use a twin needle on a conventional machine to create two lines of stitching at once.

1. Prepare your hem as usual. Because a mock cover stitch does not cover raw edges, you may want to overedge (pg 138) or otherwise protect your raw edge before folding and pressing.

2. Sew along your hem's seamline using the twin needle.

The same strategy can be used to create a plain seam (pg 66) using the twin-needle stitch. Importantly, take care to consider which needle you want exactly on your seamline, or your seam may be off by the width between your twin needles.

When sewing sweater knits, it's important that they don't get distorted. Consider sewing with a tissue paper sandwich (pg 155), or ease the fabric (pg 101) through your conventional machine. When using a serger, use the differential feed feature, if it's available.

Because sweater knits are such a loose and stretchy knit, they may require stabilization in high-stress seams, such as shoulders. This can be done by adding a stabilizing material like bias binding or elastic; edgestitching (below) the seams also adds strength and stability by attaching the seam allowance to the body of the fabric.

Tutorial Time: Edgestitching a Seam

Edge stitching is a type of topstitching that is extremely close to the edge. It's used for many situations—for strengthening seams, creating very delicate topstitching, as detailing on specialty seams and hems, and more.

1. Consider switching to an edge-stitch foot; if you do, align the guide on the foot with your sewn line to prepare for a perfectly straight line of stitches.

2. Sew very closely to the seam with a straight stitch.

Delicates

Delicate fabrics are tough to work with, not only because many of them are actually delicate, but also because they're often translucent, slippery, full of holes, or a combination of all three. Sheers almost float off the work surface, making it difficult to cut them, and inner construction methods are visible on the right side. Sleeks and shiny fabrics are slinky and slippery and clearly show marks on their delicate surfaces. Meshes and nets, which are both peppered with holes in the weave, are tough to pin and sew because of the amount of air in their makeup.

Spencer and petticoat, based on the 1821 painting *Jeanne Gonin* by Jean-Auguste-Dominique Ingres, made from silk taffeta and lined with linen

COSTUME AND MODELING BY IN THE LONG RUN DESIGNS
Photo by In the Long Run Designs

Sheers

The fabrics in this section are lightweight to the point of floatiness, are generally semi-transparent, and drape delicately. Historically, these fabrics have been made from silk or cotton, but now they are commonly blended or entirely composed of synthetic materials.

Cambric, a plain weave, is a soft and fairly crisp fabric historically made of linen or cotton. **Batiste**, which is a kind of cambric, has a slight sheen and is often printed. **Lawn** is a slightly heavier version of the fabric; it is crisp and dense and mimics linen. All three fabrics may or may not be translucent; if they aren't, refer to Lightweight and Medium-weight Wovens (pg 63) for sewing tips.

Dress made with a sheer polyester material found at a crafting thrift store; decorative rope was used to connect the dress at the top.

GARMENT AND MODELING BY CHARLIE NEBE (THE STITCHERY)
Photo by Natalie Jones

Cambric and Its Cousins

Cambric is an old textile; its name has been translated and its makeup has been modified over hundreds of years. In American English, batiste and chambray are varieties of cambric and lawn is a very similar textile, but the exact definitions of the four have become so muddled and confused that their names are basically interchangeable with each other. If you're looking for a very specific textile, especially for historical re-creations, be sure to inspect fabric descriptions and purchase swatches.

1. Organza
2. Chiffon
3. Batiste
4. Habutai silk (China silk)

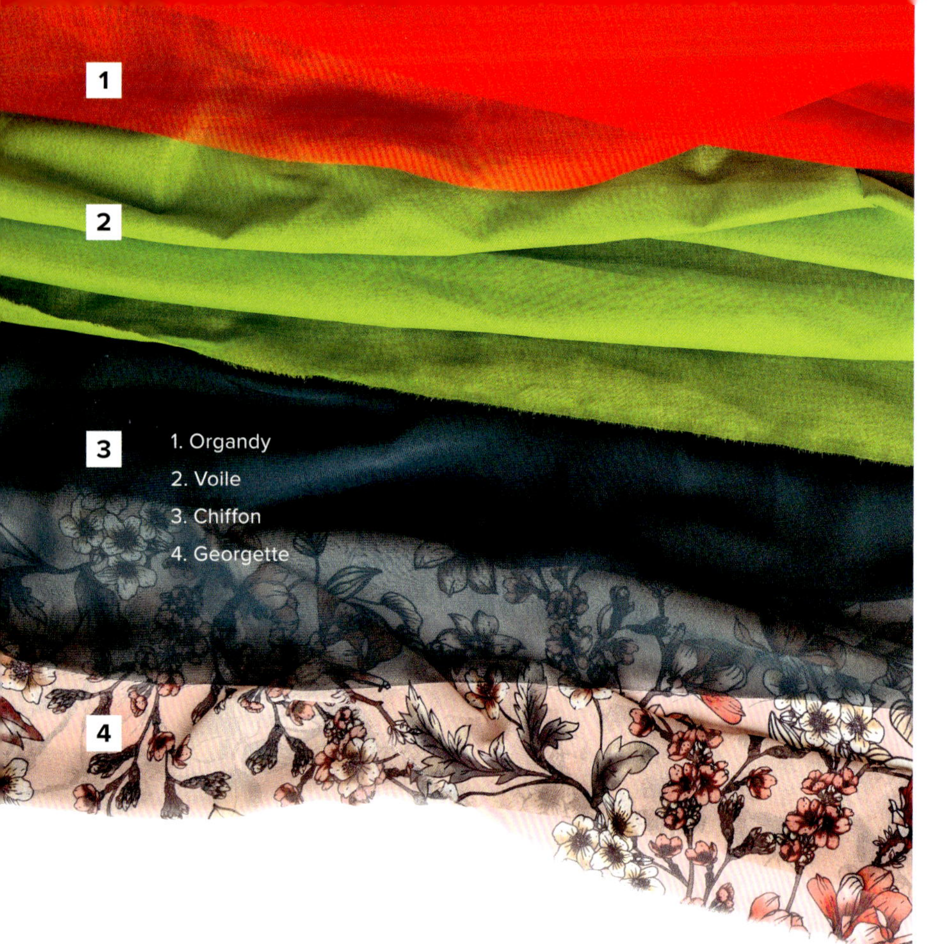

1. Organdy
2. Voile
3. Chiffon
4. Georgette

Chiffon is plain-woven with twisted threads, which gives it a slightly rough feel but also adds a shimmery finish. It has a soft hand and drape, especially when compared to organza, organdy, and tulle.

Georgette is very similar to chiffon, but the increased twists and alternating yarns in the weave give it a crepe texture. It has a matte finish and a soft hand and drape.

Habutai silk, also known as China silk, is a plain-weave silk fabric that's fairly inexpensive compared to other genuine silks. Not all habutais are sheer; if yours is not, treat it like a lightweight woven (pg 63). Other habutais are very slinky; if yours is slipping around on you, treat it like a sleek (pg 116).

Organza and **organdy** are similar fabrics that were historically made from silk and cotton, respectively. They are smooth, stiff, lightweight, and transparent. Now, they are both frequently made from polyester, making them basically interchangeable.

Voile is very lightweight and ranges from semi-sheer to sheer. It is soft and smooth and made from cotton or a cotton blend.

✸ QUICK TIP!

Remember: Silk is a material, not a weave. When sewists refer to "silk fabric," they may be thinking of a silk sheer or silk sleek (pg 116), many of which are often (or have been historically) made from silk. ●

Because these fine fabrics can be made of silk, cotton, linen, synthetics, or a combination of two or more of them, it's essential to either know your fabric's composition or do extensive swatch tests before working with it. A silk chiffon, for example, is going to react to heat much differently than a polyester one.

1. Lawn
2. Organza
3. Voile

Fabric Preparation and Care

Many of these fabrics cannot be machine washed; you may need to carefully hand wash the fabric. For those with loose plain weaves, like voile, consider overedging (pg 138) or stitching along the non-selvedge edges before washing to prevent excessive fraying of the weave.

If you prewash your silk (or have it pretreated at the dry cleaner's) you won't have to worry about water spotting (pg 10).

Cotton cambric, batiste, lawn, and voile should be prewashed; they will shrink. Polyester and other synthetic versions of these fabrics should be prewashed to remove chemicals used during the manufacturing process.

Care depends on the fiber content of the fabric; many delicates are dry-clean only. Pay attention to the manufacturer's recommendations and test a swatch if you'll be washing, especially if you intend to machine wash and dry.

Generally, organdy, cambric, batiste, lawn, and non-silk chiffon, georgette, and organza can be machine washed cold or warm on the gentle cycle and laid flat to dry, but silk and wool varieties of these materials should have particular care taken with them; they may need to be dry-cleaned or hand washed. Voile should be washed on the gentle cycle with cold water and laid flat to dry.

Habutai silk is a special case: It is washable, but it changes after washing, becoming softer. This will affect seams, so if you intend to wash your habutai silk, it's important to prewash it. Do this using the gentle cycle with cold or warm water, and tumble dry on low heat.

Pressing

Always use a press cloth on sheers. Using silk organza as a press cloth with these fabrics is particularly valuable; it is see-through and tolerates heat well, so you can be careful with your delicate fabrics. Even when using a press cloth, do not linger or use a lot of pressure. You want to minimize risks of damaging your delicate fabric.

Before steaming, always swatch to make sure your fabric is not susceptible to water spots.

Otherwise, press sheers according to their fiber content; starting at a low heat and increasing until pressing is effective is always a safe bet (and don't forget to press a swatch first!). Cotton and linen should be steamed with high heat, wool with medium heat and no steam, synthetic with low to medium heat and steam, silk with medium heat and no steam.

Because they're so delicate, pressing seam allowances can cause ridges on the outer fabric. Prevent these by finger pressing or using cardboard between the seam allowance and main fabric piece (pg 72).

Pattern Transfer/Marking

Chalk, disappearing ink, and thread are all suitable marking tools for delicate sheers. However, a tracing wheel (pg 110) is also a great option because it's a particularly delicate technique; when used without transfer paper, no marks are made on the fabric itself.

Tutorial Time: Using a Tracing Wheel

A tracing wheel uses a special kind of coated paper and a tracing tool to transfer marks onto fabric without cutting pattern pieces. When used without the coated paper, tracing tools leave subtle, gentle indents in the fabric, which can then be reinforced with a different marking method.

1. Place your fabric on a cutting mat, and then lay the transfer paper coated side down (facing your fabric) on top. Finally, lay down your pattern piece.

2. Gently roll your tracing wheel along the lines you want to transfer. You can also use another tool, like a sculpting implement. Just make sure to test first!

3. Remove your pattern and transfer paper, revealing your transferred marks.

To use a tracing tool on delicate or textured fabrics that may be damaged by transfer paper, follow the exact same process without laying down the paper. Just be sure to mark or cut your pieces before the indentations left by the wheel fall out!

Cutting

Generally sheers should be cut on the straight grain, but many patterns calling for delicate fabrics will require the fabric to be cut on the bias; make sure to respect this requirement, because drapey fabrics are particularly affected by the stretch that bias provides. Additionally, make sure to not let the fabric hang off a table when cutting or transferring pattern pieces! The fabric will warp out of shape, distorting your cut pieces.

When laying out, consider punching pins vertically into a piece of cardboard or foam (below) within the seam allowance. Alternatively, use pattern weights distributed all over the fabric when cutting to prevent shifting underneath the pattern pieces. Pins in the body of the fabric will mar delicate fabrics.

Tutorial Time: Pinning Vertically and Weighting Patterns

Pinning vertically and distributing weights when cutting both achieve the same goal: They secure the fabric, preventing it from slipping around during the cutting process. These techniques are ideal for slinky, slippery, and very lightweight materials.

Pin pieces vertically through your pattern piece and fabric into a piece of corrugated cardboard or foam. Instead of just the pattern and fabric having connection points, the pins will secure both layers to a solid surface—your cardboard or foam. Only use this strategy in the seam allowances or if your material won't be damaged by pins.

Alternatively, weight the fabric evenly, across the entire material. Weighing the center of your fabric—not just the seam allowances—will have the added benefit of gravity to help prevent fabric from slipping around during the marking and cutting processes.

Make sure you use very sharp shears or a rotary cutter with a new blade. You don't want to struggle to cut this fabric; a dull blade may damage the fabric, or (in the case of scissors) the fabric may get caught between the blades of your sheers without cutting at all.

If your sheer is a particularly slippery variety, cut it on a grippy fabric, such as one with a nap. This will prevent the fabric from moving around as much. This strategy works only when using scissors—a rotary cutter will just cut through both layers of fabric. If you have serrated-edge shears, use those; they're specially made for cutting slippery fabric.

If you find that the fabric is shifting too much and causing you great trouble with cutting or sewing, consider starching. Note that this is only an option if the finished piece will be washable, because the starch will need to be removed after construction. Make sure to straighten the grain of the fabric before starching.

✸ QUICK TIP!

If you fold your fabric, the selvages should meet in a straight line. This indicates that the fabric's grain has not been distorted during prewashing, from being on the bolt, as a result of the manufacturing process, or another reason. If your fabric is off-grain, it's very important to straighten it before transferring patterns, cutting, starching, or interfacing.

To straighten the grain of a fabric, first fold the piece horizontally so that the selvages align. Standing with the fabric, wiggle it and manipulate it until all *draglines* (large, bulbous wrinkles, which in this case indicate an off-kilter grain) have fallen out.

If this strategy doesn't work, place the fabric onto a large surface. Stretch along the bias, and then fold to check if the fabric's grain is now straight. Repeat as needed.

Finally, heat may be necessary. Fold your fabric into quarters with the selvage and a straight edge meeting. Beginning a few inches inside the folded corner, steam or press toward the raw edges. Carefully manipulate the fabric as you go to encourage it into its intended shape. Do not press over the folded sections; you want to avoid creating creases that will need to be pressed out later. •

Pinning and Alternatives

With sheers, always use fine pins or sewing clips to prevent snags. Alternatively, hand baste. Basting (pg 99) is a particularly good option with the more slippery sheers, because it will prevent the fabric from shifting during sewing. Plus, these fabrics are so delicate that pinning and ripping out seams can cause damage. Hand basting or otherwise securing seams allows you to confirm fit before committing to a row of stitches you may otherwise need to rip out.

Interfacing

Consider interfacing carefully; because they're see-through, sheers usually cannot be interfaced with normal interfacing. Experiment to find one that complements your sheer, both in color and in opacity. Self-fabric or organza may be the safest choice, but sheer nonwoven sew-in is a fine choice, too.

Fusibles, in general, are not ideal for sheer projects. They may cause bubbling on delicate fabrics, and the adhesive on fusibles commonly shows through to the front of the fabric.

Be particularly sure to preshrink interfacings and linings. If they shrink and the fashion fabric doesn't, the thin outer fabric will pucker dramatically.

Sewing

When sewing delicate fabrics, use a fine thread and a small needle. If your thread or needle are too large, your fabric may pucker or your stitches may skip. Start with a 70/10 microtex for organdy, organza, voile, and habutai silk; a 70/10 universal or microtex for georgette; a 60/8 microtex for chiffon; or a 70/10 universal for cambric, batiste, and lawn. Always make sure to have a new sharp needle when sewing with delicate fabrics, because many of them damage easily.

Generally, match your thread content to your fabric: Use polyester thread with synthetic fabrics and cotton with natural fabrics. More specifically, the best thread composition for sheers depends on the quality of your material and the stress your seams will be under. Use cotton thread with expensive fabrics; the cotton thread will break under pressure instead of ruining the fabric. Polyester thread has some elasticity, which is nice to give seams and hems a small amount of give, but it may cause your fabric to pucker during sewing. You may also consider machine embroidery thread or clear thread; machine embroidery thread is delicate and, therefore, will be less visible on translucent pieces, and, of course, clear thread will disappear almost entirely.

If you are using a straight stitch with these delicate fabrics, consider a straight stitch foot and straight stitch plate. The smaller opening in the foot and plate prevents delicate fabrics from getting pulled into the machine. Because of that small opening, however, other stitch types are not possible. A 2.5mm straight stitch is a great starting point, with or without the straight-stitch foot and plate.

If you do not have a straight-stitch foot or are not using a straight stitch, consider using a walking foot. That tool will help evenly feed the fabric through the machine, preventing slippery delicates from shifting during the sewing process.

When sewing slippery fabrics, hold the thread tails to encourage the fabric to feed through the machine. These fabrics may also get caught in your machine as you begin and end lines of stitching; prevent that from happening by starting and ending your line of stitching with the fabric sandwiched in tissue paper (pg 155). You can then tear the tissue away when you're finished.

Use taut sewing (below). Alternatively, a serger's differential feed will easily feed the fabric through your machine. Consider increasing the foot pressure on both your serger and conventional sewing machine so that the foot has more grip on the thin fabric. If the material puckers during sewing, try reducing the tension on your machine.

Tutorial Time: Taut Sewing

To taut sew, hold your fabric both in front of and behind where it feeds into the machine. Importantly, do not stretch the fabric; you want to hold it taut but not distort it. You also need to make sure you don't pull the fabric through the machine. Instead, let the feed dogs do all the work as you keep the layers taut.

Thread is put on a spool under tension, which means it releases some of that tension when sewing. On very delicate fabrics, even this small amount of contraction can cause ripples in the seamline. If you sew with your fabric taut, the thread and fabric can contract together, reducing or eliminating that rippling.

Taut sewing also encourages the fabric to feed through the machine evenly; there is less chance of the layers slipping out of place.

Facings will show through to the right side of translucent materials. To finish edges, use binding (pg 73) instead. To line, use a full lining or flatlining (pg 141). Flatlining will hide internal details (like facings and seam finishings) but will take away the translucency of the piece.

Enclosed and delicate seams are great for translucent materials. French (pg 114) and rolled-edge (pg 132) seams enclose the seam allowances so that raw edges are not visible from the right side of the piece. Overedge (with narrow zigzag or two- or three-thread overlock stitches, pg 138) and hairline (pg 122) seams sew right up to the edge of the fabric, so that there is no raw edge to show through to the front. Both options protect raw edges on fabrics prone to fraying.

Tutorial Time: French Seams and Mock French Seams

French and mock French seams enclose raw edges, creating a seam that's both delicate and protective.

1. With *wrong* sides together, sew a line of stitches outside of your seamline (within the seam allowance). These can be straight, overlock, zigzag, or wrapped stitches.

2. Clip your seam allowances up to the line of stitches you just created.

3. Press your seam open, and then fold the fabric right sides together. Press the fold.

4. Sew another line of straight stitches, this time along your seamline.

5. Press the resulting seam to one side.

A mock French seam results in a similar lightweight seam with enclosed raw edges, but it can be simpler because it doesn't rely on sewing wrong sides together first (and, therefore, can be executed on a piece that has already been fitted or constructed).

1. With right sides together, sew a straight stitch along your seamline.

2. Press the seam open, and then fold and press the seam allowances inward, *toward* the seam, so that their raw edges meet at the line of sewing.

3. Close the fabric along the seam so that the right sides are together, joining the folded seam allowances. Pin or clip.

4. Edgestitch (pg 105).

5. Press the seam allowance to one side.

Options for hems include overedging (pg 138), a rolled hem (pg 132), and binding (pg 73). A double-fold hem (pg 85) or a hairline hem (pg 122) will also work and result in topstitched detailing. Use taut sewing (pg 113) and/or a differential feed when hemming.

With sheer, delicate fabrics, it's even more important than usual to test buttonholes and other stitched details. Make sure that your machine, your fabric, and your interfacing can all handle the delicate nature of the fabric. Consider using tearaway stabilizer on buttonholes and other stitched details to support the fabrics while you stitch.

A lesbian pride suit made of a silk satin stripe with custom-printed polyester crepe lining of Sappho's poetry

SUIT AND MODELING BY MAEVE FOLEY
Photo by Ben Jennings

Shinies and Sleeks

The fabrics in the shiny and sleek category are dense, slinky, and smooth. Most were historically made of silk but are now available in polyester and other synthetic versions.

Shiny and sleek fabrics are particularly difficult to sew with because of their combination of slipperiness and delicacy. Collectively, they're often referred to as satins; many of the fabrics colloquially referred to as satins are actually satin weave (pg 17) fabrics, while others share characteristics with classic satins and are, therefore, often lumped together in common parlance.

CONFUSING TOPIC!

Confusingly, fabrics are often labeled as bridal satin, lining satin, simply satin, or other ambiguous names for shiny and wiggly fabrics. But remember, satin is:

- A weave
- A category of fabric
- A descriptor

But satin is *not:*

- A specific fabric

In the context of this book, treat anything labeled as satin or satin lining as you would *charmeuse.* If it's cheap, it's almost certainly 100 percent polyester. If you're looking for a specific fiber content, make sure to order swatches and carefully inspect fabric labels! ●

1. Sateen
2. Charmeuse
3. Generic satin lining

1. Shantung
2. Silk dupioni
3. Polyester dupioni
4. Polyester taffeta

Some satins are matte, crepe, or both on the reverse. This "wrong side" is beautiful in its own right and can be used as the fashion fabric for a piece. The contrasting sides are particularly useful for embellishing each other, as with trim or binding.

Charmeuse has the classic satin structure of shiny on one side and matte on the other, but a different ratio of over/under yarns during the weaving process gives it a fluid and slinky drape. It is lightweight and historically made of silk. **Crepe-backed satin** has a crepe reverse, while **duchesse satin** is medium-weight with a slightly duller finish and firmer hand than a charmeuse.

Sateen is the (historically) cotton version of satins; now, all satins and sateens can be made from synthetic materials. Cotton is often combined with spandex to create a stretch cotton sateen, which may be more matte than other fabrics in this section (making it easier to work with!).

Taffeta is light- to medium-weight, structured and stiff, and delicate. It is smooth and has an easily recognizable sound and sheen.

Dupioni has a distinctive slubby finish with a sheen. It has a crisp drape, is soft, and will fray easily and excessively. **Shantung** is a very similar fabric, but is lighter weight and less slubby.

QUICK TIP!

Some satins are double-faced, which means they have been manufactured in two layers. They may be the same or different on each side; they're often created so that both sides of the fabric are the shiny "right side" of the satin weave. Because double-faced satins are double-layered, they drape heavier than regular single-layer satin fabrics do.

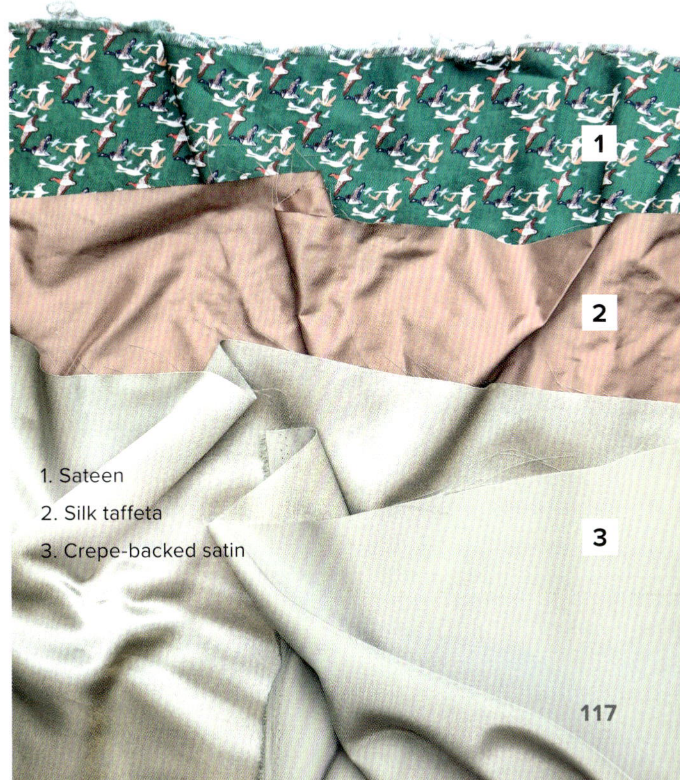

1. Sateen
2. Silk taffeta
3. Crepe-backed satin

Fabric Preparation and Care

Most shiny fabrics should be pretreated the same as they will be laundered. The silk versions of taffeta, shantung, satin, charmeuse, and dupioni are best left to the experts: dry cleaners.

Polyester versions of these fabrics can be washed in cold or warm water using the gentle cycle and then machine dried on low heat. Charmeuse should be hung to dry, and shantung should be laid flat to dry.

Shiny fabrics may be dulled by the washing process. Of course, that may be exactly the look you want! Just make sure you wash and dry a swatch before committing to your big piece, to make sure the finished sheen is the one you want.

Because many of the shinies fray dramatically, consider overedging (pg 138) along the edges of your fabric before sending them through their prewash cycle.

Creases in taffeta are very hard to get out. Always hang to store both the fabric and your completed pieces to prevent the creases from forming in the first place.

Pressing

Iron shinies carefully. Many of these fabrics have a low heat tolerance—especially the synthetic and synthetic blends. Always start by pressing a scrap with your iron on a low heat setting; increase it gradually until you hit an efficient temperature. Always use a press cloth; silk organza is a great option as a press cloth because it tolerates heat and allows for accurate pressing, because it's translucent. On fabrics that have a matte side (charmeuse, sateen, taffeta, and satin), press from that side of the fabric to protect the sheen.

QUICK TIP!
Shiny fabrics, especially taffeta, may be affected by water spots (pg 10) when washing or steaming. Prewashing the entire piece of fabric removes this risk, because the entire piece becomes a "stained" water spot! Of course, the fabric will be changed by this process—test with a scrap first to make sure the water-spotted version works for your project. •

When pressing seams open, prevent pressing ridges into the right side of your fabric by placing a piece of cardboard between your seam allowance and main fabric (pg 72). You can also consider finger pressing or roller pressing these delicate fabrics.

Pattern Transfer/Marking

Shiny fabrics are generally easy to mark, but care must be taken because they're delicate and may be affected by the water or heat needed to remove those markings. To that end, make sure you can remove chalk and disappearing ink before moving on to your larger pieces of fabric.

Tailor's tacks, thread tracing, or a tracing wheel (pg 110) may be the safest options, but care must also be taken to not mar the fabric with these strategies—you risk pricks and snags when you use sharp tools.

Cutting

When working with shiny slinkies, use weights distributed across the entire piece of fabric (as opposed to just in the seam allowance or around the edge of pattern pieces, pg 111) instead of pins. This eliminates the risk that a pin will snag the fabric and greatly reduces the ridiculous shifting that shiny fabrics do during the pattern layout and cutting process. When weights don't make sense, always use extra-fine pins, which are less likely to snag. Never let fabric hang off the edge of your cutting surface during the laying out and cutting process; the weight of the fabric will distort the grain of the fabric.

Cut with a rotary cutter or a sharp pair of bent-handle shears. Serrated edge shears are specifically made for these slinky kinds of fabric. Make sure they're very sharp, and wipe them frequently to prevent synthetic debris buildup, which dulls the blades.

Wipe down scissors frequently to prevent debris buildup.

If you choose to cut with shears, consider covering your cutting surface with a textured surface: a large piece of thick fleece, placed as a tablecloth, works wonderfully. The pile on the fleece will grip onto the slinky fabric, greatly reducing how much it moves around during pattern placing and cutting. A large piece of cork works, too, and it comes with the advantage that you don't have to worry about cutting through it.

If you're really struggling with the slippery nature of shinies during the cutting process, consider using starch, which can be washed out after construction (or, even, just after cutting). Swatch test before starching, and be sure to straighten the grain of your shiny fabric before stiffening so that you don't cut off-grain.

If you choose to cut your shiny fabric on the bias or if your pattern calls for it, make extra sure to respect this requirement. Slinky, drapey fabrics are particularly affected by the natural stretch on the bias. If you cut one piece of skirt on the bias and another on the straight grain, for example, it will show!

Otherwise, all fabrics with a shine should be laid out using a with-nap layout. The shine will almost certainly look different depending on the direction. Cut on a single layer, both to ensure you're respecting the nap and to help with the shifty slinkiness.

Pinning and Alternatives

As mentioned, slinky fabrics are particularly prone to snags; even hangnails and rough calluses can snag delicate fabric! Only pin in seam allowances with fine pins.

Interfacing

Be very careful when choosing the interfacing for your shiny, slinky fabrics. Fusibles are fine, but they may cause bubbling and may be tougher to adhere to fabrics sensitive to heat. Using self-fabric interfacing or another lightweight woven (like batiste or organza) is always a solid choice, and sew-in woven or nonwoven fabrics are easy and accessible options.

In any case, be particularly sure to preshrink interfacings. Shinies show bubbling and other mistakes very clearly; if your interfacing shrinks and pulls at your fashion fabric, it will be obvious.

Sewing

Sew shiny fabrics with microtex machine needles, which are less likely to mar the surface of fabrics while sewing. Use a 70/10 with charmeuse and dupioni, a 75/11 with shantung, and an 80/12 with sateen, crepe-backed satin, and duchess satin. Use a new sharp needle to reduce the chance of snags; change your needle if you are working on a particularly long project or think your needle may be dull.

Use a 2.5–3.5mm straight stitch with slinky shinies. A standard foot works well, but a walking foot may help avoid shifting during sewing, because it will feed the fabric more evenly through the machine. If you're using a serger, enable the differential feed feature. If your fabric is getting caught beneath your machine's feed dogs, switch to a straight-stitch machine plate and presser foot. You can also start and end lines of stitches with your fabric sandwiched between layers of tissue paper (pg 155), so that it won't get pulled into your machine.

Generally, use a fine thread that matches the fabric's fiber content when sewing with shinies. Polyester is a fine default, but consider using silk thread with silk fabrics and cotton thread with cotton fabrics.

You may want to baste (pg 99) your piece together before sewing. Not only will it help massively with slippery fabric shifting, but it will also allow you to fit and otherwise preview your complete piece. Because they are so delicate, it's even more important to practice techniques before committing. Removing seams and resewing is dangerous with these delicate fabrics, so resewing should be avoided when possible!

Sleeks are not transparent like sheers, but because they're thin and drapey, special consideration still has to be taken for inner construction; these fabrics will show construction details just because of how slinky they are! Hems on facings will show through not because of translucency, but because the fashion fabric is so thin and smooth that the imprint is visible, especially for any raw edge finishing. Consider using the selvedge as the edge of your facing, if it's clean. You can also interface your facings and then leave the interfaced raw edge unfinished (pg 120). The interfacing, cut with pinking shears (pg 66), will prevent the facing from fraying.

Tutorial Time: Interfacing as Raw Edge Protection

Fusible interfacing protecting a raw edge from fraying

If the piece you're using this technique on is not visible (the edge of a facing, for example), pinking the edge (pg 66) (after applying the interfacing) will add another layer of security.

When fusible interfacing is applied right up to the edge of a piece of fabric, it can act as a hem in the sense that it protects the raw edge from fraying.

It's not foolproof, though! Particularly fray-prone fabrics, like burlap and jacquard, will start to come apart despite the adhesive on the interfacing. And if the interfacing becomes separated from the fabric—due to either of the materials shrinking, for example—it will cease helping at all.

To reduce the chance of puckers and the appearance of puckers from the natural indentations sewing makes, taut sew (pg 113). You can also reduce the tension on your machine to reduce puckering.

Be sure to use tearaway or water-soluble stabilizer when sewing stitched details, like buttonholes. This will create a stable surface for you to sew on.

Plain seams (pg 66) work well with shiny fabrics; often the raw edges can be protected with just pinking (pg 66) or searing (pg 121). A hairline seam (pg 122) is a clean and minimal option. Use a three-thread overlock stitch to sew a plain seam or protect raw edges.

Tutorial Time: Searing

Searing melts fabric; the individual yarns fuse into one, which prevents them from fraying. Searing and other melting-related techniques only work on synthetic materials; natural fibers will burn.

To sear raw edges, rapidly pass a flame about 2″ away from your fabric's edge.

You can also cut material using a wood burner or soldering iron.

This technique does take some trial and error to determine how closely and for how long your fabric and flame should meet. Always swatch when using new techniques and new materials!

⚠ STAY SAFE!
When heating or melting synthetic materials, always wear lung protection; your mask and filters must be rated for vapors. Use care around flames and hot tools. •

Dupioni and shantung need some special consideration when seaming due to their propensity to fray; their raw edges will need protection. Overedging (pg 138), binding (pg 73), or French seams (pg 114) are the best options.

Hem options abound! You can do a basic overedge (pg 138), a rolled hem (pg 132), or binding (pg 73). A topstitched horsehair-braid hem (pg 124) provides some structure to a hem. A hairline hem (pg 122) or regular double-fold hem (pg 85) are simpler.

Tutorial Time: Hairline Hems and Seams

Hairline hems and seams are extremely low-profile. They are delicate and minimal, but they can also be hard to sew.

A single-fold hairline hem is appropriate for a fabric that does not fray, like jersey.

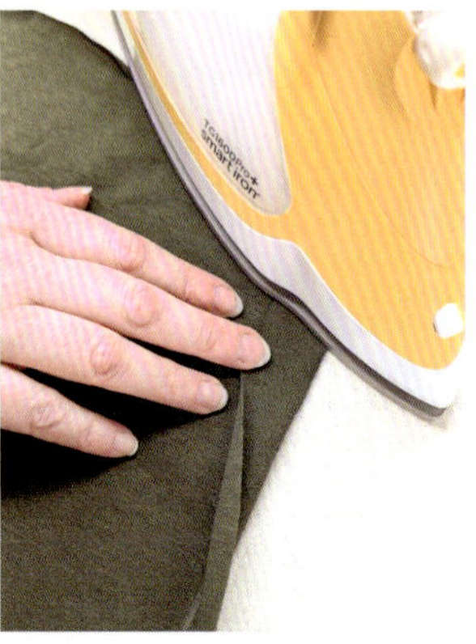

1. Fold your hem along your hemline; press.

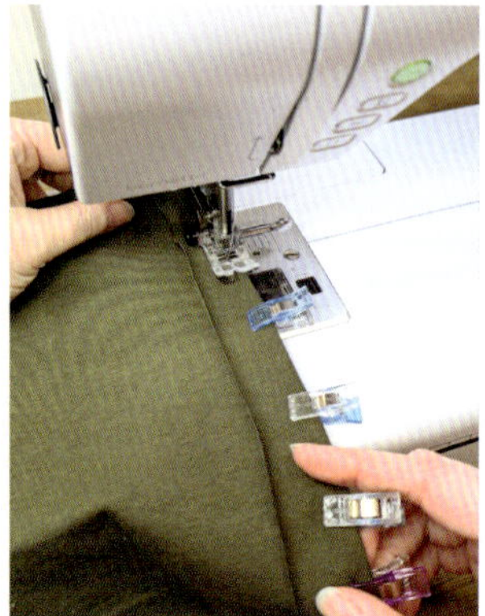

2. With or without an edge-stitch foot, edgestitch (pg 105) along the fold of the hem.

3. Carefully cut off the seam allowance, very close to the line of edge stitching.

The double-fold version works well for lightweight, translucent, and slinky wovens.

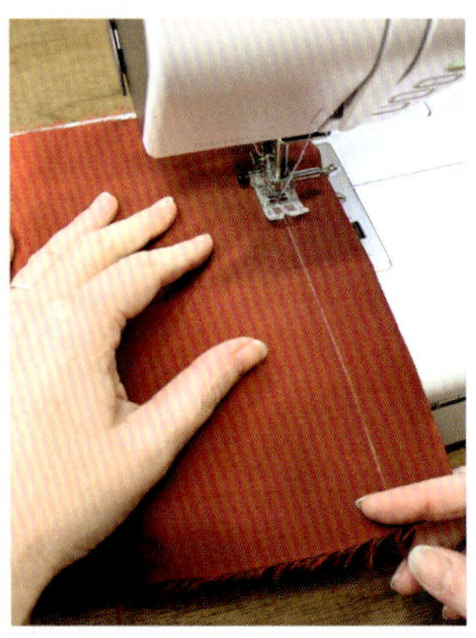

1. Sew a straight stitch along your hemline. For this step, you're only going through one layer of fabric.

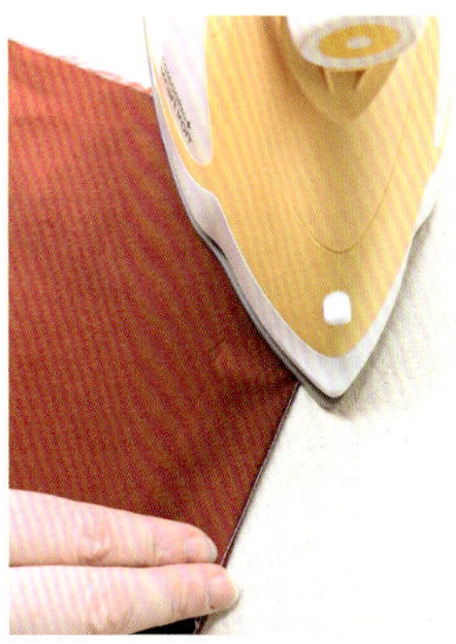

2. Fold to the wrong side along that line of stitching. Ideally, the stitching will be just barely to the inside of your piece.

3. Edgestitch (pg 105) your hem.

4. Carefully trim the seam allowance very close to your second line of stitching.

The same concepts can be used for seams.

5. Fold and press your hem once more to the inside of your piece.

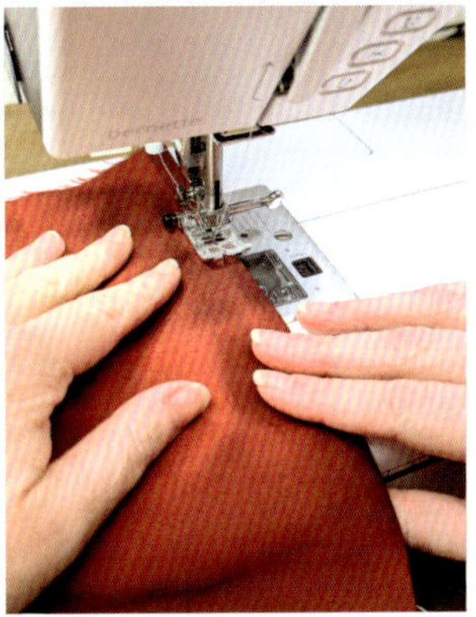

6. Then edgestitch (pg 105) once more to finish the hem, enclosing the raw edge.

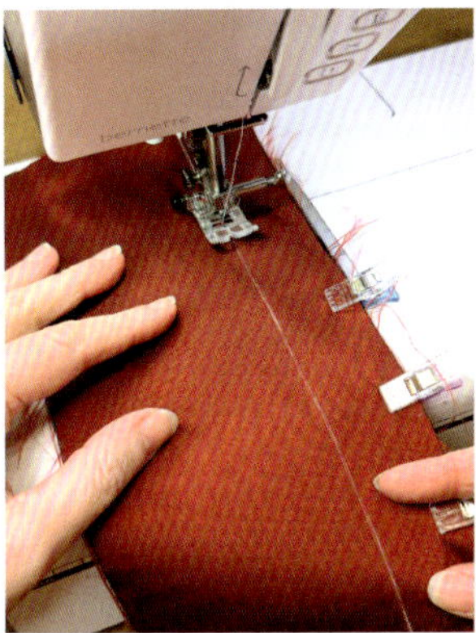

1. Straight stitch your seamline.

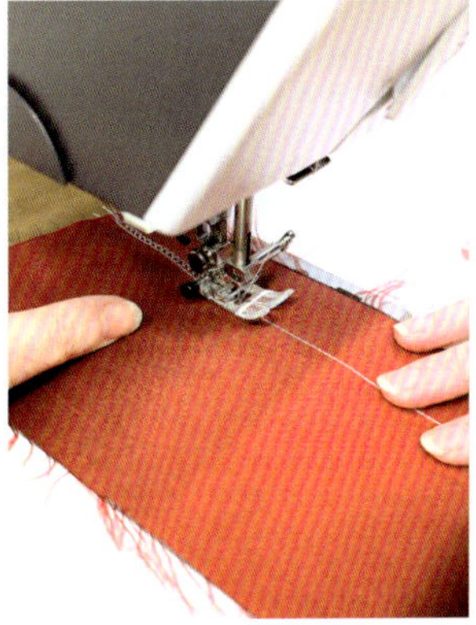

2. Stitch again with a zigzag stitch, directly next to your original seamline, but inside the seam allowance.

3. Carefully cut your seam allowance very close to the zigzag stitches.

4. Instead of using a zigzag stitch and then cutting, you can use an overlock, rolled (pg 132), or wrapped stitch, any of which will enclose the raw edges.

5. Press to one side.

Tutorial Time: Facing and Horsehair-Braid Hems

Horsehair braid is a mesh fabric, almost always made from nylon or polyester, that's very stiff and comes in long rolls of thin strips—like a utilitarian roll of ribbon. Horsehair braid works perfectly for stiffening hems, especially on those of skirts and dresses. Facing, a partial lining, is usually made of either the same fabric as the outer fabric or is a different lightweight lining fabric.

1. On the right side of your material, pin the horsehair ¼″ into the seam allowance. Sew along the hemline.

2. Flip the horsehair braid to the reverse, creating a folded hem. Press.

3. Topstitch (pg 177) the horsehair braid into place.

A facing is installed in a similar way.

1. Pin the outer fabric and facing right sides together, matching along the sew line.

2. Sew along the sew line.

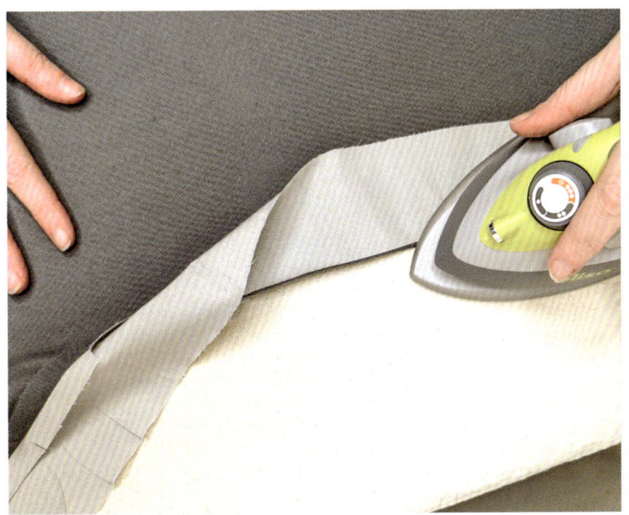

3. If the sew line has curves or turns, clip the seam allowance. Otherwise, turn the piece right side out and press.

Some facings are edgstitched (pg 105), topstitched (pg 177), or left unsewn. Many facings are understitched: The facing is edgestitched to the seam allowance but not to the outer fabric.

Corset made with a stretch mesh and embroidered lace from Bra Builders using a pattern by Madalynne Intimates

GARMENT BY NATALIE GRUENTZEL (SPARKLY SEWIST)
Photo by Natalie (Sparkly Sewist)

Meshes

Meshes are characterized by the holes incorporated into their design. These holes are often used for air and moisture flow; for that reason, meshes are popular athletic and performance fabrics.

Athletic mesh, most often used for sports jerseys, is tough and thick and does not stretch.

Power mesh is also very strong but stretchy. It's sturdy but lighter than both powernet and athletic mesh and has less supportive power than powernet. **Powernet** has a much tighter weave than the other meshes and, therefore, has the strength to support and compress, which is what it's often used for. It is durable and stretchy and may be almost entirely opaque.

Illusion mesh, sometimes called **stretch mesh**, is a finer fabric than power and athletic mesh. Most popularly it comes in a wide range of skin-tone colors and is used to create the illusion of bare skin. Illusion mesh is also often embellished with rhinestones and other detailing for performance apparel.

QUICK TIP!
Because of their similar names and structures, the names and properties of meshes aren't super well defined. If you need specific properties in your mesh, be sure to carefully read fabric descriptions and order swatches.

Fabric Preparation and Care

Athletic mesh, power mesh, and powernet can be machine washed cold and gentle. Tumble dry athletic mesh and powernet; lay power mesh flat to dry. Hand wash illusion mesh, and then lay it flat to dry.

Meshes should be prewashed as they will be washed after construction. Because they're delicate fabrics, it's important to remove debris from manufacturing that may affect the sewing process. Always use a delicates bag when machine washing meshes.

Pressing

Generally, meshes should not need to be pressed. If you must, start at a low heat and increase until effective. Always use a press cloth to prevent scorching synthetic fibers.

1. Illusion mesh/stretch mesh
2. Powernet
3. Athletic mesh
4. Power mesh

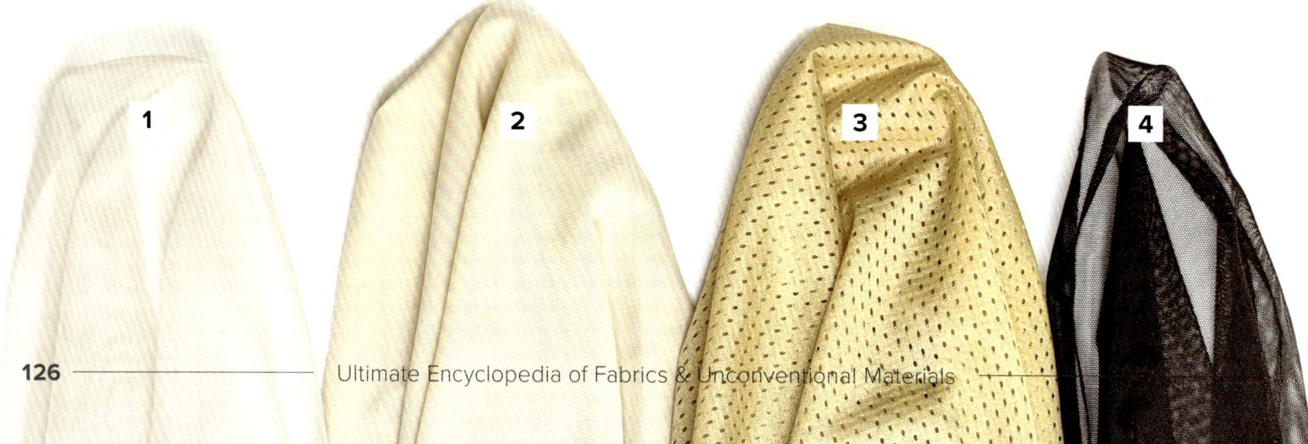

Pattern Transfer/Marking

Disappearing ink and chalk both work well on meshes. On particularly loose meshes, you may need to use tailor's tacks, safety pins, or thread tracing in a contrasting thread color in order to make your marks visible despite the fabric's holey nature.

Cutting

Meshes can be cut using regular rotary cutters and fabric shears. While athletic mesh can be cut in multiple layers, the other three meshes should be cut in a single layer; they will shift during cutting, which will affect your pieces! As with other delicate fabrics, never let the thinner meshes hang off of your cutting surface; gravity will distort them and, therefore, your cut pieces.

Cut meshes on the grain, respecting your desired direction of stretch. If your mesh has a very directional pattern of holes, consider cutting using a with-nap layout.

Pinning and Alternatives

Clips and all-purpose pins will work on many meshes, but some of those fabrics may be too open to ensure security using typical tools. In that case, install tearaway or water-soluble stabilizer, which can be removed once sewing is complete.

Interfacing

Generally, interfacing mesh isn't necessary or desired: You're negating the purpose of an open textile by adding an additional layer. However, if you want your mesh to be stiffer, there are options:

- Stiffen the mesh using a product made just for that purpose, such as Mod Podge Stiffy (by Plaid) or Stiffen Stuff (by Beacon).
- Use two layers of mesh (self-interfacing).
- If only needed temporarily, use starch, white glue, hairspray, tearaway interfacing, or water-soluble interfacing.

Using safety pins to secure mesh

Sewing

An 80/12 jersey machine needle with a 2mm zigzag stitch using a standard or roller presser foot will work well for meshes. Because athletic mesh is more substantial, a 2.5mm straight or 1.5mm narrow zigzag stitch will work better. If you experience skipped stitches, especially with delicate illusion meshes, switch to a smaller needle (like a 70/10).

For athletic mesh, use all-purpose or heavy-duty polyester thread. For powernet and power mesh, use all-purpose polyester. For illusion mesh, use all-purpose or delicate polyester thread.

Whether meshes ravel depends on their construction; generally, they do not. Whether they ravel will determine your need to protect fabric edges.

Meshes that do not ravel can be sewn with plain seams (pg 66). Meshes that do ravel can be overlocked (three-thread overlock stitch, pg 70), flat-felled (pg 81), or bound (pg 73); those options are also good for hiding the raw edges on meshes that are particularly see-through.

With very open meshes, consider stabilizing your seams or sandwiching your fabrics between tissue paper (pg 155) so the machine has something to sew through even when the needle goes between the weave of the fabric.

Many meshes will be used in high-impact applications like athletic jerseys, performance wear, and detailing on outdoor gear (such as water bottle pockets). In those cases, consider sewing with a double row of stitches (pg 100) for each seam. This will increase the number of fabric yarns caught in the thread of your seams, drastically increasing seam strength, especially on very open meshes.

For hems, consider a single- or double-fold hem (pg 85), a mock cover hem (pg 104), binding (pg 73), or overedging (pg 138). Remember to consider whether your fabric ravels when choosing a hem strategy, and stabilize the area before sewing if necessary.

Wedding gown made, in part, using tulle

GOWN AND MODELING BY MELISSA WIESS (SEWRENITY COSPLAY)
Photo by Christina Kroeker

Nets

Nets are an even looser weave than meshes—when sewing them, you'll spend a lot of time sewing air!

Medical gauze, the fabric used for bandaging, is strong but thin. It's actually one of the tighter-woven netting fabrics. **Cheesecloth** is a very loosely woven variety of gauze.

QUICK TIP!
Looking for the gauze you find at the fabric store? Head to Lightweight Wovens (pg 71).

Burlap, also known as **hessian**, is a rough, durable, open-weave fabric. It is historically made from the stalks of the jute plant, although it also comes in linen versions. Denser-weave burlaps sew like heavyweight wovens (pg 76), but many forms of burlap are a very open weave.

Tulle is a very strong and lightweight netting. The very common nylon version is inexpensive and stiff, while silk tulle (its historical makeup), is soft and much less stiff. Layering tulle is a great way to create volume when combined with other lightweight fabrics. **Bobbinet** is a specific kind of tulle woven on a machine that gives it hexagonal holes. Bobbinet is made of cotton.

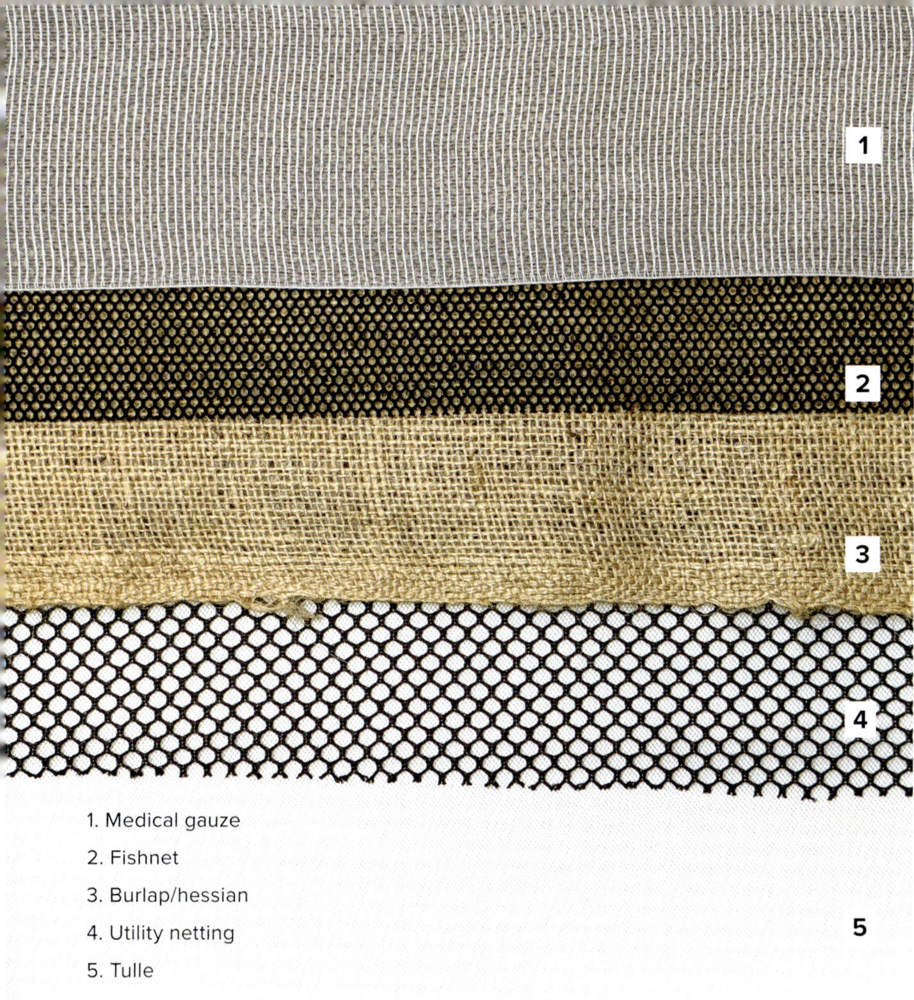

1. Medical gauze
2. Fishnet
3. Burlap/hessian
4. Utility netting
5. Tulle

CONFUSING TOPIC!
Tulle may be referred to as **crinoline**, which is also the name of a stiff petticoat. Historically, crinoline was made from cotton or linen and horsehair and was very stiff, providing more structure and support than modern tulle. If you need your tulle, bobbinet, or crinoline to be particularly structured or support other textiles, be sure to actually handle the fabric to get an idea of the way it behaves before starting your project or purchasing yardage! •

Utility netting is a catch-all term for the fabric used in laundry baskets, tent screens, and backpacks; they can also be used for garment making, especially to provide airflow in athletic apparel. Utility nettings are usually made of nylon or polyester. They may or may not have stretch. They're durable and easy to care for. A specific kind of utility netting is **fishnet** fabric, an extremely low-density knit used primarily to make tights.

Fabric Preparation and Care

Generally, netting fabrics should be treated like delicates when it comes to washing and drying. Hand wash burlap, tulle, and bobbinet and then lay them flat to dry. Gauze can be machine washed cold and tumbled dry on low. Fishnet and utility netting should be machine washed cold or warm and then laid flat to dry.

Gauze should be preshrunk, especially if it is made of cotton. The other netting fabrics are more situational. Jute, tulle, bobbinet, and crinoline should only be prewashed if they will be washed when part of a finished piece. Similarly, fishnet and utility netting should be prewashed as they will be laundered when finished.

Importantly, the edges of these netting fabrics must be protected before they go through the wash. Loose gauze, burlap, and fishnet can completely come apart during the washing process if their raw edges are not overedged (pg 138).

QUICK TIP!
Always use a delicates bag when machine washing netting! Otherwise, their holes may get caught on parts of the washing machine or on other items in the load. •

Because they are woven so loosely, after their pretreatment, these fabrics may need to be manipulated into their original weave by straightening the grain. More so than other fabrics, distorted weaves in nets will show in finished products.

Tulle and bobbinet should be stored hung (both when they're unused fabric and when they're in finished pieces); wrinkles can be particularly tough to remove. Otherwise, do not hang nettings to dry or to store. Gravity will pull at their loose weaves, distorting them.

Pressing

Gauze and burlap can both be pressed with steam on a hot setting. For all other netting materials, start at a low heat, gradually increase until you get a good press, and always use a press cloth. Polyester tulle, in particular, melts extremely easily; take care not to damage your fabric *or* your iron!

Like other loose-weave fabrics, nettings should be pressed, not ironed. The sweeping back-and-forth motion of ironing can distort a net's structure.

Pattern Transfer/Marking

Burlap and gauze can be marked with regular marking tools such as chalk and disappearing ink. Tulle, fishnet, and utility netting are tougher to mark because of how holey they are; consider tailor's tacks, thread tracing, or safety pins for a removable option.

Cutting

Net fabrics are best cut with a rotary cutter, which will minimize shifting during cutting. They should be cut in a single layer and using a with-nap layout to ensure that the grid pattern does not get distorted due to folding or shifting. Cut with care; arrange the fabric yarns very carefully during layout to ensure they're properly perpendicular to each other and in line with your with-nap pattern layout. Because netting fabrics show directionality so prominently, a single accidentally diagonal pattern piece is really going to show!

Gauze, utility netting, and fishnet can be very shifty for the cutting process; consider cutting them on a textured surface so there is more grip. (In this case, you also must cut with shears, not a rotary cutter.)

Burlap will begin shedding and fraying immediately after cutting. Not only will it make a massive mess, but you also risk the fabric fraying past the seamline. Consider overedging (pg 138) the cut edge immediately after cutting your pieces.

Additionally, when sewing with burlap, open-weave gauze, and other extreme-fray netting, consider cutting a wider-than-usual seam allowance. This will allow you extra space to protect raw edges.

Pinning and Alternatives

All netting fabrics are best secured with fabric clips; pins won't work well due to the holes in the weaves! If even clips aren't getting enough of a hold, use water-soluble stabilizer or tape to secure the fabric before sewing.

Sewing with water-soluble stabilizer

Interfacing

Because of their extremely holey natures, nets do not interface well. A stiff lining or even self-fabric can provide structure and body, but traditional sew-in and (especially!) fusible interfacing just doesn't make sense.

If you really need your netting stiffer, consider starching. This can be a temporary measure (to make sewing easier, for example) or a permanent one.

Sewing

Because their construction and fiber content vary so wildly, the machine needle and basic stitch best used for each netting fabric is also quite different.

- **Burlap/hessian:** 80/12 denim, 2mm zigzag stitch
- **Gauze:** 80/12 ballpoint, 3mm straight stitch
- **Tulle, bobbinet, and crinoline:** 70/10 all-purpose, 2mm straight or zigzag stitch
- **Fishnet and utility netting:** 70/10 jersey, 2mm straight stitch

Use an all-purpose polyester thread when sewing netting fabric. If you're creating with a particularly sturdy utility netting, consider upgrading to heavy-duty. A delicate gauze or fishnet may benefit from fine thread.

Because nettings are composed largely of holes, you may need to stabilize before sewing to ensure your machine has something to grab onto. A parchment paper sandwich (pg 155) or water-soluble interfacing are great for this task. A walking or roller foot will help evenly feed these tricky fabrics through a machine's feed dogs, helping to prevent shifting during sewing.

Care must also be taken when choosing seam and hem finishes, because the holes allow for raw edges to be visible through the fabric. Binding (pg 73) hides the raw edges and provides a clean finish. French seams (pg 114) are a good option because they result in a clean finish on the inside—an inside that may be visible from the outside of the piece. However, they aren't appropriate for substantial nets, because it creates a bulkier seam. A plain seam with a three- or four-thread overlock stitch (pg 70) allows the seam to blend into the rest of the fabric, even if it's visible on the right side.

You can topstitch (pg 177) or flat-fell (pg 81) thicker nettings like burlap and sturdy utility netting to flatten the seam and give a cleaner finish. Just consider whether you need to use a stabilizer or paper in the seam to make sure you have something other than air for the machine to grab onto!

Tulle, bobbinet, crinoline, and many fishnet and utility netting fabrics do not fray, so hemming is not required. If you do opt to hem, consider binding (pg 73), a delicate rolled hem (pg 132), or overedge (three-thread overlock stitch, pg 138).

Tutorial Time: Rolled Hems and Seams

A rolled hem, which is a very thin and delicate hem, can be created with a conventional machine using a rolled-hem foot or with a serger using a two- or three-thread rolled-hem stitch.

Although it's a simple concept, executing a rolled hem can be tricky, especially because the fabrics they're best for can be shifty and floaty! Consider starching or applying wash-away stabilizer to your hem allowance before beginning your rolled hem.

1. Switch to your rolled-hem foot. With the wrong side facing up, roll your fabric into the foot.

2. Lower your presser foot and begin sewing. The foot will guide the fabric into a rolled shape.

On a serger, a two-thread rolled hem is great for very lightweight fabrics, like sheers; the three-thread version is better for medium-weight materials.

When using a serger, the threads themselves create the roll in the hem. Set your machine for a rolled hem according to your manual; then sew with your fabric right side up on your serger. Consider switching to wooly nylon thread in the upper looper of your serger; the wooly nature of the thread will fill in the gaps in the stitches, creating a very uniform and clean finish.

To create a rolled-edge seam, replicate the process but with your fabrics' right sides together. Glue basting (pg 99) helps immensely.

Due to extreme fray, gauze and burlap must have their raw edges protected. Use an overedge stitch (pg 138) and then do a single-fold hem (pg 85).

If you have a lot of issues with netting fabrics getting sucked into the machine, consider switching to a straight-stitch foot and plate. The smaller needle holes make it much less likely that holey fabric will get pulled inside the machine. Sewing between two layers of tissue paper (pg 155) will also help prevent this issue—in that case, you can continue using the walking or roller foot recommended earlier.

QUICK TIP!

Burlap is extremely messy. Clean your machine often when sewing with it and especially after finishing a project, or the fiber dust may cause sewing issues in future sewing endeavors. Consider wearing lung protection.

Piles and Naps

Piled and napped fabrics can be tricky to work with—and not just because of their fuzzy finishes. Most of them are sensitive to pressing, their textures are at risk of damage during all points of the sewing process, they're slinky, and they're messy.

Base of Anishinaabe jingle dress is made from sky blue velveteen. This dress is a sacred cultural garment made by an Anishinaabe artist; it is not for cosplay or costuming. It was brought to the Anishinaabe people through a dream long ago and can be seen in powwows and other First Nations ceremonies across the United States and Canada. To learn about cultural appropriation, you can find a short explainer video at nativegov.org/resources/cultural-appropriation-video/

GARMENT BY ADRIENNE BENJAMIN
Photo by Adrienne Benjamin

CONFUSING TOPIC!
The words *pile* and *nap* are often used interchangeably, but they are actually two different ways of constructing a textured fabric (pg 21). Luckily, the two types have very similar difficulties and special techniques for dealing with them—those are addressed in this chapter. ●

Piled fabrics, in particular, can be very slinky and love to shift during sewing. Pin or clip densely (pg 134) to help minimize wiggliness, but be sure to remove the pins or clips before they can damage the texture. If the fabric does shift while you're sewing, you can fix it! Stop stitching, raise the pressure foot, and maneuver the fabric back in line. If you're sewing right sides together, encourage the textures to grab onto themselves in the correct orientation. Then continue sewing.

Tutorial Time: Pinning (and Clipping) Densely

When your fabric is prone to shifting during the sewing process, use many pins affixed closely together to hold the layers of fabric securely.

Use the same technique with sewing clips on fabrics sensitive to pins.

Another way to help prevent shifting is by sewing in the direction of the pile—the direction that is smooth if you run your hand across it. This will also reduce the chance of damaging the pile during topstitching. In general, it's best to always sew *with* the texture, instead of against it.

QUICK TIP!

When the pile on a fabric is a different fiber than the base fabric, the label should clearly state what each of them is. Take note of this! When you prewash, press, and care for your fabric, you'll need to know the entire fiber composition of the fabric, not just that of the base or pile. •

Topstitching (pg 177), or any time the foot moves over the front of the fabric, risks damaging the raised texture of these fabrics. If during swatching you realize that topstitching will damage your fabric, use water-soluble stabilizer on top of the textile, which can be removed once you have a successful seam. Make sure to swatch test the stabilizer, too, to make sure it doesn't damage the fabric!

Because of their raised fibers, the fabrics in this section can be very difficult to press. Luckily, you can heal a crushed texture somewhat by tumble drying or steaming and then brushing with a scrap of the same fabric.

QUICK TIP!

When sewing with piles and naps, practice taut sewing (pg 113). If you get puckers during sewing, reduce the upper thread tension. •

Piled and napped fabrics are usually extremely messy. Remember to clean your machine after sewing with them; the fluff from the texture will build up in your machine, affecting its ability to sew. If you're experiencing a jammed machine, skipped stitches, or any other machine-related issues, vacuuming out your machine should be your first troubleshooting step. It's an easy task that can solve many issues.

STAY SAFE!

If your textured fabric is particularly sheddy, consider wearing lung protection while working with it—especially when cutting, sewing, and cleaning your workspace. A simple cloth face mask will be enough to prevent you from inhaling large, floating fibers. •

Washcloths made from towel terry and backed with cotton muslin

WASHCLOTHS BY ANNYE DRISCOLL
Photo by Annye Driscoll

Cozies

Microfiber technically refers to any fabric made with ultra-fine fibers. In the context of cozies, however, microfiber fabrics are soft, lightly textured, very dense, and durable—think microfiber washcloths. They are soft and drape nicely. They make great fabrics for cleaning supplies and garments; they resist stains and are absorbent.

A common microfiber is **minky**, sometimes sold under the brand name Cuddle (by Shannon Fabrics). Minky is extremely soft but also durable and easy to care for. It is often used for baby blankets and plushies.

Another common microfiber is **faux suede**, often sold under the trade name Ultrasuede (by Toray Industries). Faux suede emulates the fuzzy side of genuine suede but is on a nonwoven backing. It is significantly thinner than all but the most lightweight leather. It is soft, smooth, and drapey.

1. Fleece
2. Faux suede
3. Minky
4. Microfiber
5. Sweatshirt fabric

Flannel is soft and warm. It is medium-weight and a twill or plain weave; it may or may not have a brushed nap. It has a natural mechanical stretch.

Fleece, often called polar fleece, is soft, napped (on either one side or both), and lightweight. It is almost exclusively made of polyester. **Sweatshirt fleece**, which may also be referred to as sweatshirting, is cozy and warm but bulky. One side is brushed and napped, and the other is smooth.

Terry is a woven or knitted fabric where protruding loops create an absorbent and soft surface. **Towel terry** is looped on both sides. It is warm and absorbent, but frays and sheds. French terry, a stretchy variety, is included in Stretch Velvet, French Terry, and Velour (pg 142).

Chenille is the name of both a fabric and the yarns it's made of. It is heavy but extremely soft, durable, and piled with no nap. Because of the way the pile is constructed, chenille has an iridescent, fuzzy quality.

Fabric Preparation and Care

Prewash your cozy fabric as you intend to care for it once your project is complete. Flannel, sweatshirt fabric, and towel terry will shrink, especially if they're cotton; make sure to shrink these fabrics before sewing with them.

Wash minky and microfiber cold and dry them with low heat. Flannel, fleece, sweatshirt fabric, and towel terry should be machine washed warm and then tumble dried.

Fleece and sweatshirt fabric are prone to pilling; turn them inside out to wash.

Chenille and faux suede can run the gamut from delicate to extremely sturdy; make sure to consult the manufacturer's recommendation when washing them. If they're not dry-clean only, consider hand washing and then tumbling on low heat to revive the pile.

Pressing

Cozy fabrics must be pressed carefully. For fleece, sweatshirt fabric, minky, microfiber, faux suede, and chenille, press with low heat from the wrong side of the fabric. A cotton terry towel, because it can withstand high heat and has a nap of its own, works well as a press cloth for these fabrics (including for other cotton terry towels!). Make sure to swatch your fabric to make sure the pile on your terry press cloth is enough of a buffer to protect your fabric. Self-fabric facing the pile is also often a great choice.

Wool, cotton, and natural blends may require higher heat.

Cotton and wool flannels can be pressed with medium heat and steam. When pressing flannel fabrics, however, take care to *press;* the sweeping movements of ironing and the natural stretch of that fabric will distort the fabric.

When pressing seams and hems, finger press or use a piece of cardboard (pg 72) to prevent damaging the body of your piece.

Pattern Transfer/Marking

Because of the texture, marks may need to be on the back and/or untextured side of cozy fabric. Disappearing ink and chalk are good options in this case. If you do need to mark on the pile or nap, confirm that chalk will stick to the pile well enough to hold up to the sewing process, or that the act of marking with a disappearing ink pen will not mar the surface of these cozies.

QUICK TIP!
Some cozies are identical on each side. In that case, make sure to properly mark wrong sides of the fabric while you're cutting out your pattern pieces, for the sake of both respecting nap and preventing confusion during construction. •

In all cases, tailor's tacks or thread tracing with contrasting thread are the safest ways to mark cozies.

Cutting

Cozies can be easily cut with either a rotary cutter or fabric shears.

Almost all cozies have directional naps and, therefore, must be laid out respecting direction. The only exception is the smooth side of sweatshirt fabric; if you'll be using the napped side of this material as your right side, make sure to cut it using a with-nap layout as well.

Cozy fabrics, especially towel terry and chenille, can be very messy as pieces of pile are released from the base material. Consider having a vacuum cleaner near your cutting space so little fluffs don't go everywhere!

Pinning and Alternatives

Most cozy fabrics work well with all-purpose pins and clips, although you may consider ballpoint pins with knitted towel terry, knitted fleece, and sweatshirt fabric. You will need long pins if your cozy is particularly thick; shorter pins may get lost in the fabric. Holes in faux suede are permanent; use clips, tape, or glue instead of pins.

Consider pinning or clipping densely (pg 134) with minky, microfiber, faux suede, fleece, sweatshirt fabric, and chenille, because these fabrics may shift during sewing.

Interfacing

Because their piles make them tricky to press, cozies are best interfaced with sew-in interfacing. Use sew-in woven or nonwoven versions for minky, faux suede, and microfiber; sew-in nonwoven or tricot with fleece and sweatshirt fabric; and tricot with chenille.

Fusible woven or nonwoven interfacing can be used with flannel, but it must be applied very carefully so as to not damage the pile. Remember: Always press flannel instead of ironing it, because flannel can be easily distorted out of shape. Also, be sure to preshrink any interfacing used with flannel (including sew-in) and only apply interfacing after preshrinking the flannel itself.

Towel terry does not generally need interfacing; if you do need to interface it, use tricot or sew-in woven, depending on whether your towel terry is knit or woven.

Sewing

Use a 3mm straight stitch for minky, faux suede, microfiber, and flannel, and a 3mm straight or zigzag for terry (if it is a knit and, therefore, has some natural stretch, a wide zigzag will allow for that stretch). A 2.5mm straight or zigzag stitch is best for fleece, sweatshirt fabric, and chenille, again depending on the stretch of the fabric.

Because their composition varies so much, machine needle choice also varies within the cozy category.

- **Minky and faux suede:** 90/14 microtex
- **Microfiber:** 60/8 microtex
- **Flannel:** 90/14 universal
- **Fleece:** 80/12 universal
- **Towel terry:** 100/16 ballpoint
- **Sweatshirt fabric:** 90/14 ballpoint
- **Chenille:** 90/14 universal or ballpoint

When sewing fabrics with texture, take care to sew with the direction of the nap or pile. This will prevent any marring of the raised fibers and allow for a more even feed through the machine.

However, if you do need to sew against the nap or are generally struggling with the even feeding of layers, a walking or roller foot is a great choice for cozies; these specialty feet help feed fabric evenly through your machine. If your fabric is thick or your layers are building up to the point that your feed dogs are struggling to move it through the machine, reduce the pressure on your machine foot to allow for more room.

✸ QUICK TIP!

With particularly large-loop towel terry and chenille, the points of the machine foot can get caught in the loops of the pile. You can prevent this by sewing over a piece of parchment paper, which you then tear away after your sewing is finished. •

Chenille, minky, microfiber, faux suede, and flannel are best sewn with all-purpose polyester thread; you may also consider 100 percent cotton for cotton flannel. All-purpose polyester will also work well for towel terry, fleece, and sweatshirt fabric, but heavy-duty polyester may be a better choice for weightier versions of those fabrics or for pieces that will be used heavily.

Minky, fleece, faux suede, and sweatshirt fabric are otherwise very easy to sew with. Their edges can be left raw; they generally will not ravel. A plain seam (pg 66) with a wide zigzag stitch works well, or overlock with a three-thread overlock stitch (pg 70) to create a strong and stretchy seam. Grade seam allowances (pg 94) to reduce bulk on more substantial varieties of the fabrics, and consider topstitching (pg 177) for a polished finish. For hems, leave edges raw, overedge (below), or bind (pg 73). Sweatshirts often use matching ribbing for their binding, see Stretch Knits (pg 95)!

Because of their propensity for extreme shedding, towel terry and chenille must have enclosed edges ... otherwise, they'll continue to make a mess until their seam allowances have worn away! Consideration must also be taken for their substantial bulk; you may consider grading exposed raw edges (pg 94) before protecting them with binding (pg 73) or overedging (below). Reversible lapped (pg 88) and plain seams (pg 66) are low-bulk options for seaming.

Hems must also be finished; overedging (below) or binding (pg 73) are best, but a double fold (pg 85) may work on thinner versions of these fabrics.

Tutorial Time: Overedging

Overedging is a great way to protect raw edges without adding bulk to the finished piece. It can function as a seam finish or as the seam or hem itself. The overedge stitches, in ascending order of protection are:

- A zigzag stitch on the conventional machine, sewn so that one side of the stitch is just off the edge of the fabric.
- Two-, three-, and four-thread overlock stitches (and the related three-thread stretch overlock stitch).
- Two- and three-thread wrapped stitches.

Raw edges protected before seaming, separately and together

Generally, zigzagging is best when you don't have a serger or don't need a significant amount of raw edge protection. Wrapped stitches provide tight, even coverage and are usually used to finish visible edges (hems), or the seam allowance on sheer fabrics. Overlock stitches are a balance between the two: They provide security to raw edges, are not bulky, and have lots of variations so you can tailor to your fabric and use case.

There are three main ways to accomplish this technique:

- Apply the stitches to the raw edges separately, after sewing and pressing the seam.
- Apply the stitches to the raw edges together, after sewing and pressing the seam; then press the seam allowances to one side.
- Apply the stitches immediately after cutting out your pattern pieces, edging the entire piece of material. (This method is great when your fabric is *really* prone to fraying, because it protects the raw edges as soon as possible.)

Flannel can be tricky. It's often quite a loose weave and, therefore, will stretch and distort as you sew. Consider basting seams (with thread, basting adhesive, or a glue stick, pg 99) or pinning or clipping very densely (pg 134). It also frays dramatically; all raw edges must be enclosed. Sew seams with a plain seam (pg 66); then finish the raw edges with overedging (above). A flat-fell seam (pg 81) is not a typical seam for flannel, but it will work well to protect raw edges and keep bulk down. Hems should be overedged (above), bound (pg 73), or double folded (pg 85).

Velvet, Velveteen, and Corduroy

Velvet, velveteen, and corduroy all have delicate short piles.

Velvet has a particularly dense pile and a luxurious drape. It is very soft and often lustrous. Historically, velvet was made from silk.

Velveteen, the cotton version of velvet, is stiffer, more durable, and less shiny than velvet. Like velvet, it has a thick, dense pile. It can be light- to medium-weight.

In **corduroy**, the weft yarns are cut to create long ridges of pile, which run along the length of the fabric. Corduroy is durable.

✸ QUICK TIP!
Velvets often come in nonstandard widths. Before you buy, make sure you convert your pattern so that you don't end up with too much or little material. •

Chair, an 1800s Victorian frame painted in black, upholstered with royal purple short pile upholstery velvet

UPHOLSTERY BY WHIMSY & WOE FURNITURE CO.
Photo by Whimsy & Woe Furniture Co.

Crushed and Embossed Velvet

Velvet and velveteen can be crushed (by either smashing the pile or twisting the fabric) or embossed (by heat-stamping designs into the pile), both of which create texture in the pile. Crushed and embossed velvet should be treated like standard velvet.

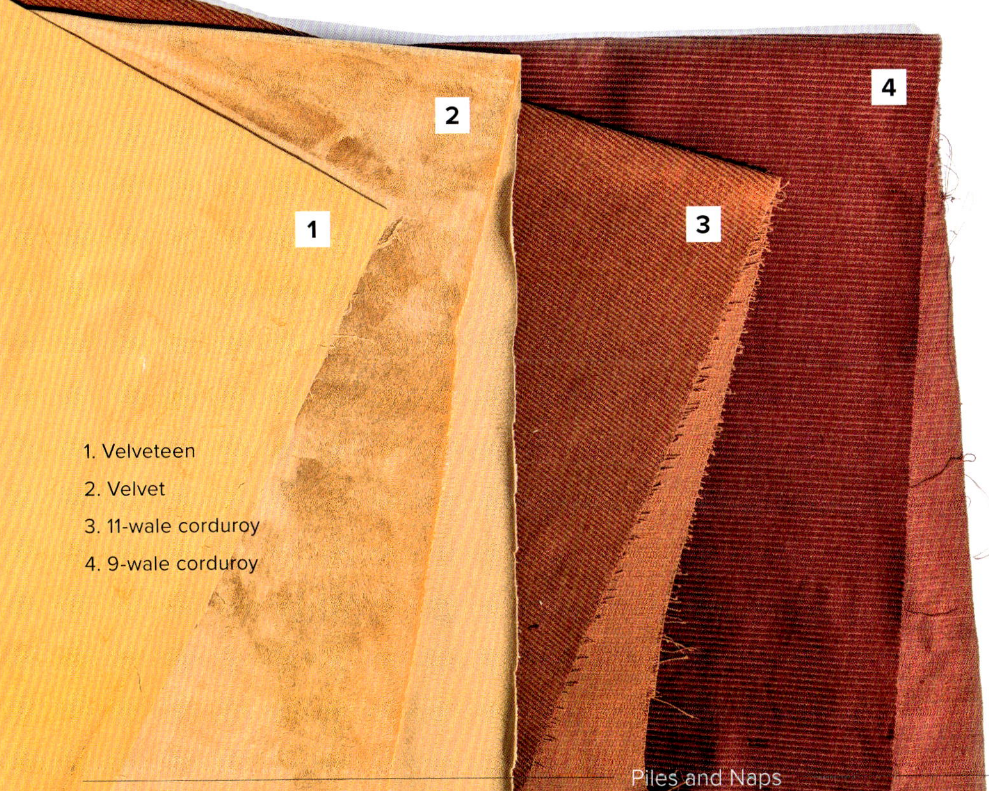

1. Velveteen
2. Velvet
3. 11-wale corduroy
4. 9-wale corduroy

✸ QUICK TIP!

11-wale corduroy versus 9-wale corduroy

When buying a corduroy, you may notice it comes with a wale count. *Wale* is the technical term for the piled rows, so a wale count is describing the row density of the fabric. •

Fabric Preparation and Care

Generally, velveteen, corduroy, and non-silk velvet fabric should be preshrunk, especially if it is cotton or a cotton blend. Machine wash on gentle with cold or warm water, and then lay flat to dry. If the pile has wilted, a quick trip through the tumble dryer on low heat will fluff it back up.

If velvet is silk it should be very carefully hand washed or dry cleaned.

Because these fabrics can be both delicate and tough to press, consider storing them rolled or hung instead of folded. This will prevent harsh creases from developing and will prevent the pile from getting marred on those crease lines.

Pressing

Woven piles are tough to press due to their delicate piles and (often) silk and/or synthetic fiber content. Always press on the wrong side of the fabric with a *needle board* (a flat board with dense rows of upright needles, which provide a textured surface to press onto), plush terry towel, or self-fabric facing the right side of the fabric. When possible (especially when pressing seams and hems), finger press. Use a piece of cardboard between the seam allowance and the main fabric (pg 72) to prevent creasing the front of the piece.

Pattern Transfer/Marking

When you can, mark on the wrong side of velvet, velveteen, and corduroy to protect the pile. When you must mark the right side, use tailor's tacks or thread tracing. Disappearing ink and chalk are usually safe options, but disappearing ink must be tested to make sure it can be removed, and chalk may rub out extremely easily, making it risky to use for important marking.

Cutting

Velvet and its siblings must be cut using a with-nap layout. When working with corduroy, don't forget to consider the direction of the wales.

All three are best cut in one layer, because they can be very shifty during the cutting process. A rotary cutter is best for cutting them; again, this prevents excess shifting during the cutting process.

These fabrics also fray dramatically. For that reason, never cut *into* notches—this risks the notch fraying all the way past the seamline. Instead, cut notches out, away from the seamline.

✸ QUICK TIP!
These fabrics will make a mess as you sew. Have a small vacuum handy, and wipe your cutting tools so their cutting power isn't affected by fiber dust. •

Pinning and Alternatives

All-purpose pins are fine for velvet and its siblings, but consider fine pins instead because of their delicate natures. Even fine pins should never be left in the fabric for a long time; they'll leave permanent marks in the pile. Clips are fine in the seam allowance but will very quickly damage the pile.

These fabrics are slinky; pin densely (pg 134) or even hand baste (pg 99) to prevent shifting during the sewing process.

Interfacing

Because of their delicate structures and contents, woven piles should not be interfaced with fusible interfacing. Instead, use sew-in woven or nonwoven interfacing or tricot.

Because these fabrics are so tough to press, consider flatlining (pg 141) for wrinkle prevention; tricot is a great option for interfacing. Zigzag or overlock these two layers together, which will also prevent fraying edges.

Sewing

Use a 70/10 microtex machine needle with velveteen and velvet; corduroy, which is usually more substantial than those fabrics, will perform best with an 80/12 denim needle. Use a 2.5mm straight or zigzag stitch. Use all-purpose cotton or polyester thread with velveteen, all-purpose or heavy-duty cotton or polyester thread with corduroy, and all-purpose cotton or silk thread with velvet (according to its fiber content).

A walking or roller foot will help feed the fabric evenly through the machine, preventing it from shifting as it moves under the feed dogs. Especially with the thicker velvets and corduroy, lowering the pressure on the machine foot may help evenly feed the fabric through the machine.

Fabric Preparation and Care

Generally, do not prewash or machine wash faux fur or teddy fur; these are hand-wash-only materials, which should be hung to dry and then brushed back into shape.

Especially when talking about stuffed animals, these materials will *need* to be machine washed at some point: Washing them on gentle with cold water, in a delicates bag, and then tumble drying on low will be your safest bet. Make sure you send a swatch through this process before machine washing and drying a beloved teddy.

Pressing

Faux teddy and faux fur should not need to be pressed, and the acrylic fur fibers will not tolerate the heat of pressing at all. Luckily, the pile will hide most wrinkles. If necessary, send your faux fur on a quick trip through the dryer on low heat; then brush to revive the pile.

Pattern Transfer/Marking

Chalk or disappearing ink work on many faux furs and teddy furs. If the pile is too long for these tools to work, a long tailor's tack in a contrasting thread color is your best bet.

Because they are so thick and substantial, most faux furs and teddy furs can be marked on the reverse with any regular writing utensil, including permanent marker. Swatch test to make sure your choice is not visible on the front.

Cutting

Faux furs have a very obvious direction and, therefore, must be cut using a with-nap layout. Especially with very long furs, think about which way the fur will lie on your piece; consider gravity when laying out your pattern pieces.

Faux fur and teddy fur are not hard to cut—they just require a very specific technique! With the fabric pile down on your cutting surface, outline your pattern pieces with a pen or marker. Using the very tip of a craft knife or box cutter, cut through just the base fabric of your faux fur. Your knife shouldn't hit the cutting surface at all; we're trying to avoid damaging any of the pile fibers! When the base material is fully cut, you can pull your pieces apart, leaving the pile intact all the way to the edge of your cut fabric.

Cutting through the backing of faux fur using only the very tip of a knife

QUICK TIP!

Getting clean cuts without damaging the pile of faux fur is possible with scissors, but much more difficult. Manipulate the very tip of your scissors between the pile fibers so that you're cutting as few of them as possible. This is best accomplished with pointed-end scissors, but ideally not your sewing shears because the heavyweight synthetic base material of faux fur will dull your blades.

Pinning and Alternatives

Generally, faux furs can be secured with regular pins or clips. More substantial furs, however, will need long pins with contrasting pin heads so they can be found in a very long pile. Consider hand basting (pg 99) if your fabric is very thick.

Interfacing

Generally, faux fur is a sturdy fabric that will not need to be interfaced. However, you can use sew-in woven or nonwoven interfacing. If you need your fabric very stiff, a structural material like EVA foam (pg 194) or Kobracast (pg 210) can be glued to faux fur with hot glue or contact cement (pg 204).

Teddy fur can be interfaced with sew-in woven or nonwoven interfacing.

In either case, because you'll be sending the front of the fabric through your sewing machine, sandwich the layers of your project between two layers of tissue paper (pg 155) so that the pile doesn't get caught in your machine.

Sewing

Use an 80/12 standard or denim machine needle with faux fur and a standard 80/12 machine needle with teddy fur. A long 3.5mm straight stitch and all-purpose polyester thread work well. A standard machine foot feeds these fabrics well, but you may want to decrease pressure or switch to a walking foot if your project gets very thick.

✸ QUICK TIP!
When you begin working with faux fur, you'll realize very quickly that the pile fibers love to get stuck in your stitch lines. You can prevent this somewhat by brushing the faux fur toward the body of the piece as you pin, but you may find it easiest to just use a comb or long needle to pull the strands out of the seam *after* you've finished sewing. •

Using a long hand-sewing needle to pull faux fur fibers out of a seam

Plain seams (pg 66) work well with faux furs; their base fabrics will not fray, and the pile often completely hides the seam from the right side, so nothing complicated is needed. Of course, specific situations may need more complex solutions.

✸ QUICK TIP!
Whenever possible, but especially when sewing the front of faux fur, sew in the direction of the pile. This will reduce the damage to the fibers and, because the feed dogs won't be working against the grain of the pile, will lead to a smooth feed through the sewing machine. •

A flatlock seam (pg 147) on a serger or an abutted seam (pg 171) on a conventional machine reduces seam allowance bulk to nothing. You can then reinforce the seam with fusible tape or fabric glued to the wrong side. Do not use the cutting feature on your serger—the fur's pile will jam the machine and dull the blades.

Tutorial Time: Flatlock Seams

A flatlock seam is a modified abutted seam (pg 171), so stitches will be visible in the final product. Those stitches look different on each side, but either can be the right side. If you prefer the loops visible, sew with your fabric's wrong sides together. Sewing with the right sides together will result in the ladder stitches showing on the front.

1. Adjust your serger for a flatlock stitch as instructed by your manual; then sew. Your seam allowance should be short enough to allow half of the width of the flatlock stitches to hang off the edge of the seam.

2. When the seam is complete, gently pull your fabric pieces apart.

3. Because this is an abutted seam, it may need to be reinforced on the reverse. Use fabric, fusible interfacing, or even glue to help keep the seam intact and strong.

If you want the look of a flatlock seam but your fabric frays or ravels, you can create a flatlock seam that has protected edges—simply finish your raw edges as appropriate for your fabric and project before executing a typical flatlock seam.

Hems can be single folds (pg 85) or faced/lined (but with lining fabric, not the same fabric). You may choose to sew your seams and then glue or hem tape your hems. Faux furs are very receptive to glue; consider hot glue for any faux fur, or contact cement (pg 204) for those with more substantial base fabrics.

Sewing with teddy fur comes with an additional complication: the pile isn't generally long enough to hide bubbling seams. Consider gluing down the seam allowances to get a clean front, or very carefully press or topstitch (pg 177) the seam allowance (but only after testing and practicing!).

If you're generally struggling with the bulk of faux fur seam allowances, remove part or all of the pile with hair clippers or scissors. Just have a vacuum handy, and wear a mask to protect your lungs.

In general, always clean your workspace and machine thoroughly after sewing with faux furs. No matter what you do, you'll have little acrylic hairs everywhere. It's like cat hair—but plastic!

Embellished and Embroidered Fabrics

Embellished and embroidered fabrics have been modified somehow from their base material. Not only do you need to know how to handle the foundation fabric, but you also must manage the additions. Those with added detailing such as glitter, sequins, and beading may be delicate, and they definitely will make you think about where you place your seamlines. Lace, embroidery, and eyelet present the same issues, with the added difficulty of holes built into the materials.

The Chimera, inspired by Thierry Mugler's original 1997 gown, made with thousands of scales sent from viewers around the world

GARMENT AND MODELING BY ARIEL HAZ
Photo by Hazariel

Embellished

Embellished fabrics are base fabrics (of any kind) that have been added onto with **sequins**, **beads**, **rhinestones**, or **glitter**. They can be difficult to sew because you have to consider both the properties of the base fabrics (which are often delicate, stretchy, or both) and how to navigate the embellishments themselves.

Sequins, beads, and rhinestones on fabrics can be adhered, sewn individually, or sewn in sections.

Fabric Preparation and Care

Fabrics that have already been embellished should not be pretreated. If you're doing the embellishment yourself, make sure to preshrink and otherwise clean your base fabric before bedazzling. Glitter fabric can be pretreated as it will be laundered; some are machine washable, but more often they're hand-wash or dry-clean only. Most other embellished fabrics are dry-clean, hand-wash, or spot-clean only. They should be laid flat to dry.

Because these fabrics are very difficult to iron and to repair, make sure to store them in a way that prevents wrinkles and other damage to the base fabric. Ideally, they should be stored hung and in a garment bag.

Drag bodysuit made from stretch mesh and a lot of sequins and rhinestones

GARMENTS AND MODELING BY LEVI TRACY
Photo by Levi Tracy

1. Beads and sewn sequins
2. Glitter
3. Sewn sequins
4. Sewn sequins
5. Adhered sequins

Pressing

Embellished fabrics can be very difficult to press or remove wrinkles from. Some are steamable, but steam will ruin the finish of many sequins, beads, and metallic threads, so do a thorough swatch test (including letting the swatch fully dry) before committing to steaming your fabric or finished piece.

✸ QUICK TIP!
If your embellished motif is sparse enough, you can iron or steam around the decorations. In that case, use heat and steam according to the base fabric. ●

Adhered sequin and glitter fabric is a little easier to press than sewn versions. Press on the wrong side (opposite the glitter or sequins) using a thick terry cloth as a mat so that the embellishments aren't damaged by your ironing surface. Start at low heat and gradually increase until you get an effective press. Always use a press cloth, especially when your material's base fabric is synthetic.

Pattern Transfer/Marking

If you can mark around your embellishments or on the back of your fabric, use the marking tool best for your base fabric. Otherwise, tailor's tacks, thread tracing, and chalk are always safe choices—just make sure your chalk washes out of your embellishments easily.

Masking or washi tape are also great options; they will easily come off of plastic embellishments.

Cutting

Generally, use craft scissors (when cutting through actual sequins), fabric shears (when cutting through just fabrics), or a rotary cutter when cutting embellished fabrics.

✸ QUICK TIP!
If your sequins want to fly around as you cut (or break, pg 151) your embellishments, tape the outline of your pattern piece with masking or washi tape; then cut through the tape along your cutline. The tape will secure the cut sequins, which can then be thrown away. ●

Cutting over a taped cutline

Always cut embellished fabrics using a with-nap layout—they do not have a traditional nap, but their decorative elements almost always have direction. (The exception is glitter fabric, which is usually applied in a flat, even layer all over the fabric. Take a moment to make sure your glitter fabric looks the same from all directions before cutting using a puzzle-piece style or on-the-grain layout, according to the base fabric.)

In addition to considering the nap, take a moment to make sure gravity is going to work with the sequins and beading. Imagine a dress where strings of beads hang away from the body because it was cut and sewn upside down! Similarly, consider carefully your pattern layout. Will the pattern be symmetrical on your piece? In the case of a garment, will it lay in a flattering place on the body? Take a moment to consider your pattern layout before you commit to cutting into expensive fabrics.

Sequins hanging with gravity and against it

QUICK TIP!
If you're using sewn sequins, immediately stitch over your seamlines or right outside of them (but within the seam allowance) once your fabric has been cut out. This will prevent your sequins from unraveling from their connection points.

Embellished fabrics should be cut in one layer. This will help ensure a logical layout for the decorations and make it easier on your hands and scissors: You won't be cutting through multiple layers of plastic sequins, for example.

If you're using a sewn beads fabric, remove the beads from the seam allowance before cutting. Instead of clipping them out one by one, use a hammer to break beads; this will leave securing stitches intact, and make sure entire lines of beads won't come free from your fabric.

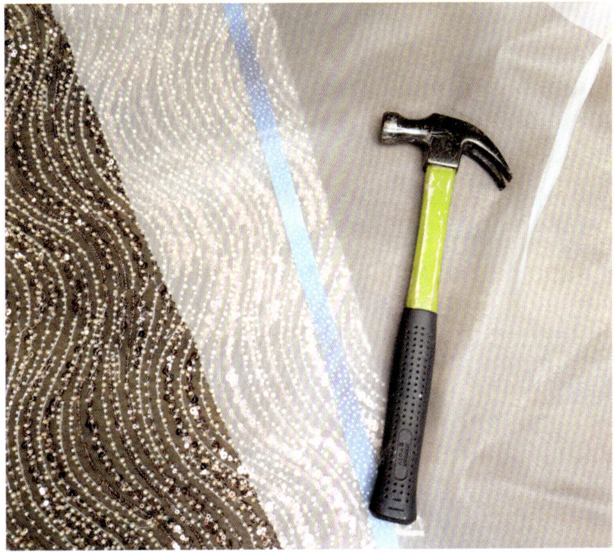

Breaking beads with a hammer. The washi tape marks the sew line; the press cloth prevents broken pieces from flying everywhere.

STAY SAFE!
When cutting, sewing, and (especially!) hammering embellishments, always wear eye and lung protection. If your machine needle shoots a sequin into your eye or you inhale a shard of glass, that will be a bad time.

Pinning and Alternatives

Use pins appropriate for the base fabric of your embellished material. Do not pin through beads, rhinestones, or sequins; you risk bending or dulling (and, therefore, ruining!) your pin or even damaging the embellishment. Glitter material may need slightly thicker pins to pierce through the glitter coating on the material.

Clips are also an option if they are appropriate for the base material. Do not leave clips on sequins for a long amount of time; they will dent the decorative elements.

Interfacing

Embellished fabrics should be interfaced according to their base fabrics. However, make sure to always use sew-in interfacing, because these fabrics shouldn't generally be ironed. Before sewing the interfacing in, remove embellishments from your interfacing seamline if they can't be sewn over.

If you must stiffen embellished fabrics—either temporarily or permanently—consider starching. A spray starch in a key area, like a collar or button placket, is an alternative to tricky commercial interfacing. As always, though, make sure to swatch first, and make particularly sure that your embellishments aren't damaged by the stiffener you choose.

Sewing

Before sewing, you may need to remove embellishments—especially sewn beading—from the seam allowance (if they weren't removed in the cutting step). Use thread snips (with pointed ends) or seam rippers. Make sure that removing the embellishments won't cause the entire section to unravel; if it will, you may need to remove fewer embellishments, fill in the section after you've sewn, or hammer the embellishments (pg 151) instead.

Generally, choose your needle and thread for machine sewing embellished fabrics according to the base material. However, here's a good starting point:

- For beading, choose entirely based on the base fabric because you will not be sewing through any beads.
- An 80/12 microtex needle, when using sequined fabric, will allow you to pierce sequins. A stretch needle when using stretch sequin fabric is appropriate. If you remove sequins from the seam allowance, choose entirely based on the base fabric.
- Glitter is a coated regular fabric; an 80/12 stretch or universal needle (according to the fabric's stretch) will probably be strong enough to deal with the coating. If you get broken needles, upgrade to a microtex or denim needle for extra power.

Regardless of the needle you choose, make sure to have plenty of extras. Sewing with embellished fabrics always risks bent and broken needles, and you want to be able to continue sewing even after you have a casualty! Your starting stitch should also be tailored to the base material, but using a longer (3.5mm) straight stitch is a good start; with a longer stitch, you'll risk fewer bent and broken needles.

✸ QUICK TIP!

Sew slowly when creating with embellished fabrics. You want to be able to react to issues—whether that's a broken needle, a bead in your machine, or wiggling expensive fabric—very quickly. •

Generally, use all-purpose polyester thread for adhered sequins and glitter fabrics (which are likely light- to medium-weight polyester fabrics) and fine thread for delicate nets, which many beaded and sewn-sequined fabrics are on.

A walking foot is great for these fabrics, which will bunch and slip while feeding through your machine. If your embellishments create a thick layer of fabric, consider decreasing the pressure of your presser foot so that the substantial material can more easily move through your machine.

Glitter fabric can be seamed and hemmed according to the specifics of its base fabric.

To hem sequins and beading, you may need to remove more embellishments; a single-fold hem (pg 85) may work well for your base fabric but will be impossible to execute without taking out beads! Consider if using hem tape, glue, or hand sewing a hem is an easier and cleaner solution.

Is It Worth It?

Because many of these fabrics require you to remove embellishments for every sewn line, consider: Is it worth it to take out a great deal more embellishments to create a seam with hidden raw edges (like a French seam or overedged seam), or will your piece will be okay with just the seamline removed, and then pinked edges (or a lining!) protecting the raw edges?

Whatever your finishing choices, consider that embellishments can be added back after your piece is finished: Collect some of the embellishments you removed from the seam allowance and sew them back onto your fabric to fill in gaps! Then make sure to keep a small collection of extras stashed for future repairs.

Embroidery, Lace, and Eyelet

In **embroidery**, a decorative element is added with thread or yarn to a base material.

Some laces are embroidered, but not all embroidery is lace. Generally, **lace** is created by knotting or weaving yarns into an open, airy format. That is, where a woven fabric would be woven and a knit fabric would be knit, a lace fabric is knotted, braided, crocheted, knit, or even—yes—embroidered! Lace *is* a fabric, whereas embroidery is *done* to a fabric. That said, because both feature decorative stitched elements with (often) relatively thick lumps of thread, they sew similarly.

Eyelet, also called cutwork, is somewhat lace's opposite construction technique: Holes are cut into fabric and then reinforced with decorative stitching. In eyelets with small holes, you may be able to avoid them entirely and sew using techniques relevant to the base material.

A-line skirt embellished with a layer of black lace

SKIRT BY JONA GIAMMALVA, FROM *THE ESSENTIAL A LINE* (C&T PUBLISHING)

1. Embroidery on a netting 2. Eyelet 3. Embroidery on a conventional woven fabric 4. Lace

1

2

3

4

Fabric Preparation and Care

Generally, prewash eyelet, embroidery, and lace as they will be washed on their final piece—of course, this is made tricky when you'll be using these materials *as* embellishments, because they'll be added to another fabric. In that case, consider sending a swatch of your base material and your lace, embroidery, or eyelet through the wash together to make sure they both survive the trip.

Lace and eyelet are usually delicate fabrics—they may be dry-clean only, they may be hand-wash only, or they may be able to be machine washed cold and laid flat to dry.

If you'll be doing your own decorative stitching, prewash your base fabric before beginning that process.

Pressing

Press the wrong side of your material gently on a padded surface; you don't want to mar the embroidery detail or the fibers themselves. Always use a press cloth; that will ensure you never catch the point of the iron on sewn details. Start at a low heat and increase until effective, especially if you don't know the fiber content of your base material.

✷ QUICK TIP!

Many eyelets are identical on both sides. In that case, make sure you mark which side will be your wrong side and then always press from there—if you damage threads, they'll always be on the same side. •

Pattern Transfer/Marking

Some laces and many eyelets will be woven densely enough to use chalk, disappearing ink, and other conventional marking tools; just swatch test to make sure the tool you choose can be removed from your delicate and expensive fabric. If your lace or eyelet is too holey for a written mark, tailor's tacks or lines of washi tape may be your best option. For very delicate fabric, press and remove your washi tape on a sturdy fabric before placing it on the lace or eyelet to remove some tackiness.

Embroidered fabric can be marked with a technique appropriate to the base material. If you need to mark through the embroidery itself, chalk is probably a safe choice—just swatch to make sure it will wash out, because it may get caught in between the decorative threads.

Cutting

Use fabric shears, a rotary cutter, or serrated shears to cut lace. Generally, use cutting tools appropriate to the base material to cut eyelet and embroidered fabrics. Heavy-duty scissors may be required to cut through very dense stitching. Cut on the grain, unless the fabric has a directional element that requires a with-nap layout.

Lace and embroidered fabrics often have large motifs that repeat infrequently and, therefore, will need special consideration when it comes to layout. Will your lace be laid out on your pattern pieces the way you intend? If you want to use a certain element as a hem, is it properly aligned? Always cut in one layer so you know you're getting the designs and details you intend and also so you're not risking a ragged edge by forcing a cut through multiple layers of thick decorative threads.

Pinning and Alternatives

Some laces and eyelets will be dense enough for fine pins, clips, and glue sticks to function effectively. Others may need to be secured with hand basting (pg 99) or spray baste glue, especially those used solely as a decorative element on another material.

Do not pin through thick elements of embroidery and lace; you risk dulling or bending (and, therefore, ruining) your pins. Instead, pin around these elements. Use clips and glue when you do need to secure the thick elements, but don't leave your clips in for too long—they will leave dents in the decorative stitching.

Interfacing

Eyelet fabric and dense lace can be interfaced—sparingly—to stabilize hems and seams. In those cases, use fusible woven or nonwoven interfacing or organza.

Otherwise, lace should not generally be interfaced, especially very airy versions. If it needs to be stiffened temporarily, starch it. Flatlining (pg 141) with tulle can provide significant sturdiness without adding bulk, and may even be nearly invisible underneath the lace.

Interface your embroidered fabric according to its base fabric.

Sewing

Sew eyelet, embroidered fabric, and lace with a 2.5mm straight stitch, all-purpose or fine polyester thread (according to the delicacy of the material), and a walking foot. Consider decreasing the pressure of the walking foot if your fabrics shift during sewing or if embroidered seams start to layer up and become thick.

Use a 60/8 universal or stretch needle with eyelet (according to its stretchiness) and a 60/8 universal machine needle with lace. When you'll be sewing through embroidery and not just around it, start with an 80/12 denim needle. The denim needle will be strong enough to push all the way through thick, layered threads. If you experience broken or bent needles, either increase the size of your needle (therefore, increasing its strength) or switch to a microtex needle.

Many of these fabrics will be built on a net or mesh base fabric, and many eyelets are far enough apart that their holes don't need to be considered significantly when choosing seams and hems. When you're not manipulating the appliqué portion of these materials, treat the fabric as just the base fabrics; choose seams and hems that are appropriate for that material.

You may find that your lace or eyelet, particularly very lightweight versions, get pulled into your machine when sewing. In that case, sew using a tissue-paper sandwich (right) or a straight stitch plate.

QUICK TIP!

Sewing with the help of tissue or parchment paper can make creating with sticky, holey, and very lightweight materials a breeze. Simply sandwich the materials in between two layers of the paper and sew! You can then tear the paper away, leaving a clean and easy seam.

Sewing with a complete tissue-paper sandwich

You may find that you need only one layer of paper when working with certain materials: A layer on top allows the presser foot to easily slide across an otherwise sticky material, while a layer on the bottom prevents very delicate fabrics from getting sucked below the presser plate. Experiment to find out what your application needs!

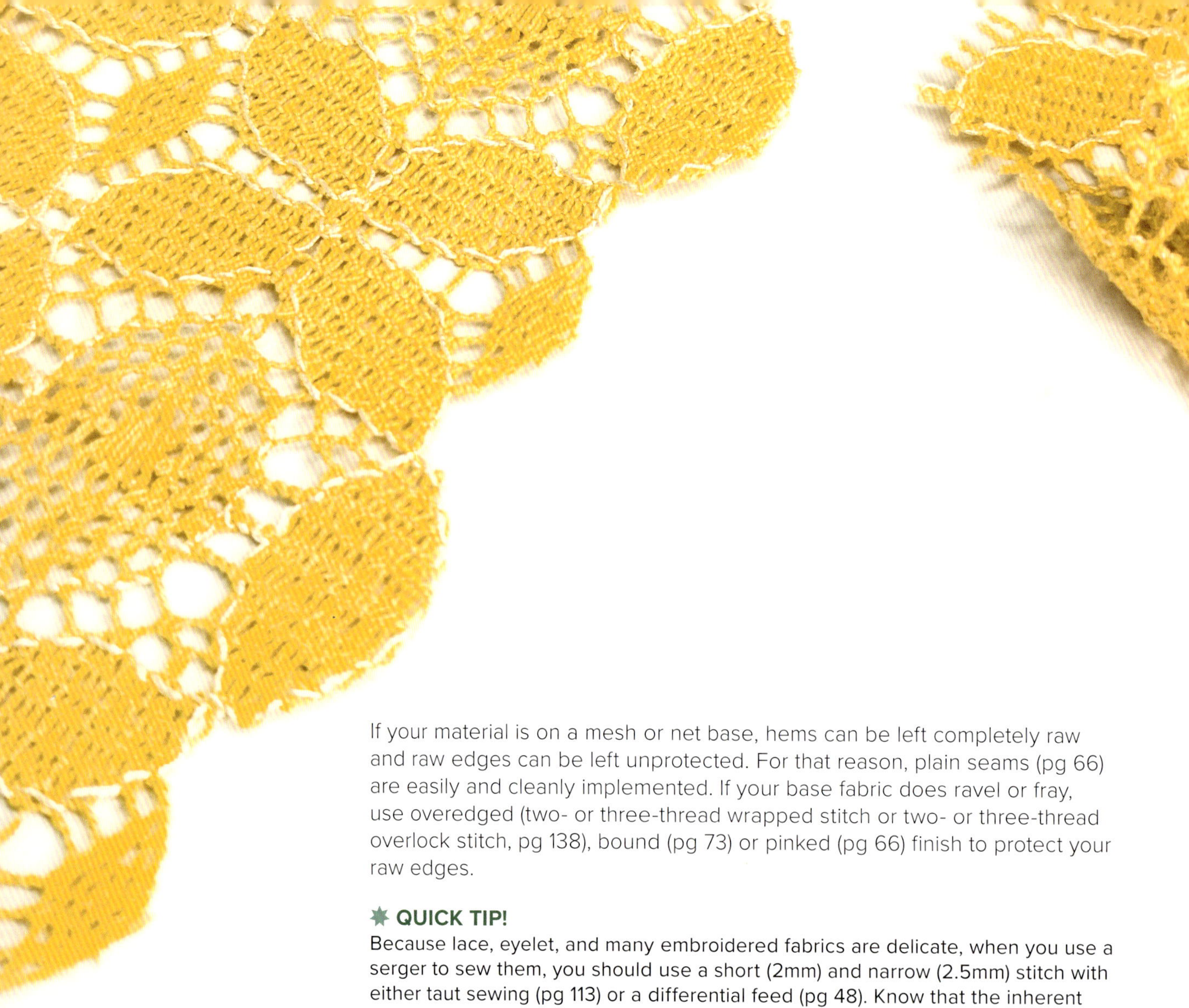

The raw edge of lace, closely clipped, suitable to be used as a hem or the top of a lapped seam

If your material is on a mesh or net base, hems can be left completely raw and raw edges can be left unprotected. For that reason, plain seams (pg 66) are easily and cleanly implemented. If your base fabric does ravel or fray, use overedged (two- or three-thread wrapped stitch or two- or three-thread overlock stitch, pg 138), bound (pg 73) or pinked (pg 66) finish to protect your raw edges.

QUICK TIP!
Because lace, eyelet, and many embroidered fabrics are delicate, when you use a serger to sew them, you should use a short (2mm) and narrow (2.5mm) stitch with either taut sewing (pg 113) or a differential feed (pg 48). Know that the inherent bumpiness of their embellishments can cause stitching issues with a serger; if you can, plan your seams and hems to avoid prominent motifs. •

Lapped seams (pg 160) are a surprising addition to the options. Using a pair of sharp thread snips, cut around the decorative stitching on the seamline edge of one of your two fabric pieces, making sure to account for the needed overlap in a lapped seam. You can then sew along the clean lace, embroidery, or eyelet, creating a seam that's very clean—and often, invisible.

You can also use lace and embroidery itself to hem: Using a sharp pair of thread snips, carefully cut around the edge of the embellishment closest to your piece's hemline, and then leave it raw. Similarly, eyelet can be used as a hem if the holes are close enough together. You then may want to stabilize the hem to strengthen the raw base fabric edge.

QUICK TIP!
For the same reason that lace can be used as a hem, lace and embroidered appliqués can be removed completely from their connective fabric to be used as embellishments on other fabrics. •

Specialty Fabrics

Specialty fabrics have particular construction or fiber content that make them tricky to sew. Lamé, latex, leather, and cork have unconventional fiber contents—metal, rubber, skin, and bark, respectively. Felt is a more typical fabric, but its unique construction means it can be treated a bit differently during the sewing process.

Catrina de Papel Picado dress made with laser-cut felt fabric panels and decorative fabric flowers

COSTUME AND MODELING BY MELANIE JASMINE (MJASMINE DESIGN)
Photography by David Ngo

Coat made from dead-stock buffalo check recycled melton in a wool blend

GARMENT AND MODELING BY TAI HICKS (BASMA SHIMMIES)
Photo by Tai Hicks (Basma Shimmies)

Felt, Boiled Wool, and Melton

Felting is the process of pressing fibers together to create a solid textile. There are different kinds of felting *and* different products created from felting.

The fabric we know as **felt**, which we may buy in sheets from the craft store or off of typical fabric bolts, is a stiff and textured fabric with no grain. Wool felt is very warm and wrinkle resistant; acrylic felt is inexpensive and accessible. Felt has a great body, as it is very structured. Felt comes in multiple thicknesses and is, therefore, suitable for different applications.

Fulling is a specific kind of felting where the yarns of an existing fabric are matted together with hot water and agitation. **Boiled wool** is similar to felt fabric and is made by fulling knits. **Melton** is made by fulling a twill wool and has a more pronounced nap. Both are wrinkle and moisture resistant.

Although felt is a nonwoven, boiled wool is made from a knit, and melton is made from a twill weave, all three can be treated like a dense woven fabric during the sewing process, which makes them fairly easy to work with. Not least of all because, due to their dense and knotted fibers, felts do not fray.

Making Felt

Felting wool is an easy project that you can do yourself. Wool shrinks and fuzzes when wet, which means that the yarns become tangled with each other and obstruct the weave or knit of the fabric. This can be extremely undesirable if you've accidentally felted a prized sweater, but if done on purpose, it can be a great creative exercise. Create your own textile!

1. Boiled wool
2. Melton
3. Felt
4. Felt

Fabric Preparation and Care

Boiled wool, felt, and melton are tough to wash and prewash because they may felt or full more. If they will be washed once complete, they should be prewashed—all three materials will shrink—but make sure to swatch your wash and dry technique first, to make sure your finished material (possibly more felted or fulled than before) is still to your liking.

Generally, boiled wool and felt can be machine washed on gentle in cold water and laid flat to dry. Melton is more delicate: Consider spot cleaning, dry cleaning, or hand washing in lukewarm water with gentle detergent.

Remember: If your boiled wool, felt, or melton is wool (not acrylic), make sure to store it protected from moths and other wool-eating critters!

Pressing

Because all three of these materials are textured, they should be pressed with a press cloth. For 100 percent wool varieties, use a wool setting with steam (but make sure the fabric has been preshrunk first). If they are synthetic or a synthetic blend, start at a low pressing temperature and increase until pressing is effective.

Pattern Transfer/Marking

Chalk works extremely well on boiled wool, felt, and melton. Because they're completely opaque materials, you can also mark on the reverse with conventional pens and markers.

Cutting

Boiled wool, felt, and melton can be cut with scissors or a rotary cutter. If they are a thick fabric, consider cutting just one layer at a time. Make sure your cutting tool is sharp; because these fabrics are so dense, a dull blade will just pull at the fabric instead of cutting it.

If your boiled wool, felt, or melton is acrylic or an acrylic blend, consider using (sharp) craft scissors instead of your nice fabric shears to prevent them from being dulled by the thick plastic fabric.

Pinning and Alternatives

All-purpose pins and clips work well with boiled wool, felt, and melton. With thicker fabrics or when layers begin to build up, you may need long pins so that they aren't lost in the bulk.

Interfacing

Sew-in or fusible woven or nonwoven interfacing work well with these fabrics. Remember to always preshrink interfacings before using them with preshrunk fabrics such as these.

Sewing

Boiled wool, felt, and melton are fairly easy to sew with. They do not fray, so edges can be left raw, and they can even be glued instead of sewn if desired.

Use a size 80/12 needle for melton, a 90/14 for boiled wool, and a 90/14 or 100/16 for felt. A universal needle will work for many applications, but if you experience broken or bent needles or are struggling to get your needle through these bulky fabrics, switch to a microtex.

A 2.5mm straight stitch is a good starting point, but consider lengthening that to 3mm for thicker fabrics and as layers build up. A walking, roller, or nonstick machine foot will help feed these substantial fabrics through the machine. Use all-purpose cotton or polyester (according to the fabric's fiber content) thread. Heavy-duty thread may be necessary for thicker fabrics, especially those that will be under stress when the piece is complete.

Lapped (pg 160) and abutted (pg 171) seams work well for these fabrics; because they don't fray and can be quite thick, minimal seams are elegant and appropriate. Topstitching (pg 177) adds a nice finish and flattens bulky seam allowances. Hems are not necessary, but a single fold (pg 85) works well for a finished edge.

Tutorial Time: Lapped Seams

Lapped seams are minimal and beautiful, but they are complicated by their asymmetrical seam allowances.

1. Decide which of your pieces will be the top of the lapped seam. Only on that piece, carefully cut the seam allowance entirely away.

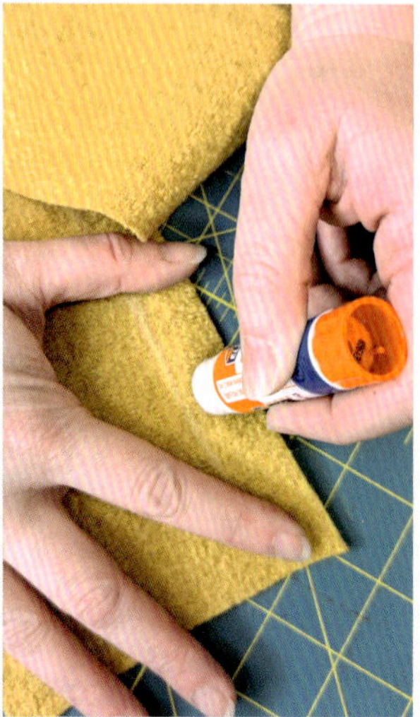

2. Align the pieces, matching seamlines. Baste the two layers together (pg 99); pins will distort the seamline, creating a wobbly and inaccurate seam.

3. Edgestitch (pg 105) along the seamline. If desired, topstitch (pg 177) down the bottom seam allowance.

When sewing with felted and fulled fabrics, the feed dogs may get stuck in the surface of the material. If this happens to you, sew your fabric between two layers of tissue or parchment paper (pg 155), and then tear the paper away once sewing is complete.

QUICK TIP!
Glue works particularly well with felted and fulled material because adhesive can easily bond to the dense, textured material. All seams and hems can be achieved with hot glue or PVA glue (regular white glue or tacky glue). If you're using PVA glue on a plain seam, use clips or weights within the seam allowance to secure the seam while the glue cures. •

Because of their construction, felted and fulled materials will create a lot of dusty fibers in your workspace and, importantly, your machine. A dusty machine can cause sewing issues, so make sure to clean it often when working with these materials; a small vacuum works great for this task! Additionally, consider wearing a mask to protect your lungs.

Leather

Lightweight **leather**, which is the skin of an animal that's been refined for use in clothing, crafts, and home goods, is durable and soft and has a beautiful drape. It is insulating and breathable. **Suede** is a specific finish applied to leather that gives it a pleasant fuzzy nap. It is generally less durable and harder to clean than other leather finishes, but it is softer.

Creating with leather and suede introduces some difficulties: They can be expensive to acquire, are difficult to clean, and require some specialty techniques. They have some advantages over traditional textiles, though! Because you can use a puzzle-piece style layout with most of them, there is almost no waste of material, and—best of all—they don't fray.

Third Fleet Master *(Monster Hunter)* waist sash is a goat skin cincher that has been overlaid with a veg tan leather cincher and a silk dupioni sash.

COSTUME BY WIGTALL AND WIGSMALL OF WIG-WIG COSPLAY
MODELING BY WIGSMALL OF WIG-WIG COSPLAY
Photo by Brett Bauer

What about Heavyweight Leather?

Leather comes from different animals, with different finishing types, and in many different thicknesses, not all of which can be sewn on a conventional machine. Leather craft is its own art form with specific techniques and challenges. Entire books have been written on the subject!

The techniques included herein are appropriate for thin leather (around 3 ounces or less, see Quick Tip below), which are accessible for most home sewists and their machines.

QUICK TIP!

The United States and Europe measure leather differently. In the United States, a leather's thickness is denoted in ounces per square foot: 1 square foot of 1-ounce leather weighs 1 ounce. In Europe, actual thickness of the leather in millimeters is used: a 1 ounce leather is about 0.4mm thick.

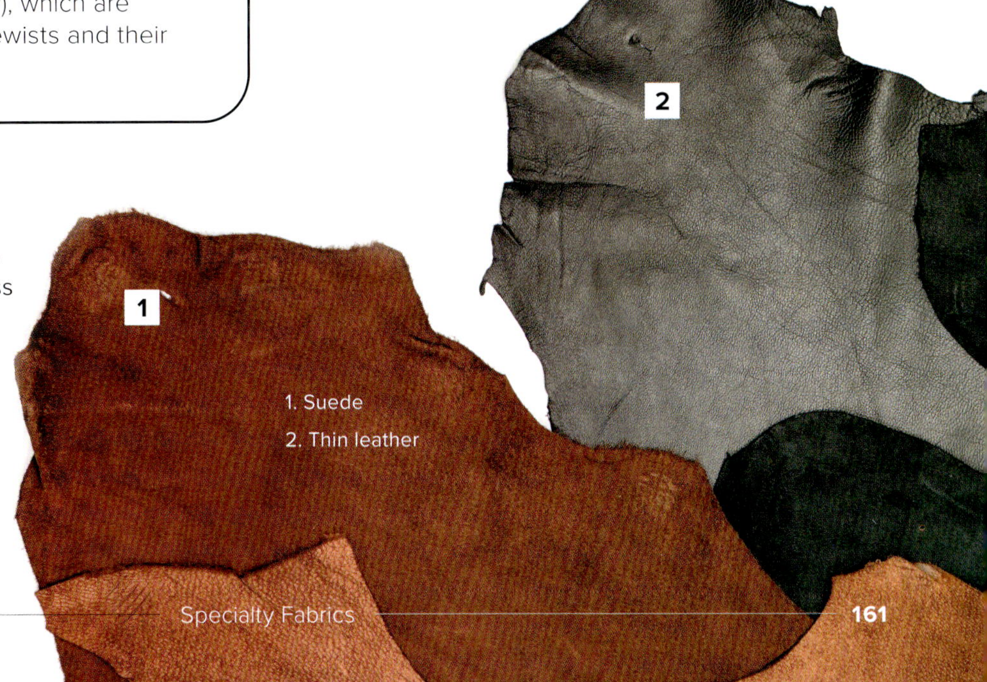

1. Suede
2. Thin leather

Is My Leather Real?

It's *usually* easy to tell if a material is leather or not: Just look at the reverse side! If it looks like suede or skin, it's leather. If it looks like fabric or plastic, it's vinyl.

If you still can't tell, though, use the burn test (pg 15) on a scrap or inconspicuous part of your material. Leather will brown, then burn. Faux leathers will melt; they're plastic!

Stretch Leather

Some lightweight leather has natural stretch—it is skin, after all! Others have a fabric backing, which includes spandex fibers; these not only allow for the natural stretch of the skin, but also ensure its recoverability. When sewing with these materials, make sure to use a zigzag stitch and a walking foot. You may want to experiment with your machine needle: A stretch needle may get you better results than a leather one.

If your stretch leather has a fabric backing, consider the direction of its stretch and grain and be sure to cut your pattern pieces with respect to them, instead of using a puzzle-piece style layout.

Fabric Preparation and Care

Some leather is machine- or hand-washable. If it is, always make sure to prewash it; it will shrink.

Most leather, however, must be either dry-cleaned or cleaned and conditioned using products specifically made for that purpose. Don't use fabric or hand soaps with leather; they'll wear out the material.

Suede can be brushed to revive its fuzzy nap with a suede brush or another piece of suede (suede to suede).

Do not store leather materials or finished creations folded; folds can become permanent creases. Use padded hangers or roll to store. Keep leather out of heat and sunlight when it's stored; those elements will dry it out, making it stiff and brittle.

Pressing

Leather can be pressed but won't necessarily need it. Usually, wrinkles can be hung out—leave your material hanging, and the wrinkles will fall out. If they don't, press at medium temperature using a paper press cloth and no steam. Make a particular effort to always swatch test pressing! Specialty and embossed leathers, especially, may be damaged by heat, because their finishes may have been applied with heat.

When constructing leather pieces, you'll often use a hammer or seam roller instead of pressing. For example, when pressing open a seam or preparing to secure a hem, you'll want to use one of those tools instead of a hot iron.

Seam rolling a leather hem

As with other napped fabrics, pressing suede can ruin the texture. Press on a plush terry towel or another piece of suede with the textured surfaces facing each other.

Pattern Transfer/Marking

On the right side of leather, mark with chalk or a leather marking tool after confirming that your choice of tool can be removed safely. On the reverse, regular marking tools will not show through to the front of your piece.

Any sueded material needs to be cut using a with-nap layout. Certain other types of leather—such as those that still have hair, or *top grain* versions, which haven't been sanded smooth—should also be laid out with nap. When in doubt, examine your materials under different lighting conditions and from many angles and see if it looks different.

Even conventional hides have grains—though it's not based on yarns and weaves! Skins stretch in different directions and are thick or thin in different sections. Generally, the part of the leather nearest and running parallel to the spine will have the most consistent thickness and density, and as you move away from the spine, the leather will thin. That thinner leather at the edges is usually going to be stretchier.

For that reason, cut pattern pieces along the grain of the spine, and place important, substantial pieces parallel and next to the backbone so that they'll drape nicer and have more consistent thickness. Additionally, make an effort to match symmetrical pieces of your creation in thickness—you want both of the side fronts of your dress to be the same thickness, for example.

If your piece of leather has been cut so small that you can't tell how you'd cut along the grain, a puzzle-piece style layout is fine and preserves precious material.

QUICK TIP!

If you run out of material on your hide, you can't just run to the fabric store to buy more; even a skin from the same kind of animal and finished the same way will have subtle differences. Laying and cutting out your pattern pieces carefully and correctly is crucial.

If your project will take more than one skin, buy them at the same time and plan your pattern pieces so that the differences between the two are symmetrical (or, at least, intentional).

Finally, sewing with leather often involves unconventional seams like lapped (pg 160) and abutted (pg 171). While laying out your pattern pieces, consider that you may need to modify your seam allowances to account for those choices.

QUICK TIP!

Because of its nature—it came from an animal, who had a moving body and lived a life—leather hides may have more natural imperfections than fabric. Before you cut any leather piece, carefully inspect for holes, scars, divots, or natural wrinkles (such as on the neck). Mark those marred areas with chalk or a leather marker.

When laying out pattern pieces, consider where on your piece you want these imperfections to be; maybe they'd work best as the bottom of a bag or the underside of a collar.

Cutting

Cut leather using a rotary cutter or very sharp scissors. If you'll be using scissors, consider investing in a pair of heavy-duty sewing sheers so that your everyday ones don't take a beating. Because leather can't be folded, you must cut on one layer.

When cutting, aim for one smooth, continuous cut to prevent ragged edges and dangling pieces. This is especially important if you'll be leaving your hems and other edges raw.

Finally, if your leather looks the same on both sides, label the reverse with a regular writing utensil so you don't make mistakes in your construction later on in the sewing process.

Pinning and Alternatives

Holes in leather are permanent. Use sewing clips, a glue stick, or water-soluble sewable tape instead of pinning or basting with thread. If your leather is too thick for sewing clips, consider using binder clips instead. These are also great for clamping seams while adhesive cures.

When transferring patterns, use weights instead of pins.

Interfacing

Woven sew-in, nonwoven sew-in, and organza are the simplest options for interfacing leather.

However, fusible is also a great choice if your leather can handle the heat; in some ways, it's a safer choice, because attaching it won't add perforations to your material the way sew-in will. Err toward low-temperature fusible varieties, and always swatch test.

If your leather is naturally stretchy, you can use a fusible stabilizer to prevent difficulties with stretch and in high-stress areas (like shoulder and crotch seams) to strengthen.

Sewing

Sew leather using heavy-duty polyester thread, a 2.5–3mm straight stitch, and a nonstick, walking, or roller foot. Consider that a roller foot may leave marks in delicate leather and suede. If your foot or the feed dogs are damaging the leather, sew with a tissue-paper sandwich (pg 155) to protect your material.

With very lightweight leathers, an 80/12 universal needle may do the trick. However, thicker leathers will need more substantial needles: Use a 90/14 up to a 110/18 leather needle depending on the weight you're sewing and the number of layers in your stitch line. Change needles if you at all suspect that your needle is damaged or getting dull; you do not want to risk marring leather's delicate surface with a substandard machine needle.

You may need to reduce presser foot pressure or use a seam jumper (pg 77) to allow thicker leather or bulkier seams to feed nicely through your machine. Conversely, when sewing right sides together, the faces of very smooth leather may slip against each other. Baste (with glue or water-soluble sewable tape, pg 99) or increase presser foot pressure to help resolve this slippage.

✸ QUICK TIP!

Because holes in leather are permanent and the material is expensive, mock-ups are essential. Denim, canvas, heavy muslin, and felt are all appropriate materials; choose the one that's closest to the weight and drape of your chosen leather. ●

Instead of backstitching at the beginning and ends of seamlines, leave thread tails long and then tie them after you're done sewing. The long tails can then be clipped (and the knots secured with a dab of glue) or tucked into the glued or stitched seam allowance.

Plain (pg 66), lapped (pg 160), welt (pg 165), and flat-fell (pg 81) seams are all appropriate for leather. Seam allowances will bubble up; to secure them, use a seam roller or hammer to flatten and then either glue or topstitch them down. When topstitching, increase the stitch length.

Hammering a seam allowance before topstitching

Tutorial Time: Welt Seams

A welt seam is beautiful and decorative but does not, itself, protect raw edges. It can be done when raw edges have already been protected, especially with low-bulk options like pinking (pg 66) and overedging (pg 138).

1. With right sides together, sew a straight stitch along the seamline.

2. Press the seam open and then to one side. Traditionally, this should be the side away from the center front of the body, when making garments. Topstitch (pg 177).

Single-fold (pg 85), faced (with lining fabric, pg 124), and bound (pg 73) hems work for leather ... or the edge can be left raw! To create a single-fold hem in leather, mark your hemline, fold and hammer, and then glue or sew to secure.

Contact cement (pg 204) can be used to secure seam allowances, seam, and hem. Just be sure to wear proper personal protective equipment.

Above all, take your time when creating with leather. Mark, cut, and sew slowly! It's a delicate material, but the lightweight versions aren't that much different than typical fabrics; they just need extra patience and consideration.

Tissue Lamé

Tissue lamé is an extremely lightweight shiny metallic fabric. The wefts are made of metal—historically, they were silver, gold, or copper, but now Mylar is often used instead. The warps are regular threads, which makes the fabric particularly reflective. Lamé frays like wild and exposed metallic yarns can be very scratchy.

Lamé is notably difficult to sew with. It is sensitive, requires special techniques, and can be downright frustrating. If you decide to create with lamé, buy extra material, practice with swatches, and take breaks.

QUICK TIP!

Not all metallic fabrics are tissue lamé!

If it's fabric-backed, stretchy, or both, it may be a metallic-coated polyester, polypropylene, or polyurethane; basically, a typical nonwoven faux leather fabric covered in a shiny coating.

Other fabrics—like many jacquards—have real metal fibers and, therefore, need special consideration, but they do not generally have the extremely fiddly nature of tissue lamé.

Finally, some actual lamés are fabric-backed, often with tricot. This fabric backing gives tissue lamés structure, stability, and a soft reverse, which makes them *significantly* easier to both work with and wear. If your project could work as well with a fabric-backed lamé as it would with an unbacked version, seriously consider taking the easier route. ●

Barbecue Leona *(League of Legends)* gold detailing on dress and belt made with tissue lamé

COSTUME AND MODELING BY MAKER FISHMEAL
Photo by Sydney Newland (Cinnamon + Birch)

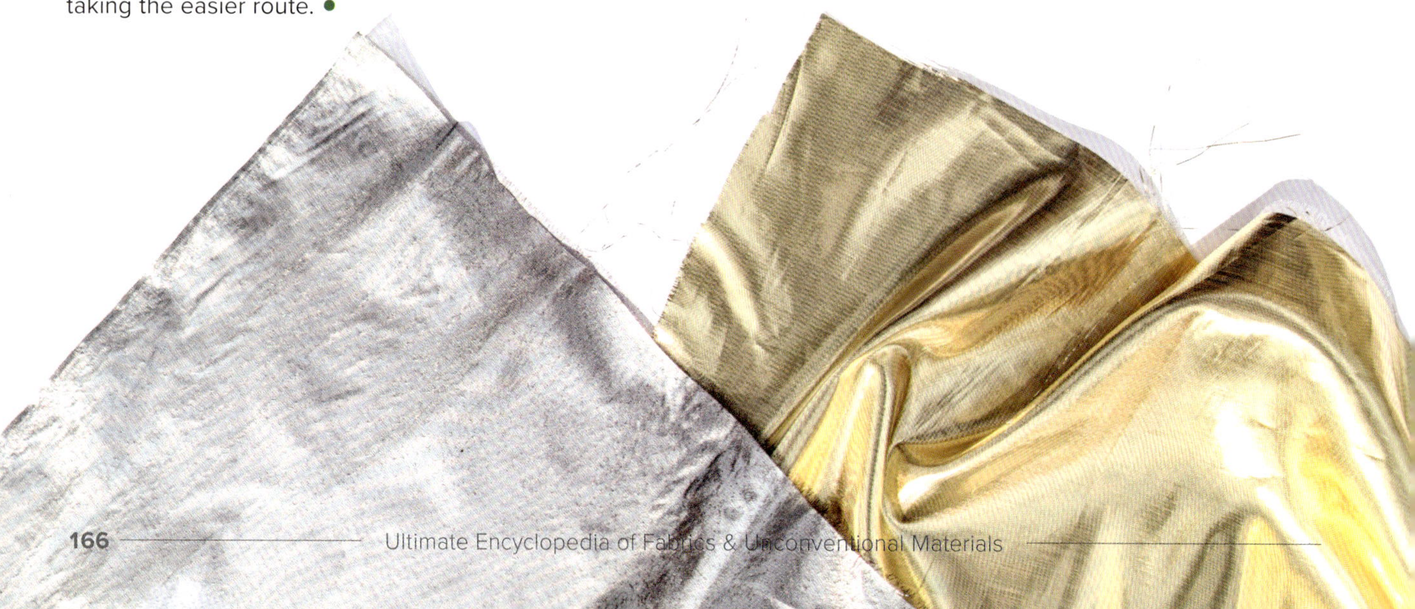

Conductive Fabrics!

Traditional fabrics with genuine metal incorporated into the structure (such as actual tissue lamé) are naturally conductive due to their metal content. But other fabrics are made *specifically* for conducting electricity and used for medicine, artwork, and sporting.

Conductive yarns can be added to any fiber or structure but are commonly added to a polyester or nylon woven base.

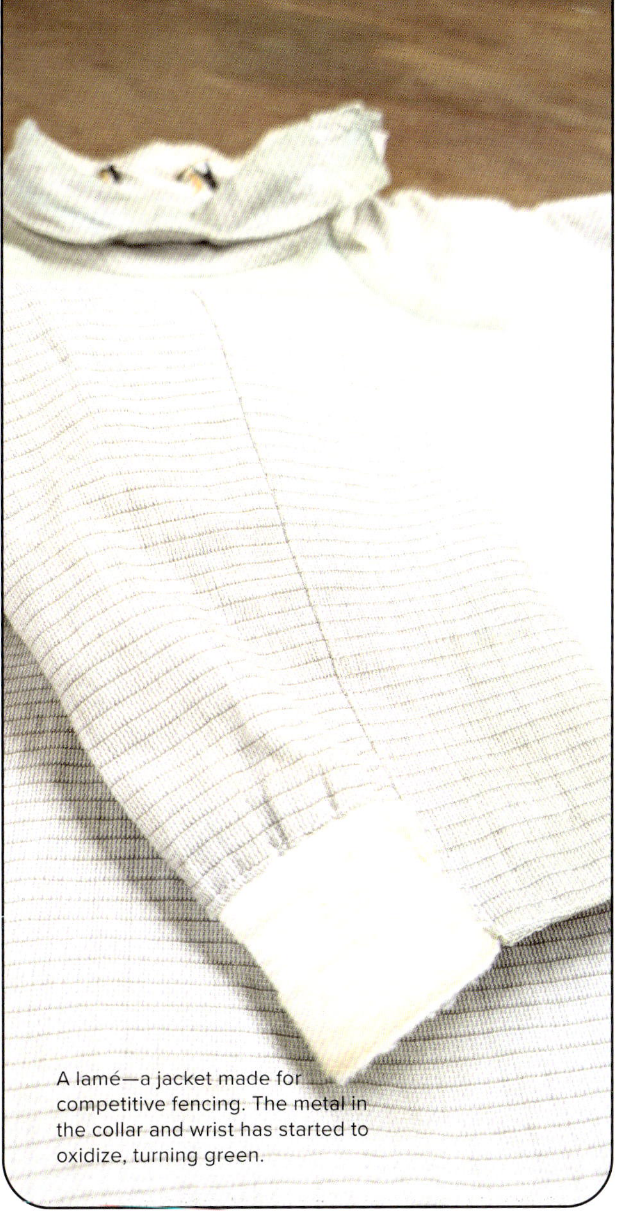

A lamé—a jacket made for competitive fencing. The metal in the collar and wrist has started to oxidize, turning green.

Fabric Preparation and Care

Unsurprisingly, lamé is tough to care for. It is almost always dry-clean only. Metal fibers will tarnish or rust, so creations must be kept stored away from moisture. Lamé is difficult to press, so it needs to be stored hung, but it also snags easily, so you should use only padded hangers.

Lamé is very susceptible to staining. Even products meant for fabric, like seam sealants (pg 56), will spread and stain on this sensitive material.

Pressing

Never steam lamé; the intense moist heat will ruin the finish of the metallic yarns. Press very carefully on low heat, on the wrong side, and using a press cloth.

Pattern Transfer/Marking

Disappearing ink is best for lamé; chalk will rub off of the slick fabric, and thread tracing and tailor's tacks will mar yarns. Test on a scrap to make sure your particular marking tool doesn't damage the sensitive material.

Cutting

Cutting lamé is a bit of a balancing act. It's best cut with extremely sharp blades, so freshly sharpened fabric sheers or a new rotary blade are a must. Unfortunately, lamé also dulls blades considerably and quickly. If you have the means, sharpen your fabric sheers both directly before *and* after completing a lamé project.

Another option is to buy a brand-new pair of craft scissors; they'll be as sharp as they come, but dulling them won't hurt as much as using your nice expensive fabric scissors. If you do pursue this route, test first to confirm that your new craft scissors are capable of making an adequate cut.

Pinking shears (pg 66) are tempting; they'll help control fraying while you sew. Consider whether it's worth the damage to your scissors to use them on metal.

Lamé is very lightweight and slinky; always cut on just one layer. It also has a slightly different sheen from each direction due to the metallic yarns, so cut using a with-nap layout.

Pinning and Alternatives

Pins will snag lamé badly and may even break metallic yarns, causing runs. If you do need to use pins, use sharp, fine pins. Otherwise, stick to clips. When transferring patterns, weight them down instead of pinning.

Interfacing

Because lamé is both difficult to sew and uncomfortable to touch, you may want to consider some dramatic interfacing options:

- Back the entirety of your piece with a very lightweight fusible nonwoven interfacing. This will add strength to the material, making it easier to manipulate and less prone to runs. When using fusible products, always fuse on as low a heat as possible through a very damp towel in order to not damage the metallic yarns in your material. Always swatch test first; even low heat may cause the moisture in the towel to damage the metallic threads.
- Flatline your entire creation. With this solution, you get to choose the fabric that will be touching your skin (if you're making a garment), and gain the advantage of having a sturdier material in the seamlines. Batiste, organza, and sew-in nonwoven interfacing are classic options, but any typical lining material will work, depending on the support you want to give your lamé.
- Add stabilizer tape along the entire seamline, which will contain fraying coming from the seam, reduce runs somewhat, and allow you to pin or clip more densely (pg 134) to reduce slippage during sewing.

Alternatively, purchasing lamé that's already fabric-backed (pg 166) solves many issues, and allows you to interface with conventional techniques and materials.

Sewing

When sewing with lamé, needle choice will drastically affect your outcome. Always use a new needle and change it frequently; remember, lamé dulls blades! Start with a 70/10 microtex and test on scraps. If you get runs, switch to either a smaller needle or a ballpoint needle. If you're sewing with metallic thread, use a metallic needle. If none of your experimentation gives good results, reconsider your stabilizer and stitch length.

Use all-purpose polyester thread and a standard presser foot to sew lamé. Start with a 2.5mm straight stitch; a longer one (up to 3.5mm) may reduce runs. Like other delicate materials, lamé tends to get sucked below the stitch plate; if you have this problem, sew with a tissue-paper sandwich (pg 155) or switch to a straight stitch plate.

If you get puckers, taut sew (pg 113).

✸ QUICK TIP!
Holes often show in lamé once seams and pins are removed; those same holes may fray into the body of your creation. Because it's so tough to cleanly remove lines of stitches, proper mock-ups and swatching are essential when working with lamé. If you do end up with a needle or pinhole in your material, rub it with a finger to massage the yarns back into place. ●

Because lamé is so scratchy and because it frays excessively, enclosed seams are necessary: French (pg 114) and flat-fell (pg 81) seams are good options. While a double-fold hem (pg 85) is fine, a rolled hem (pg 132) with a rolled-hem foot is more delicate and is achieved with just one line of stitches, reducing the chance of runs.

✸ QUICK TIP!
Do not use a serger with lamé: The high speed of a serger introduces risk of damage, its dense stitches will likely cause runs, and lamé's metallic yarns will quickly dull the blade. Stick to a conventional sewing machine! ●

Pouches made from cork fabric.

BAG BY JESSICA KAPITANSKI FROM *CREATE WITH CORK FABRIC* BY C&T PUBLISHING

Cork

Cork is a layer of bark that is harvested from live trees. Thin cork adhered to a fabric backing makes an excellent material for bags and other accessories. It is soft and flexible, durable, lightweight, and easy to clean.

Thicker cork, which does not have a fabric backing, is still sewable (up to a certain thickness) and can also be glued.

1. Cork fabric
2. Thick cork

Fabric Preparation and Care

Cork does not need to be prewashed; it should be spot cleaned with soap and water.

Pressing

Pressing cork is not usually necessary, because it does not wrinkle or crease. However, it is possible; cork does not melt, so you should press according to the fiber content of the fabric it's adhered to.

QUICK TIP!
Steam will relax cork; if you have a roll of cork you wish to flatten, steam the roll gently and then leave it to set under weight. •

Pattern Transfer/Marking

Chalk works great on cork, as do leather markers. Mark on the adhered fabric according to what's safe for it; chalk is usually a safe option, but make sure to swatch before committing to large marks!

Because cork is opaque, conventional marking tools work well on the reverse. Permanent markers make obvious, bold lines.

Cutting

A rotary cutter works very well on thin cork and fabric-backed cork. Craft scissors will also work on both fabric-backed and thin cork, but thicker cork will require a box cutter (pg 200). In all cases, using a very sharp blade will result in edges that are clean and beautiful and can be kept raw.

Cut fabric-backed cork on the grain. Thicker, unbacked cork can be cut puzzle-piece style.

Pinning and Alternatives

Cork is best secured with clips; pins will struggle to flex through the thick material and will leave holes. You can also baste with a glue stick or basting spray (pg 99).

Interfacing

Cork is very stiff, so interfacing is not generally necessary. Fleece batting, foam, or another layer of cork is usually the best option. These can be sewn in, but permanent spray adhesive or contact cement (pg 204) are good options for adhering stiffeners to cork, especially if your sewing machine can't handle multiple layers of these substantial materials.

Sewing

Thin and fabric-backed cork is surprisingly easy to sew! If your machine can handle the thickness of material you're sending through it, the actual techniques used won't be trouble for you.

Start with an 80/12 universal, microtex, or topstitch machine needle, but thicker material may need a thicker needle. Use a roller or nonstick presser foot, a 2.5mm straight stitch, and either all-purpose or heavy-duty polyester thread, depending on the weight of your cork and the application you're sewing for.

Cork does not fray. With lighter-weight cork, a plain seam (pg 66) with topstitched seam allowance is easily executed and beautiful. If your cork is thick enough that a regular seam won't bend well enough to make a good finish, instead sew an abutted seam (pg 171). Consider reinforcing the join with a fabric strip glued or sewn into the back of the cork pieces. A lapped seam (pg 160) will be strong but will result in a bump in your cork.

Tutorial Time: Abutted Seams

Abutted seams connect your material without any overlap at all—perfect for very bulky materials and very minimal seams.

1. To begin, cut your pieces all the way up to the seamline. Align them at the seamline; then use fusible interfacing or stabilizer to baste the pieces together. (To create an abutted seam in one step, you can stop here!)

2. Use a wide zigzag stitch to connect the pieces. You can sew from either the right or wrong side of the piece.

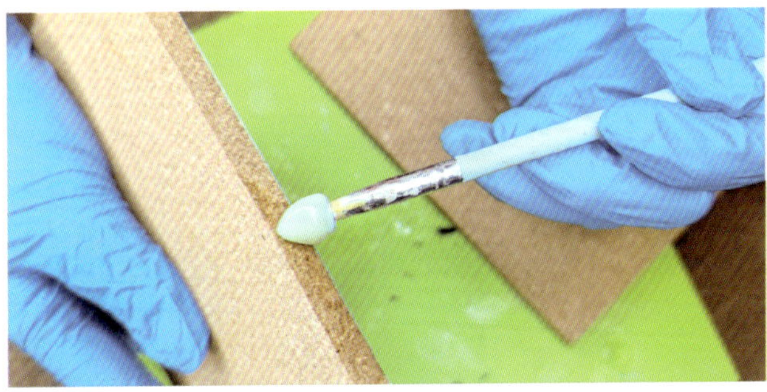

Abutted seams are even easier to create with thick materials and glue.

After cutting both pieces to the seamline, adhere with glue.

For both sewn and glued abutted seams, the reverse side of the abutted seam can be reinforced with interfacing, fabric, tape, fusible interfacing, or glue.

Because it does not fray, cork doesn't need to be hemmed and raw edges don't need to be enclosed. An overedged (zigzagged or four-thread overlocked, pg 138), bound (pg 73), or (if the cork is thin enough) single-fold hem (pg 85) will also work. If your cork is thick enough, consider beveling the edge (pg 198) with a rotary tool to create a more finished look.

Cork pieces can also be constructed using glue. Contact cement (pg 204) and permanent high-strength spray adhesive are good options. Use the same seam and hem options as with sewn seams, although abutted seams (above) with thin cork will need additional reinforcement; glued abutted seams on their own will not be particularly strong.

Latex

Latex rubber is made from the sap of a tree, which is processed into sheets that can be used as a textile. Latex is stretchy and usually shiny. It is unique among fabrics because it *cannot* be conventionally sewn—the tiny holes created by sewing needles will rip the material, causing creations to completely fall apart. Instead, a latex creator uses glue and latex-specific sewing techniques to make costuming, apparel, and accessories.

Latex comes in different thickness, ranging from 0.2–1mm. The thinnest latex can be slightly translucent; thicker versions have substantial body and can be used for outerwear and bags.

Fabric Preparation and Care

Latex cannot be machine washed or dried. Instead, gently hand wash your fabric and creations in warm water with classic blue Dawn dishwashing soap; then hang dry. Never store your latex on metal or cloth hangers, as these materials can damage your fabric—stick to plastic! Latex creations should also be stored out of the sunlight, because UV rays also damage the material. Finally, latex is very susceptible to color transfer; do not let latex pieces touch during storage. Garment bags help immensely in this regard.

When you first get your latex sheeting, it will be covered with a powder that prevents it from sticking to itself. Do not prewash this powder away! Your latex being nonstick will make it much easier to construct with.

Latex should also be stored with a nonstick coating—apply either talcum powder or a latex shiner after washing and before putting your piece away.

Pressing

Latex cannot be traditionally pressed. Instead, use a seam roller and adhesive to flatten seams and hems.

Pattern Transfer/Marking

Regular and gel pens work very well on latex and can be easily removed with acetone or, for a more effective result, a heptane-based thinner like Bestine Solvent and Thinner (by Speedball).

Cutting

Because latex does not fray, lapped seams are the norm, and raw edges will often be left unhemmed. For that reason, you really want clean raw edges; they'll be visible!

More important, any ragged edges in latex constructions introduce weak points, where the latex is more likely to tear.

Little black dress made from embossed latex

GARMENT BY ARCANE TECH, MODELING BY MAGGY COSPLAY
Photo by Arcane Tech

0.5mm latex sheeting

For these reasons, a rotary cutter is simply the best option for cutting latex. Cut carefully in single, smooth motions, and clean up any ragged cuts before manipulating the fabric more.

Latex does not have a grain or directional stretchiness, so pattern pieces can be arranged puzzle-piece style.

Pinning and Alternatives

Latex should never be pinned; small holes risk future tearing. Instead, use clips or washi tape to prepare your fabric for construction.

Interfacing

Latex does not interface or line. If you need more substantial latex, you're better off buying a thicker sheet.

Sewing

Once you have your pattern pieces cleanly cut, you're ready to start gluing the latex. First, clean the seam allowance with acetone; you don't want any powder interacting with the glue. You may prefer to mark the seamline with a gel pen or washi tape first; this will also help you properly align your pattern pieces when it's time to adhere them. Don't forget to clean both of the pieces you're going to be adhering. You may see your latex curl as you apply acetone—don't worry! When the acetone dries, the latex will uncurl.

Latex curling as its adhesive gasses off

STAY SAFE!

Don't forget to wear safety gear when working with chemicals! Your mask should be rated for solvents, not just particles. Wear gloves and eye protection when using acetone and high-powered adhesive.

Next, apply glue. You can use solvent-based or ammonia-based glue; both work well, with slight differences in how they interact with water and the latex itself. Apply a very thin layer of the glue—make sure to remove any excess, as it can both cause lumps in your seams and reduce the power of the glue. Wait for the glue to fully dry; then carefully press your latex seam together. Apply a thin layer of talcum powder to your seamline.

QUICK TIP!

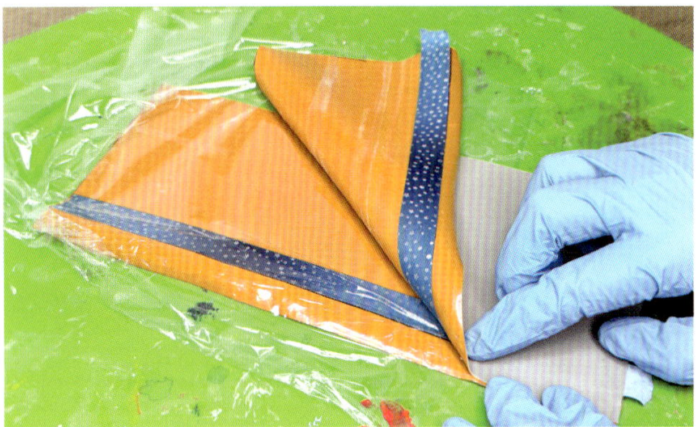

If you're having trouble with your glue touching and adhering before you're ready, cover the parts you're not ready for yet with cling wrap; then reveal just the portions you're actively working on.

Finally, use a seam roller to seal your latex sheets to each other. This step welds the adhesive and latex and presses out minor air bubbles.

QUICK TIP!

Gluing latex together can be tricky! The fabric is wiggly and loves to stick to itself. Luckily, if you make a mistake, it can be corrected! Just gently pull apart the seam—carefully, so as not to cause a tear—and re-press the seam.

Hems are not necessary, but a single-fold hem (pg 85) gives a particularly clean edge; glue it with the same process you used for the seams. Alternatively, a strip of latex glued to the inside of your raw hem significantly strengthens the material and is much easier to implement than a folded hem.

You may be surprised that your completed latex piece does not have the shine you expect from the material. That's because it's still covered in powder! Carefully applied silicone oil—most commonly, a product sold with the brand name Vivishine—will get you the gorgeous luster you're looking for.

Vinyls

The fabric commonly call **faux leather, upholstery vinyl**, or just **vinyl** is actually two main types of fabric: PVCs (polyvinyl chlorides, actual vinyls) and PUs (polyurethanes). Some have spandex added for stretchiness, others are completely clear, many have textured added, many are waterproofed—the list goes on!

For the sake of brevity, I will refer to all varieties as vinyl, even though PUs are not technically classified as such.

Some sewing techniques work universally for all vinyl varieties. In particular, holes are permanent: Pinning and sewing create weaknesses in the materials that cannot be repaired. For that reason, it's best to use clips, tape, or glue instead of pins. Even more important, do your best to not sew over the same spot in a project multiple times, because those tiny holes may combine to create larger ones. This includes backstitching at the beginning and end of stitching lines; instead of backstitching, leave your thread tails long and then tie or glue them down.

Additionally, vinyls dull blades and needles very quickly. Have extra needles and rotary cutter blades ready, and switch often for best results.

Vi *(League of Legends)* jacket, belts, and shoes all made from vinyl

DOLL CUSTOMIZATION BY ENCHANTERIUM
Photo by Enchanterium

Non-Stretch Vinyls

Non-stretch vinyls are durable, easy to clean, and usually heavyweight. They can be difficult to sew, especially thicker varieties. They may have a knit, woven, or foam backing, which increases stiffness and thickness. They're often used for upholstery (especially for outdoors), bags, outerwear, and utility purposes.

Heavyweight PU vinyls have some natural elasticity and drape much better than PVC vinyls. They are often matte, and when used to emulate leather, they have a more natural appearance. They're less durable and more expensive than PVC vinyls.

Lightweight PU laminates, commonly known as PU fabrics or PULs, are conventional woven fabrics that have been coated with a clear layer of polyurethane. That clear layer allows the base fabric's pattern to show through the film and makes the fabric durable, waterproof, and very easy to clean. They may be labeled as laminated cotton and laminated linen when the base material is those fibers, but often the base fabric is polyester.

PVC vinyls are often shiner and stiffer than PU vinyls. In faux leather form, they often appear less realistic. They're more durable than PU vinyls and are, therefore, better suited for outdoor and heavy-use upholstery.

Oilcloth, also known as enameled cloth or American cloth, is duck or canvas coated with PVC.

CONFUSING TOPIC!
Marine vinyl has been coated with UV and moisture protection. Otherwise, it is the same material as other upholstery-weight vinyl fabrics. •

The *Ruffle Heart Ita Bag* is a stash-buster made from thrifted satin and holographic faux leather.

BAG BY DAEMERYS
Photo by Annye Driscoll

Fabric Preparation and Care

Most vinyls are tough to machine wash or even hand wash. Oilcloth, heavyweight PU vinyl, and PVC vinyl are best spot cleaned with gentle products.

Lightweight PU vinyl is usually machine washable—because it's often used for cloth diapers, it has to be! Machine wash it hot; then machine dry.

Because they're prone to creasing and are difficult to press, vinyls should be stored carefully. Store fabric in rolls, not folded, and hang finished pieces.

1. Heavyweight PU vinyl
2. Oilcloth
3. Lightweight PU laminate
4. PVC vinyl

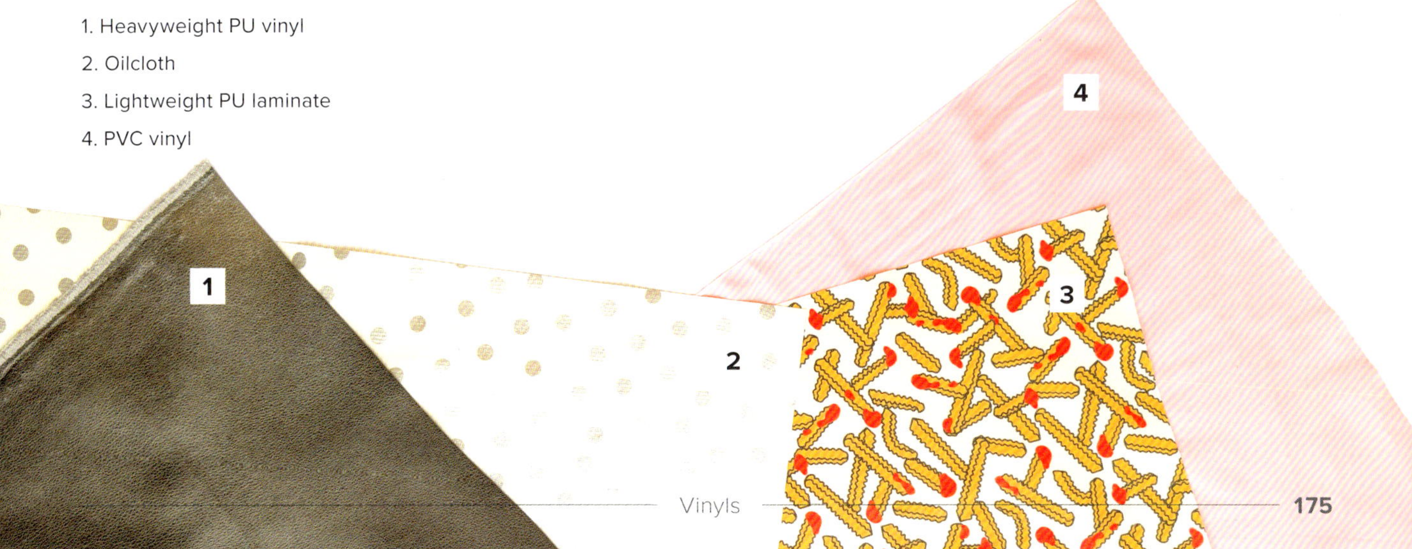

Pressing

Press vinyls from the wrong side—that is, the side with the fabric backing. Start at very low heat; the fabric backing may, itself, be made of a synthetic material and, therefore, sensitive to heat. Use a press cloth.

If pressing with an iron does not remove wrinkles, consider carefully using a steamer or heat gun on your vinyl fabric to remove wrinkles and, especially, tough creases. Make sure to practice on scraps first to make sure your heat is low enough; vinyl will melt.

⚠ STAY SAFE!

Vinyl is dangerous when inhaled. If you're heating the material, especially with a heat gun, always wear a mask with filters that are effective on vapors. •

Pattern Transfer/Marking

Vinyls are easy to mark because they're completely opaque; with many, you can use permanent markers on the wrong side without any ill effects. Disappearing ink, chalk, or a regular pen are safer options. On the right side, a dry-erase marker is a great temporary option on vinyls. Just swatch first to make sure it will come out of your material completely!

Cutting

A rotary cutter works great on vinyls, although the tough plastic coating will dull blades faster than fabric. For that reason, never use your fabric shears on vinyl; if you can, have a tough and sharp pair of heavy-duty scissors reserved for these types of fabrics.

Because vinyls almost never have a grain or nap, you can usually completely puzzle-piece pattern pieces without respecting direction at all. The exception is a highly textured or patterned fabric; a crocodile skin faux leather, for example, will need to be cut using a with-nap layout so that the texture looks as natural as possible. Some fabric-backed vinyls should be cut on the grain because that backing will affect how it performs; when in doubt, drape large sections hanging on each grain and see if you can detect a difference.

✸ QUICK TIP!

If you'll be leaving hems raw take extra effort to cut cleanly. A sharp rotary cutter helps a lot with this task! •

Pinning and Alternatives

Pinholes in vinyls are permanent. Instead of pinning, use clips, a glue stick, or basting tape (pg 99). Be sure to take out clips when you're done; over time, they will leave indentations in the vinyl, permanently damaging it.

Interfacing

Because heavyweight vinyls are so substantial, their interfacing must also be stiff. When used in bags and costuming, foam is a great option. Otherwise, use a sew-in woven to avoid the struggle with pressing vinyls.

Thinner vinyls can be interfaced using more typical methods. Again, sew-in is always the safer choice with these heat-sensitive materials, but fusible can be used with caution. Choose woven or nonwoven generally, or knit or stretch if your lightweight PU vinyl has stretch that you need to preserve.

You can also use your fabric's backing material as a sort of self-interfacing (pg 45). Using canvas oilcloth? Self-interface with canvas! Using a lightweight PU and linen vinyl? Self-interface with a medium-weight linen!

Sewing

Sew PVC vinyl and heavyweight PU vinyl with a 90/14 leather or microtex needle and a 3.5mm straight stitch. Oilcloth performs best with a 90/14 denim or microtex needle with a 3mm straight stitch, and lightweight PU vinyl works well with an 80/12 universal or denim needle and a 3mm straight or zigzag stitch (according to its stretch). Have extra needles ready: When layers begin to build up, your needles may break. If that happens, consider increasing your needle size by one. You can also sew very slowly—even using the handwheel to control your machine exactly.

Use all-purpose or heavy-duty polyester thread. If you're using a particularly thick vinyl or when the layers start adding up, you may need to reduce the pressure on the machine foot so that your fabric can feed easily through the machine.

Vinyls can be very sticky fabrics, which causes difficulties during sewing. It makes it difficult to feed them evenly (or at all!) through a sewing machine; use a walking, roller, or nonstick machine foot. Sandwiching them between two layers of tissue paper (pg 155) solves that problem entirely: Just tear away the tissue paper once your sewing is complete. Consider buying a nonstick version of the machine needle.

QUICK TIP!
Struggling to get your presser foot over thick layers of vinyl? Buy or make a seam jumper (pg 77)!

Seam and hem options abound with vinyls; because they don't fray, their raw edges can be left unprotected. Topstitched plain (below), welt (pg 165), and flat-felled (pg 81) seams are classics. With thicker fabrics, lapped seams (pg 160) work well. Hems are not necessary at all; binding (pg 73), overedging (zigzag, three-thread wrapped, or four-thread overlock, pg 138), or single-fold (pg 85) hems keep the bulk down while leaving a clean finish. Hems and seams can also be glued.

Tutorial Time: Topstitched Seams

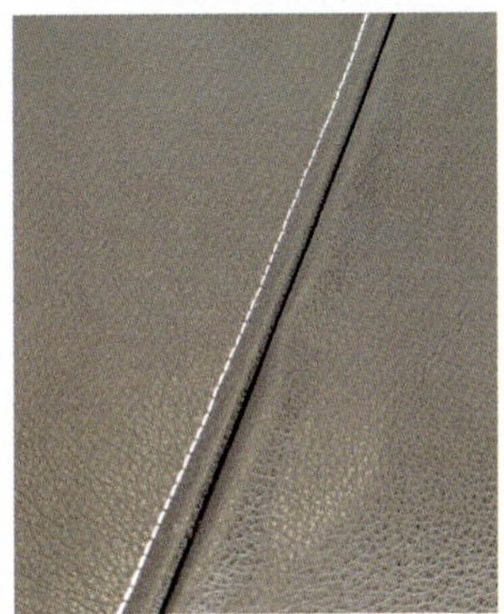

Topstitching seams protects raw edges somewhat, but it is more often used for either decorative purposes or to flatten the seam on materials that don't easily press. On this example, the left seam allowance is sewn down; the other is glued.

1. On conventional materials, press the seam open, or press them together and to one side to create a welt seam (pg 165) (a version of a topstitched seam).

2. Topstitch the seam allowance down, flattening and decorating the front of the piece.

With more substantial materials, adhesive (contact cement, (pg 204); hem tape; and the like) will prevent bubbling seams without adding extra lines of stitches.

Because they're so bulky, topstitching or otherwise securing seam allowances on heavyweight vinyls may be necessary to get a clean look. However, this process makes a stiff fabric even stiffer, which will affect the piece's drape. Make sure to consider that change when planning your piece.

QUICK TIP!
Increase your stitch length when topstitching vinyl! This will both decrease the amount of holes in the material and make it easier for your presser foot to move along the sticky material.

The best glue to use on vinyls is contact cement (pg 204). You can also use a glue made specifically for vinyl, like 3M Rubber and Vinyl Spray Adhesive 80 (by 3M).

QUICK TIP!
Many lightweight PU vinyls, which are on a base of interlock, have some natural stretch. If you're struggling with the stretch properties of your PU vinyl (even if it does not have spandex added), treat it like a stretch vinyl (pg 178).

Sleeves, collar, and skirt made with faux stretch leather and decorated with double-cap rivets

GARMENT AND MODELING BY SADIE STEELHEART
Photo by Julie Soto

Stretch Vinyls

Faux stretch leather, which is much lighter, drapier, and (of course!) stretchier than upholstery vinyl, is often made of a mix of PU, polyester fabric, and spandex. Stretch vinyls are used for apparel, costuming, accessories, and home goods.

Fabric Preparation and Care

Stretch vinyls do not need to be prewashed. They should be spot cleaned with gentle products or machine washed cold or warm on a gentle cycle and then laid flat to dry.

Like other vinyls, stretch vinyls crease, and those creases are difficult to remove. Store stretch vinyl fabric and creations rolled or laid flat.

Pressing

With stretch vinyl, always press from the wrong side of your piece while using a press cloth. Start at a very low temperature and increase it only until you get an effective press; this fabric is made of spandex, vinyl, and polyester—all of which are sensitive to heat!

Pattern Transfer/Marking

Use disappearing ink or regular pen and marker on the wrong side of stretch vinyls and either chalk or a dry-erase marker when marking the right side. Swatch test to make sure these options are all removable before committing.

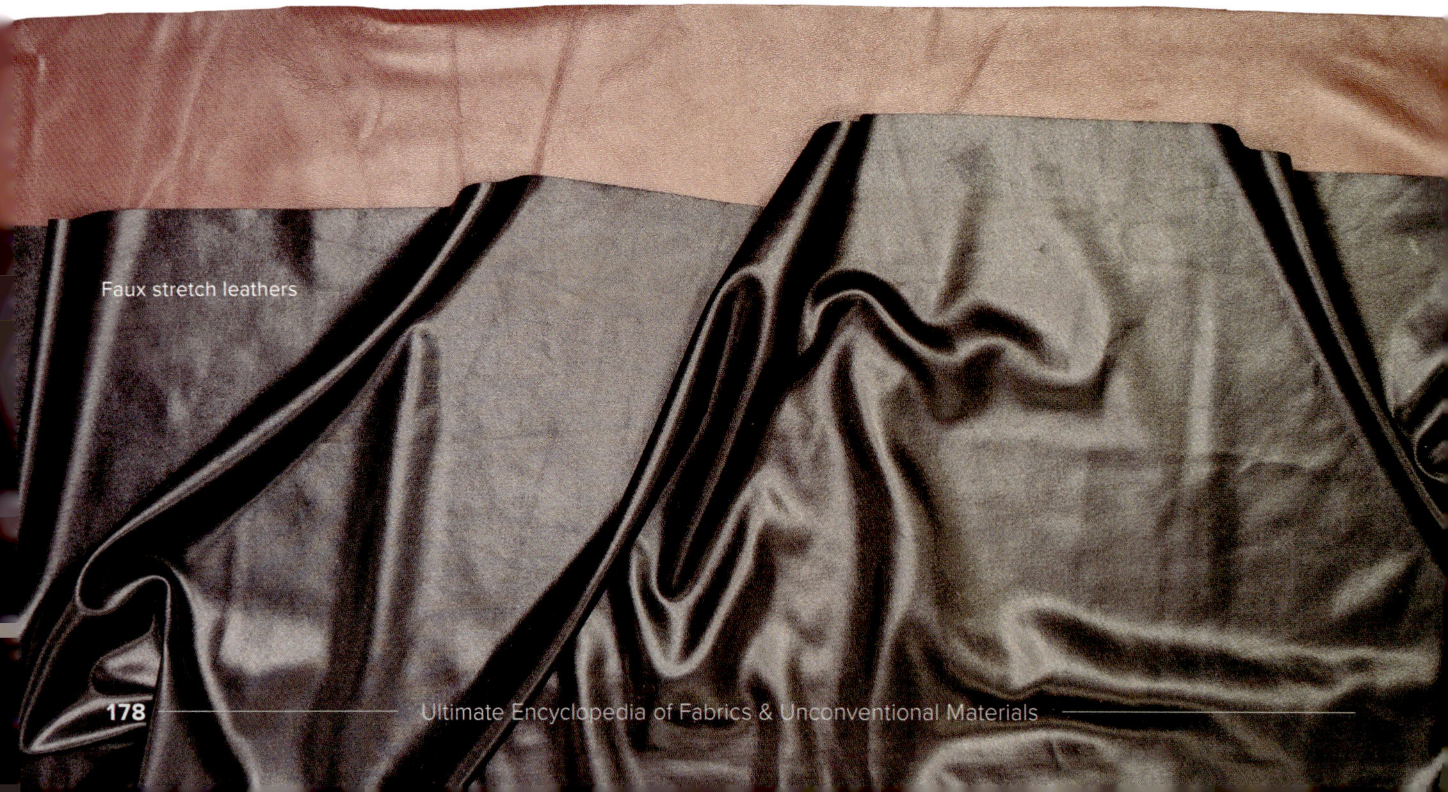

Faux stretch leathers

Cutting

Use a rotary cutter or craft scissors to cut stretch vinyl; the plastic in the fabric will dull fabric shears. Make sure to think ahead to your seam and hem finishes: If you'll be leaving edges raw, take extra effort to cut clean edges (best done with a sharp rotary cutter!).

Stretch vinyl can be a very slinky, shifty fabric. Cut in just one layer to minimize movement during cutting. Use weights distributed over the entire surface of the fabric, not just in the seam allowance (pg 111); this will reduce shifting and prevent pinholes, which are permanent in stretch vinyl.

Do not let stretch vinyl hang off the side of your cutting surface while you transfer and cut pattern pieces; the pull of gravity will distort your layout.

Don't forget to consider the direction of stretch when laying out your pattern pieces! This material does not have a nap, but it will stretch more or less lengthwise, crosswise, and on the bias. Choose which direction you want the most amount of stretch (around your body, for example), and then lay out all pattern pieces with respect to that decision.

Pinning and Alternatives

Pins create permanent holes in stretch vinyl. Clip, glue baste (pg 99), or tape your fabric instead. Before sewing, clip or otherwise secure very densely (pg 134); this will help prevent shifting during sewing, which happens often with this wiggly fabric.

Interfacing

Because it doesn't handle heat well, sew-in interfacing is best for stretch vinyl; a substantial jersey or interlock fabric is perfect for this purpose.

Sewing

Sewing with faux stretch leather can be very tricky. It's sticky due to its vinyl coating but stretches and wiggles like a flimsy jersey. Before sewing, clean and lubricate your machine, get a fresh needle, and take a deep breath.

Begin with a 70/10 nonstick denim or microtex machine needle, a 3mm zigzag stitch, and a walking, roller, or nonstick presser foot. All-purpose polyester thread is fine; you may find you need heavy-duty for high-stress seams, like crotches and bag straps. If you have trouble with skipped stitches, try upgrading to a more expensive thread; thread quality can really make a difference with tricky fabrics like these.

If changing the presser foot doesn't solve your sticky *or* wiggly fabric issues, sandwich your faux stretch leather between two layers of tissue paper (pg 155). This will cut down on wiggling, allow the fabric to feed evenly through your machine, and even prevent it from stretching out of place during sewing. Paper can be torn away when the sewing is complete.

Luckily, because it doesn't fray or ravel, choosing seams and hems for faux stretch leather can be quite easy. Just make sure to account for the stretch!

A plain seam (pg 66) using a stretchy stitch (zigzag or three-thread overlock stitch, pg 70) works well. If you want to hide the raw edge, consider a flat-fell (pg 81) using a wide zigzag stitch. Especially for bulkier stretch vinyls, you may want to topstitch the seam allowances down (pg 177); don't forget to either use a zigzag stitch or stretch sew (pg 100).

For hems, leave the edge raw, use a three-thread overlock or wrapped stitch (pg 138), or do a single fold (pg 85) with a stretchy stitch. You can also sew a mock cover hem (pg 104), a professional-looking and stretchy hem.

Glue is an option for stretch vinyl, but most glues will not stretch as much as the fabric, so choose both your glue and your application wisely. Contact cement (pg 204) is the best option in this case; it is a very strong glue that also has natural flexibility. If you do want to glue your hems, consider (carefully!) adding fusible interfacing first; this will make the fabric more stable, meaning there will be less stress on the adhesive.

Gelatinous Cutie made with lime green transparent vinyl with a muslin lining and bone inclusions

COSTUME AND MODELING BY GINNY DI
Photo by Ginny Di

Clear and Tinted Vinyl

Clear vinyl, true to its name, is vinyl produced without any backing or printing. It may be tinted lightly to give color without removing its transparent quality. Because the materials are translucent or transparent, they need special sewing consideration.

Clear and tinted vinyls are often used for bags, accessories, and utility purposes.

Fabric Preparation and Care

Like their opaque cousins, clear and tinted vinyls should not be machine washed; spot clean them only. However because they aren't bonded to a traditional fabric, cleaning is actually much easier: Just wipe your clear or tinted vinyl with a damp cloth!

Clear and tinted vinyls are susceptible to permanent creases. Store both fabric and completed creations rolled, not folded.

Pressing

Clear and tinted vinyl cannot be pressed; the material is 100 percent plastic, and will melt under an iron. Instead, use steam or a heat gun to carefully remove wrinkles or add heat for finger pressing.

STAY SAFE!
Don't inhale vinyl fumes! Wear a mask suitable for vapors when heating plastic; the chemicals that gas off of vinyls are very bad for your brain and lungs.

1. Tinted vinyl
2. Clear vinyl

Pattern Transfer/Marking

A dry-erase marker works well on clear and tinted vinyl; once you're done with construction, just use a cloth to wipe away the marks. Because it's easily removable, however, care must be taken to not erase marks before you're ready. For a more robust option, use masking or washi tape.

Cutting

Do not use fabric shears on clear or tinted vinyls; the plastic will dull your nice scissors. A rotary cutter or craft scissors work best. You should also cut clear and tinted vinyl in just one layer; these materials don't fold well enough to cut in two layers at once.

Remember, your raw edges will almost certainly be visible in your completed piece. Take the time to clean up any jagged edges so that the inner construction of your finished piece, showing through, presents a nice finish.

Pinning and Alternatives

Pinholes are permanent in vinyl. Use clips, tape, or a glue stick instead.

Interfacing

Clear and tinted vinyl cannot be interfaced. If you need your material to be stiffer, either double up the fabric (self-interfacing, pg 45) or combine it with another fabric to create a new textile—just keep in mind that the material you choose will be visible through the clear or tinted vinyl.

Sewing

To sew clear and tinted vinyl, use a 90/14 leather or microtex nonstick machine needle; a walking, roller, or nonstick machine foot; and a 3mm straight stitch. You may also want to reduce the pressure on your machine foot so that these substantial materials can move more easily through the machine.

A mark visible inside a finished hem

All-purpose or heavy-duty polyester thread works well for sewing with clear and tinted vinyl. Clear thread is also an option, but it is not as strong as heavy-duty versions; make sure you don't use it on any high-stress areas of your project.

Clear and tinted vinyl don't fray, so a plain seam with topstitched seam allowances (pg 177) is a clean and easy solution. Lapped (pg 160) and flat-fell (pg 81) seams also work well—plus, they enclose raw edges that may be sharp against skin.

Hemming is not necessary, but a single or double fold (pg 85) is easy to achieve.

Adhering clear and tinted vinyl can be a bit tricky, because the best glue for vinyl—contact cement—is tinted and will be visible within the finished piece. 3M Rubber and Vinyl Spray Adhesive 80 is the best clear option for rubber and vinyl. Clamping also makes a significant difference when gluing vinyl: If you can weight or clip your seam while the glue dries, you'll end up with a much stronger bond.

When choosing enclosed seams and hems, don't forget to remove your markings before sewing the seam allowance into your piece! Little bits of dry-erase marker will show through to the front of your finished seam.

Paper

Paper is a great craft and art material, and most versions of it are sewable, too! In most papers, tears and holes are permanent, however, so care must be taken when sewing with the material.

I've separated papers into five categories; each is treated differently when sewing.

Thin papers are very delicate, and may do better glued rather than sewn because the risk of tearing is so great.

Standard papers sew well, though care must still be taken to prevent tearing and protect seams.

Washable papers/fabric papers are specifically made for sewing; they are more tear resistant, are often washable, and are sometimes even bonded to or blended with actual fabric.

Thin cardboard is easier to sew than standard paper because it has greatly increased strength, but it does not naturally drape like some standard-weight papers do.

Thick cardboard is very strong—there's a reason we send it through the mail! It is generally considered unsewable not because we can't pierce it with a needle, but because it won't bend enough to fit in our machines.

Stitched card made with various weights of paper

CARD BY ALISON BENYON FROM *STITCHED PAPER ART FOR KIDS* (C&T PUBLISHING)

Thin Paper

Washi (origami) paper, tissue paper, classic sewing pattern paper, and crepe paper are extremely delicate and often translucent. They're most often used for decor and utility purposes.

Fabric Preparation and Care

Thin paper is not washable and does not need to be prepared before sewn or used for crafts. Protect your thin paper from water; unless it's specifically coated for water protection, it will completely collapse if drenched. It cannot be cleaned.

Pressing

Thin paper can be pressed using low heat and a press cloth. Increase heat as needed to remove wrinkles, but deep creases may be permanent. Do not steam paper.

Dark Waters Diana *(League of Legends)* sword is made out of cardboard, which has been covered with newspaper and tissue paper using papier-mâché.

COSTUME AND MODELING BY THEMCMEGAMUFFIN
Photo by Yvonnografie

1. Pattern paper
2. Tissue paper
3. Tissue paper
4. Crepe paper

Pattern Transfer/Marking

Chalk and regular writing tools work on paper. However, colored chalk may be permanent, pencil can be tough to safely remove, and heat-erasable pens may reappear when subjected to cold. Washi tape is an okay removable option; press and release it from your pant leg or sleeve a few times before adhering it to delicate paper to reduce the amount of tack on the tape.

Ultimately, thin paper is extremely delicate and, therefore, tough to mark in a temporary way. It may be best to use a regular writing tool in a color close to that of your paper and make sure all marks are within the seam allowance of the piece you're creating. Make sure to consider the translucency of your paper: Will that mark be visible through to the front of your piece after construction?

Cutting

Thin paper is easy to cut with regular scissors—just don't use your nice fabric shears, as paper will dull them. It can be cut in layers, but remember: Creases may be permanent! Pattern pieces that call for an on-the-fold layout may be best mirrored and then cut as a whole piece.

Paper does not have a nap or grain; unless your paper has a printed pattern, cut using puzzle-piece style.

Pinning and Alternatives

Pins leave permanent holes in paper, which weakens the strength of an already delicate material. To baste, consider a glue stick or washi tape instead (pg 99). Even conventional sewing clips can leave marks in thin paper.

Interfacing

Generally, fusible interfacing works extremely well on thin paper—just make sure to swatch test to confirm that adhesive won't seep through the paper and show from the front side. Do not use sew-in interfacing; the holes introduce unnecessary risk.

You may also consider using a self-interfacing or a thicker piece of paper, but only adhere those options with a glue stick around the edges of your piece.

✸ QUICK TIP!
Want your paper sewing patterns to last longer? Use fusible interfacing on them immediately after cutting! They'll gain some rigidity (making them easier to lay flat on fabric) and become much more tear resistant. ●

Sewing

This delicate material is quickly weakened by the holes made by sewing, and, because it's often transparent, care must be taken to hide seam allowances. Use a long stitch length, fine polyester thread, and a thin machine needle (60/8 universal). A standard machine foot with increased pressure (to better feed the thin material through your machine) is a good starting point; if your paper gets caught under the feed dogs, switch to a straight stitch foot and plate.

Because paper does not fray, you don't need to protect raw edges. A plain (pg 66) or lapped (pg 160) seam works for thin paper, but you may consider instead a seam with two seamlines: flat-fell (pg 81), French (pg 114), or just a reinforced seam (pg 100) with two straight stitches. This will distribute the pressure of the seam across two lines of holes instead of one, decreasing the chance of ripping. A French or flat-fell seam also encloses the raw edges, so that a finished seam is visible through what is often a translucent material. Just make sure that your lines of stitching, in all cases, are far enough away from each other that the holes made from stitching won't rip into each other, creating larger holes.

It is not necessary to hem paper; a clean cut or even a decorative cut (using specialty papercrafting scissors, for example) are fine finishes. However, a double- or single-fold hem (pg 85) is easy to implement and will strengthen the hem somewhat.

When gluing lightweight paper, a gentle adhesive such as a glue stick or tape roller is best; both will dry clear (and, therefore, won't show through the thin paper) and neither will seep through the material. Lapped seams (pg 160) are easiest to implement with glue, as are single-fold hems (pg 85).

Standard Paper

In the context of this book, I'm using *standard paper* to mean those that are around the same weight as printer paper. This includes:

- Standard printer and notebook paper
- Wax and parchment/baking paper
- Wrapping paper
- Construction paper

These papers are opaque or nearly so, resist tearing, and are much easier to sew than lightweight papers. Among the traditional paper categories, they are the most like fabric, although they generally will not drape the way lightweight papers do.

Fabric Preparation and Care

Paper is not washable and does not need to be prepared before a project.

Pressing

Standard paper is easy to press, although it should never be steamed, because water will ruin most versions of the material. (Some papers, such as watercolor papers, are meant to absorb water well. Steaming is still not necessary to press these materials.) Start at medium heat and increase until you achieve an effective press; high-quality cotton paper may need higher heat to remove wrinkles.

When pressing open seam allowances, you risk pressing a crease into the front of the paper. Use a piece of cardboard between the seam allowance and front of the paper (pg 72) to prevent that damage.

Xie Lian *(Heaven Official's Blessing)* hat made from a cardboard and newspaper papier-mâché base and then covered in reed grass

COSTUME AND MODELING BY KENZUMII
Photo by Kizlumi

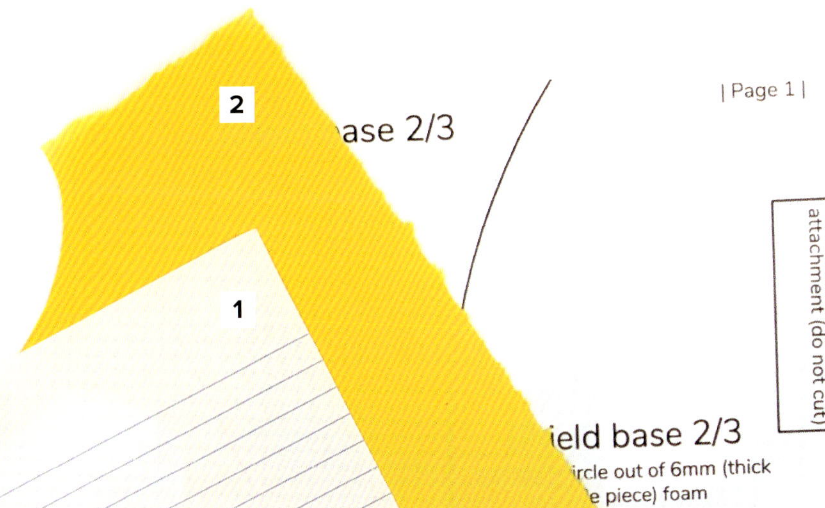

1. Lined paper
2. Construction paper
3. Printer paper
4. Wrapping paper

Pattern Transfer/Marking

Chalk and regular writing tools work well on paper. Washi tape is also a great marking tool that is easy to remove; just press and remove it a few times from your pants leg or sleeve before applying it to your paper to reduce the tack. Most standard papers are opaque, so marks made in the seam allowance don't need to be worried about. Lightweight printer and notebook papers will show dark marks through to the reverse, though, so make sure to swatch your marking strategy before committing.

Ultimately, a light-colored chalk or a de-tacked washi tape are your safest choices for removable mark making.

Cutting

Standard paper is easy to cut with any scissors—but don't use your fabric scissors, because they'll dull quickly on paper. A rotary cutter will slide through paper like butter. Paper does not have a nap or grain, so pattern pieces can be laid out in puzzle-piece fashion. It doesn't tend to shift much while working, so it can also be cut in multiple layers—just make sure to consider where your folds are in your material, because deep creases can be very hard to remove.

Pinning and Alternatives

Pinholes in paper are permanent and weaken the material dramatically. Instead, use clips, tape, or a glue stick.

Interfacing

Fusible interfacing works extremely well with standard-weight paper. Use woven or nonwoven, because paper does not stretch. Interfacing also makes paper much more resistant to tearing, which eliminates many of the risks associated with sewing with it. If you can interface your paper without drastically altering its behavior, do so. It will make sewing more fun and more successful.

Sewing

Because paper doesn't fray and standard paper is opaque, it's a fairly easy material to work with ... as long as you account for a risk of tearing.

✸ QUICK TIP!

If you do tear your paper, fusible interfacing can come to the rescue! Cut a piece large enough to cover your entire tear with wiggle room on each side. Fuse to the back of your piece while keeping the front of the tear as tidy and matched up as possible. If you don't have fusible interfacing or your paper is heat-sensitive, you can achieve the same result with a thin piece of paper and a glue stick. ●

Use a 60/8 universal machine needle, a long 3.5mm stitch length to increase the distance between (tear-risking) holes, and a standard machine foot. You may need to increase the pressure on your machine foot in order to feed your paper through the machine evenly. Use fine polyester thread.

Seam options abound! Plain (pg 66) and lapped (pg 160) seams are simple; flat-fell (pg 81) and welt (pg 165) add strength because they have multiple lines of stitching. Consider reinforcing all seams with a second round of straight stitches (pg 100) in order to distribute the pressure on the connection and, therefore, reduce the risk of tearing. Just make sure your seams are far enough away from each other that the holes made by the needle don't meld into each other, creating larger holes.

Hems are not necessary, but a single or double fold (pg 85) will create a clean finish. You can also use decorative papercrafting scissors to create a more interesting raw edge.

Adhesive works incredibly well on paper! A glue stick, glue roller, or tape roller are always safe choices, using any of the seam and hem options listed above. More substantial standard papers can tolerate a spray adhesive to get an even, wide application; just make sure to swatch test first to make sure your glue of choice doesn't seep through your paper. Rubber cement is a great safe option, too, but it's removable, so it's best for hems or basting. Don't forget to wear lung protection when using rubber cement and spray adhesives.

Fabric Paper

Fabric papers are much more durable than conventional paper, but they are also more expensive and tough to get. They're great for bags, accessories, utility purposes, and even adventure gear.

The two most common types of fabric-like paper (or paper-like fabric) are:

Tyvek (by DuPont): Made from polyethylene (PE), Tyvek is an extremely sturdy and rip-resistant material that you may know from festival wristbands and foot race bibs. Tyvek comes in different forms and may be more fabric-like (Tyvek interfacing) or paper-like (Tyvek envelopes). The photographs in this chapter are of Tyvek printing and crafting paper.

Washable paper: Washable paper is usually made of a combination of a kraft paper bonded to a nonwoven synthetic base. It is often advertised as an eco-friendly alternative to faux leather. The photographs in this chapter are of kraft-tex (C&T Publishing) and paper fabric (MB Cork).

Because fabric paper—within both the Tyvek and washable paper categories—can be manufactured in multiple ways, making broad generalizations about the materials is tough to do. As always, make sure you practice and swatch your fabric before manipulating it in any way.

Backpack made from kraft-tex (C&T Publishing), a washable fabric paper

CHARLIE KRAFT-TEX BACKPACK BY GAILEN RUNGE (C&T PUBLISHING)

1

2

3

4

1. kraft-tex
2. Tyvek
3. kraft-tex
4. Paper fabric

Fabric Preparation and Care

Both washable paper and Tyvek are machine washable. Use mild detergent with warm water for washable paper and cool water for Tyvek; then lay flat to dry. They do not need to be prewashed, but you may want to. Washable paper will crinkle, creating a wonderful textured material, and Tyvek will soften significantly for a much more pleasant sewing experience.

Pressing

Like conventional paper, washable paper is pressable; generally, start at medium heat and increase until you get an effective press.

Tyvek is very heat sensitive. If you need to press out wrinkles, do so carefully with a baking paper press cloth. You can use heat to add a scrunched, crinkly texture to your Tyvek; just make sure you don't add this texture accidentally!

⚠ STAY SAFE!
Heating PE is dangerous. Wear lung protection that's rated for vapors when pressing your Tyvek! ●

Pattern Transfer/Marking

Conventional marking tools work well on all fabric papers, although dark marks may show through to the front on light-colored or lightweight versions of the materials. Chalk, disappearing ink, and washi tape are safe options for marking the front of the material as well.

Cutting

Use a rotary cutter or craft scissors to cut fabric paper; they will dull fabric scissors.

Because fabric papers don't have conventional grains, they can be cut using a puzzle-piece style layout—but don't forget to consider any printed or textured details, which may demand on the grain or with-nap layouts.

Pinning and Alternatives

Because holes are permanent in these materials, use sewing clips or a glue stick instead of pins.

Interfacing

Washable paper can be interfaced with conventional fusible interfacing; woven fusible is a great option. Sew-in is an okay option but will introduce extra holes in the material, weakening the fabric paper.

Tyvek is tough to stiffen because it's so sensitive to heat. One option is to use spray adhesive on the faces of your materials to completely double up on your material, creating a self-interfacing (pg 45) without sewing. Another is spray starch (pg 47), which is a particularly good option on projects that won't be regularly washed.

Sewing

Both Tyvek and washable paper are rippable, though they both resist it much more than conventional paper. Still, consider that aspect when sewing with fabric paper.

Use an 80/12 microtex needle, a 3.5mm straight stitch, and all-purpose polyester thread. A standard presser foot is fine, but consider increasing the pressure if your fabric papers are particularly thin.

Neither types of fabric paper fray, making seaming and hemming a breeze. A plain (pg 66) or lapped (pg 160) seam is easy to execute; seam allowances can be topstitched (pg 177), glued, or finger pressed (pg 34). Flat-fell (pg 81) and welt (pg 165) seams provide more bulk for an industrial look, which is great for bags and other accessories. For hems, leave them raw, cut them with decorative paper scissors, or create a single- or double-fold hem (pg 85). An overedge edge finish (three-thread overlock or zigzag, pg 138) will introduce weakness in seams but is a clean hem finish.

You can also use glue on washable paper and Tyvek! Contact cement (pg 204) works well on both; with lighter versions, you're better off using a glue stick or glue runner. Contact cement has the advantage of creating waterproof seals, so if you're using your waterproof Tyvek to create camping gear, for example, you can put a light coat of the adhesive over your seams to fully seal them.

Thin Cardboard

Thin cardboard, cardstock/scrapbooking paper, and kraft paper are significantly sturdier than standard paper, making them much more resistant to tearing; sewing is, therefore, a safer endeavor! However, they don't take curves or drape at all; you're going to end up with a much stiffer and more structural piece when creating with thicker paper.

The Wanderer *(Genshin Impact)* accessories made from thin cardboard—ice cream and popsicle boxes!

COSTUME AND MODELING BY AZURIMI
Photo by Sun Orenji Photography

1. Packing paper
2. Cardstock/scrapbooking paper
3. Thin cardboard

Fabric Preparation and Care

Thin cardboard does not need to be prewashed or prepared. It's not washable, but it can be very gently spot cleaned with water.

Even more so than lighter papers, thin cardboard permanently creases. Creations made with thin cardboard should be stored carefully so that they don't acquire flaws that can't be pressed out.

Pressing

Cardboard can be pressed, although it may need a lighter touch than paper, counterintuitively, due to a lower cotton content. Start at a low temperature and increase until effective; do not steam.

Pattern Transfer/Marking

Chalk and regular writing tools work very well on cardboard. Washi and masking tape are also great for marking and should release from cardboard very easily. Don't forget to swatch to make sure your chosen marking tool doesn't stain or otherwise mar your paper, if you aren't just marking within seam allowances or on the reverse.

Cutting

Cardboard and thick paper are generally easy to cut with craft scissors. If you're struggling to get clean cuts, switch to a craft knife or box cutter (pg 200). Just make sure to keep your blades sharp; paper dulls blades. And don't use your fabric shears!

Cardboard and thick paper do not have grains. Use a puzzle-piece style layout unless printed patterns necessitate otherwise.

Pinning and Alternatives

Clips work very well on thick paper and thin cardboard, though they will mar the surface of the material if left for long. Glue sticks and tape are also great for basting these materials (pg 99).

Interfacing

Thin cardboard and thick paper are easy to stiffen—just double them up! Glue won't seep through them, so a light layer of spray adhesive works great to get an even layer for a "fusible" paper experience.

Fusible interfacing works well on thin cardboard but won't add much structure to an already sturdy material. Instead, use it to make the paper safer to sew, because it adds a significant amount of tear resistance.

Sewing

Sew thick paper and thin cardboard with a 60/8 universal machine needle. If the needle is getting caught on the layers of paper, try a microtex or leather version instead. Use a standard machine foot and all-purpose or heavy-duty polyester thread.

Plain seams (pg 66) work well with thick paper and thin cardboard, though you may need to glue or sew your seam allowances down (pg 177) to get a clean finish. A lapped seam (pg 160) works, too, though it may result in an unsightly bump in your piece. An abutted seam (pg 171), sewn with a zigzag stitch and then reinforced with tape on the reverse, is a perfectly flat seam option.

Hemming is not necessary with thick paper and thin cardboard, but a single fold (pg 85) will keep bulk down and provide a clean edge.

Gluing is a great option with thick paper and thin cardboard. A glue stick, while great for basting, may not be strong enough for seams; instead, consider contact cement (pg 204) applied in very thin layers. Always wear lung protection when working with contact cement.

Thick Cardboard

Thick cardboard, like that used in shipping boxes, is satisfying to sew because it's sturdy enough to tolerate the holes made in sewing quite nicely. Like thin cardboard, however, it does not drape at all.

Corrugated cardboard bending along the corrugation

Corrugated cardboard bending against the corrugation

Almost all thick cardboard is corrugated. That means that a layer of ridged, wrinkly cardboard is sandwiched between two layers of flat cardboard. Corrugated cardboard folds easily parallel to the corrugated ridges; the ridges provide strength when pressure is applied perpendicular to them.

Witch-king of Angmar *(The Lord of the Rings)* cosplay armor made from cardboard covered in tissue paper

COSTUME AND MODELING BY SANIT KLAMCHANUAN
Photo by Morgan Clicks Cameras

Fabric Preparation and Care

Cardboard does not need to be prepared in any way. It's not really washable, but it can be gently spot cleaned with water. Thick cardboard, once creased, cannot be pressed out; store completed cardboard creations very carefully to prevent damage.

Pressing

Cardboard can be pressed, but the corrugation will, in many cases, prevent creases from being ironed out. Use a medium heat with no steam.

Pattern Transfer/Marking

Chalk and regular writing tools work well on cardboard. For a temporary marking option, washi or masking tape works well. Thick cardboard is substantial enough that tailor's tacks and thread tracing will also work for mark making ... though it may not be fun to hand sew!

Cutting

Scissors aren't going to deal with thick cardboard well. Instead, switch to a snap-off box cutter (pg 200), which you can extend so that it's long enough to cut through the entire cardboard thickness at once. You can also easily and quickly sharpen box cutters as the material dulls it—which is important because one smooth, sharp cut is vital to get a clean edge in thick cardboard projects.

Cardboard has an atypical grain due to the corrugation. Before you cut your pattern pieces, consider how your sewing will interact with the corrugation and whether you need to consider it when laying out. If you decide it doesn't matter, a puzzle-piece style layout works just fine.

Pinning and Alternatives

Cardboard can tolerate the permanent holes pins create, but the sturdy material just doesn't work with the flex that pins require. Instead, use clips or glue. I love a glue stick, but you may need something stronger even for temporary use with thick cardboard. Consider rubber cement or gaffer tape, both of which have a quicker and stronger hold than a glue stick. Just make sure they can be safely and cleanly removed from your material!

Interfacing

Thick cardboard is so sturdy that you probably won't need to stiffen it. If you do, just self-interface (pg 45) or use thicker cardboard. This material is substantial enough that you can use permanent spray adhesive in order to create an even hold when gluing two pieces of cardboard face to face. If you want a super-rigid option, glue your two pieces with their corrugation ridges running in opposite directions; because thick cardboard flexes best along its corrugation, putting them perpendicular to each other will make your resulting material particularly sturdy.

Sewing

Cardboard can be tough to sew because of its thickness, but in many ways its sturdiness makes it much easier to work with than lighter papers.

Use a 90/14 microtex or leather needle, a heavyweight polyester thread, and a walking foot to evenly feed the material through your machine.

Because it will not roll up to fit between your needle and the body of your machine, seam options are limited to those that don't have both pieces of material spread across the seam. A plain seam (pg 66) works well if your thick cardboard is thin enough to fold; the seam allowances will then need to be glued down (pg 177) for a clean finish. Again, if folding is possible, a single-fold hem (pg 85) works in a standard machine, although a hem is not necessary with thick cardboard. You can also overedge (three-thread overlock, pg 138) cardboard edges, but don't use the cutting action of your serger with this material; it will dull your blades.

✸ QUICK TIP!
Don't forget how your cardboard's corrugation affects its ability to fold. Consider putting your seamlines along the corrugation so that the seam allowance will fold down more easily, or orient your hems along a line of corrugation so you can fold them under cleanly. It's worth taking a moment to consider how the structure of the material will affect your creation! ●

Thick cardboard is much easier to glue than it is to sew, because you aren't limited by the machine's throat (the area of the bed plate between the needle and the body of the machine). Contact cement (pg 204) works very well on the material; just make sure to wear proper protective equipment. Hot glue and permanent spray adhesive are fine options, but getting even, wide coverage with them is tougher. Lapped (pg 160) and abutted (pg 171) seams are best; abutted seams should be glued with hot glue, which can fill in the gaps in the corrugation. Make sure to also reinforce these seams on the inside of your piece with duct tape, thinner cardboard, or fabric.

Foam

In the context of this book, *foam* is a plastic that's been pumped full of air, creating a squishy, soft, moldable material. The amount and size of air holes determine the density of the foam: Low-density foams (with numerous or large air holes) are squishy, while high-density foams (with few or small air holes) are sturdy.

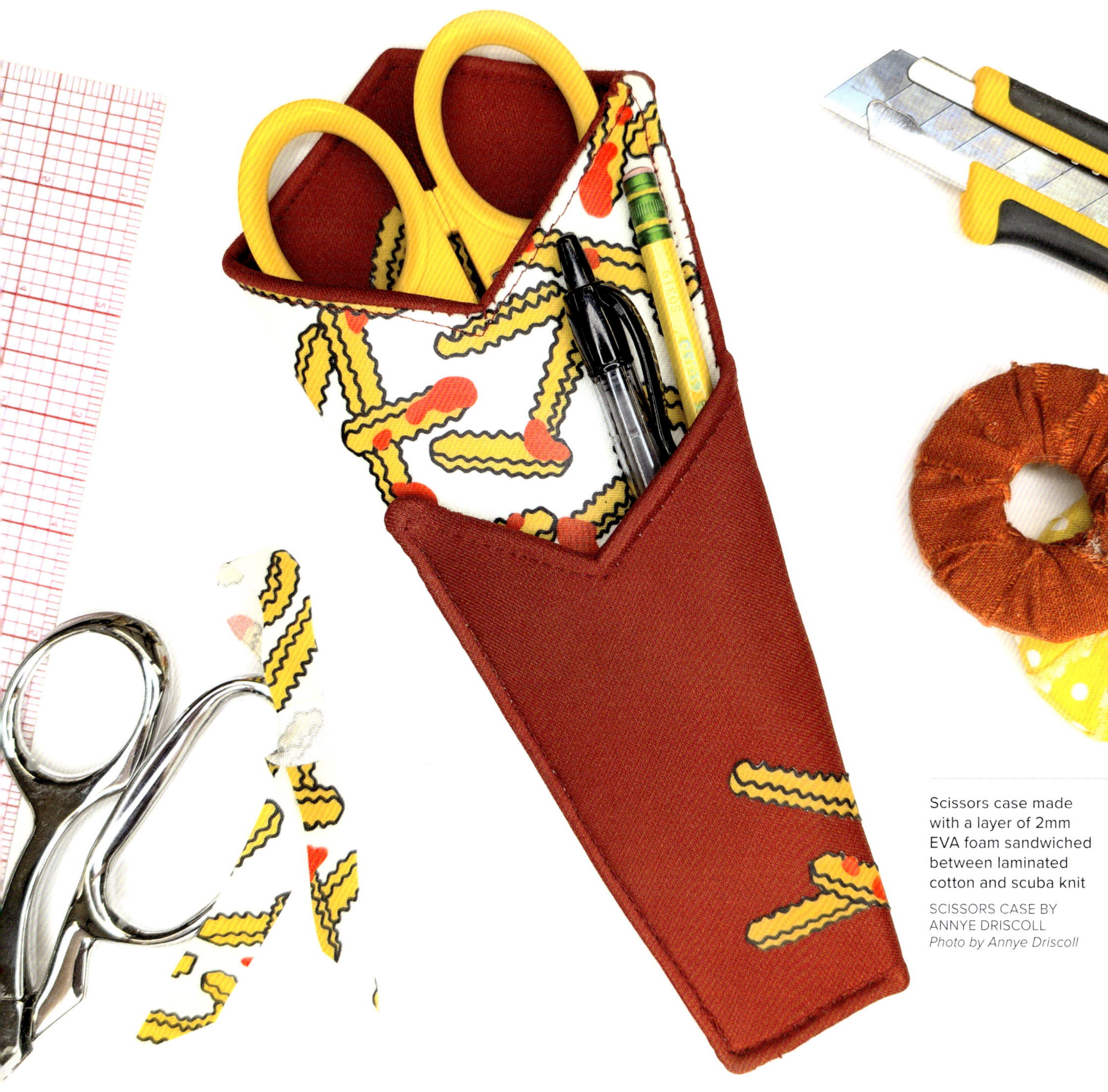

Scissors case made with a layer of 2mm EVA foam sandwiched between laminated cotton and scuba knit

SCISSORS CASE BY ANNYE DRISCOLL
Photo by Annye Driscoll

There are three kinds of foam commonly used in crafting:

Upholstery or **cushion foam** is a low-rigidity form of foam; it's squishy and very flexible. It's often described by its density and thickness. It is made of polyurethane (PU).

EVA foam (ethylene-vinyl acetate) often described as **craft foam** or **floor mats**, is a much more rigid form of foam but still soft and flexible. It is durable and inexpensive. EVA foam comes in different densities and thicknesses.

PE foam (polyethylene) is less durable than EVA foam because it doesn't have the added vinyl component that gives EVA foam its elasticity. PE foam is also less dense and rigid than EVA foam, which makes it a better squishy cushion and can make it easier to work with. PE foam also has a scratchy texture that EVA does not.

QUICK TIP!

EVA and PE foam are both thermoplastics, which means that, when heated, they will maintain a shape (though not as stiffly or dramatically as the thermoplastics in Structural Materials, pg 210). This is an advantage when sewing with them; wrinkles can be removed with a heat gun, seam allowances can be flattened somewhat with heat and finger pressing, and (most excitingly!) complex shapes can be created using just the materials, which will remember that shape.

All three of these types of foam can be sewn with a home sewing machine in their thinner forms; thicker ones will need to be glued. However, foams are tearable and holes are permanent; sewing (especially when going over a spot multiple times) introduces significant risk to your project. Before sewing foam, consider whether glue may be a better option. Additionally, confirm your fit before sewing so that you don't have to seam rip and then resew, creating more holes.

A final kind of foam, **neoprene**, is usually foam and fabric bonded together, which makes it both strong and squishy. Importantly, it's also less risky to sew through, because the fabric strengthens the foam.

QUICK TIP!

Foams dull tools very quickly but also require a sharp blade; for substantial foam projects, consider buying multiple blades or a blade sharpener. For that reason, never use your nice fabric shears on foams; they will dull extremely quickly.

STAY SAFE!

Foam lets off gas when you heat it, which is very dangerous for your brain and lungs. Always work in a well-ventilated area and wear a mask that's effective against vapors when heating these materials.

1. Thin PE foam
2. Thin PE foam
3. Thin EVA foam
4. Thin EVA foam
5. Thin upholstery foam

Thin Foam

In the context of this book, thin foams are those that are 3mm thick or less. Ultimately, though, whether your foam is machine sewable will depend on your sewing machine and the application you're using the material for. Two layers of 3mm foam may not fit under your presser foot (despite them being listed in the thin foam category and, therefore, considered sewable), but a layer of 3mm foam and a layer of vinyl will easily sew together. Use the guidance in the Thin Foam and Thick Foam (pg 199) sections if they make sense for your project!

Thin foams are often used for structure, costuming, and padding.

Yone *(League of Legends)* vest made with vinyl, which has been flatlined with 2mm EVA foam

COSTUME AND MODELING BY MAKER FISHMEAL

Photo by Sydney Newland (Cinnamon + Birch)

Fabric Preparation and Care

Foams do not need to be prewashed. Generally, these materials are spot-clean only; a machine wash will tear them apart.

Upholstery foam, because it is so absorbent, can be particularly difficult to clean; when spot cleaning doesn't do the trick, hand wash it by submerging it in cool water with gentle soap. Lay it flat to dry.

Pressing

Thin PE and EVA foams can be pressed with an iron on very low heat using parchment or tissue paper as a press cloth.

The easiest way to manipulate thin foams is with a heat gun. To remove wrinkles from EVA and PE foam, lightly pass a heat gun over the surface and then bend the material outward, opening the wrinkles, to encourage them to fall out. To press seam allowances or otherwise create creases, heat with a heat gun and then finger press.

✸ QUICK TIP!

Foams are sensitive to heat, which can be useful but makes them tricky to press. Take care not to melt foams as you're heating them.

If you're unsure how much heat it will take to melt your foam, test on a scrap. Place an extra piece of foam on a safe surface—your cutting mat will melt, but cement, wood, and brick surfaces will not—and then blast it with your heat gun until it melts away. It's extremely important to wear lung protection when performing this experiment! ●

Upholstery foam resists creasing; it does not wrinkle easily, but creating folds and flattening seam allowances is tough. If your upholstery foam does crease, steam it to release the wrinkles. Steam and then finger press to create folds. Seam allowances will need to be sewn or glued down instead of just pressed.

Pattern Transfer/Marking

If your foam will be covered, markers (especially metallic ones, which will show up on dark foams) and other regular writing tools are fine for marking the material. Chalk is a removable option, but it can stain lighter-colored foams; make sure to swatch test if your foam will be visible in your final piece. Washi or masking tape is a safe and removable option that will not stain.

Cutting

Thin foams can be cut with scissors, but you'll get cleaner edges at all thicknesses by using a craft knife or box cutter (pg 200). Because foams do not need to be hemmed, the cut on your piece may be your visible edge; it's worth it to take the time to make it beautiful!

Thin foams can be cut out puzzle-piece style.

Pinning and Alternatives

Use clips, glue, or tape to secure thin foams. Pins will leave permanent holes, which weaken the strength of the foam. Don't leave clips on for too long; they will leave creases, especially on PE and EVA foam.

When securing large pieces of foam face to face, spray basting glue is a great option because it can cover larger areas quickly.

Interfacing

Foams do not generally need to be traditionally interfaced; they're sturdy materials often used *as* interfacing. If you do need some extra sturdiness, they can be interfaced with themselves or with thicker foam glued to the reverse. Sew-in woven or nonwoven interfacing may help, but a very sturdy fabric interfacing, like buckram stiffener (pg 210), will provide significant structure to thin foams. Don't forget, though, that every time you sew something to foam, you're introducing weakness!

Ultimately, if your thin foam needs to be stiffened, it's easiest to upgrade to a thicker foam, a higher-density foam, or a different *kind* of foam (switch from upholstery to EVA, for example).

Sewing

Sew thin foam with a 4mm straight stitch, a walking foot with the pressure reduced to account for the material's thickness, and heavy-duty polyester thread. A 100/16 denim is a good needle to start with, but you may discover the need to experiment with your needle; a larger one will pierce the material more easily but leave larger holes.

You don't want to make any more holes than necessary when sewing with foams, and that means no backstitching at the beginning and end of stitch lines. Instead, tie off the tails, trim them, and then secure them with a dab of glue.

Thread tails tied off and then secured with glue

Because foams do not fray, you actually have quite a few options for seams. Abutted (pg 171) are a clean and simple option; thinner foams may need to be reinforced with tape, fabric, or more thin foam on the reverse of the seam, because the bonding area is so small. Lapped seams (pg 160) create a bump, but they are also very strong and easy to achieve with either glue or a line of stitches. A plain seam (pg 66) is always a safe bet, although a bubbly seam will need to be corrected with either topstitching or glue on the seam allowances (pg 177).

Hems are not necessary on foams and not possible except with the thinnest materials. Overedging (pg 138) works on thin upholstery foam but will shred PE and EVA foam. A single-fold hem (pg 85) is fine on thin foams, especially if it's glued. Perhaps the cleanest hem on foams is a slightly beveled edge on a very clean cut, which you can achieve with a rotary tool (pg 198).

Tutorial Time: Edge Finishing with a Bevel

A bevel is a soft-angled edge. It adds a finishing touch on atypical creative materials that don't need their raw edges protected. It can be added with sandpaper, but a rotary tool is faster and results in a cleaner final product.

Using a rotary tool to add a beveled edge to a piece of EVA foam

When using a rotary tool, you want to move your tool so that the bit is rotating *with* the movement. For most rotary tools, that means that righties move the machine away from them; lefties sand toward themselves. If you move the tool against the movement, it will skip and jump around; that's dangerous and will result in subpar sanding results.

You may have to experiment with different bits to find the one that works best for your material. I like starting with the stone bit for EVA foam; it creates a gentle texture that blends into the foam's original finish.

Gently run the rotary tool along the edge of your material, patiently sanding in the amount of bevel you desire.

Don't forget! Stay safe when sanding: Always wear lung and eye protection.

Thick Foam

In the context of this book, thick foams are those 4mm or greater in thickness. They're great as structural materials in bags, costumes, and props.

Fabric Preparation and Care

Do not prewash your thick foams; if they have surface dirt, they can be spot cleaned with gentle cleaners. If you need to do a more thorough clean, submerge your foam in cool water and carefully agitate it with a gentle cleaner (like Dawn dish soap). Lay it flat to dry.

Pressing

Remove wrinkles from EVA and PE foams by heating them with a heat gun. Then bend the foam to open the wrinkle and encourage the foam to remember its new shape. Always wear lung protection when heating foam.

Upholstery foam will react better to steam than a heat gun; lightly steam the material to remove creases.

Sailor Strange (*Sailor Moon* and *Doctor Strange* mashup design by Gladzy Kei) shoulders and cuffs made from stretch velvet sewn over two layers of ½″ (12mm) upholstery foam

COSTUME AND MODELING BY LORE ROBERTS (LOREBUILDS)
Photo by Adam Watney

1. Thick EVA foam
2. Thick PE foam
3. Thick upholstery foam

Pattern Transfer/Marking

Markers work particularly well on foams, because the materials are usually opaque and will often be covered with another material (like fabric or paint). Chalk will easily wash off of most foams, but darker ones may stain, so be sure to test before committing. Washi or masking tape is always a safe option for marking.

Cutting

A box cutter (below) is the best way to cut thick foams; the blade on a craft knife is probably not long enough. Scissors, if they can cut through thick foams at all, will result in messy and jagged edges. Make sure to get a retractable-blade box cutter; this will allow you to extend the blade far enough to cut through very thick materials. Plus, you'll be able to snap off dull sections as needed.

Thick foams can be cut out puzzle-piece style.

Tutorial Time: Cutting with a Box Cutter

Cutting foam and other thick material cleanly can take some practice, but it's worth it to be able to use those raw edges as hems. Don't forget: Plastics dull blades, and only a sharp blade will get a very clean cut. When you feel your blade pulling at your material, either sharpen or change your blade.

1. Begin with your blade long enough that it can cut through the material in one pass.

2. Cut with the edges of the blade perpendicular to your material; you don't want to tilt it to the left or right, unless you're trying to cut a bevel (pg 198). Smoothly pull the blade along your marked line while pressing firmly. You should be able to cut all the way through the foam in one pass, resulting in a perfect edge.

Pinning and Alternatives

Tape is great for securing foams, especially if you're preparing an abutted seam (pg 171). Spray adhesive is another option, although weaker forms may not be strong enough to hold substantial versions of these foams.

Even if your pins are long enough to secure these materials, don't. They'll leave permanent holes, which will weaken the foam and introduce an opportunity for tears.

Interfacing

For thicker foams, interface with self, a thicker foam, or a denser foam. Because they're already substantial materials, traditional sturdy interfacings like buckram stiffeners are not likely to provide much, if any, support.

Sewing

Thicker foams are not going to go through a typical home sewing machine. Instead, use glue. An abutted seam (pg 171) works perfectly, especially because its thickness provides plenty of area for the edges to bond. Use hot glue on upholstery foam, contact cement (pg 204) on EVA foam, and either on PE foam. If your abutted seam needs reinforcement, add a line of fabric, tape, or thinner foam to the back.

Hems are not possible on thick foams. Instead, finish with a bevel, which you can make with a rotary tool (pg 198).

Circle skirt made of 1.5mm neoprene

GARMENT AND MODELING BY ANNYE DRISCOLL
Photo by Zeke McLean

Neoprene

Most **neoprene** fabrics are foam and fabric bonded together, which creates a spongy and flexible textile. Neoprene is strong and warm. It comes in a wide range of thicknesses, most commonly from 0.5mm to 7mm. The bonded fabric is almost always either nylon or polyester, but neoprene also comes naked; that is neoprene may be bonded with fabric on either one or both sides—or neither!

CONFUSING TOPIC!

Neoprene (left) and scuba (right)

Don't forget! Neoprene and scuba are very different kinds of fabric. Scuba, a thick and spongy double knit, does not include neoprene fabric's defining bonded foam. •

You're probably familiar with unbonded neoprene; it's commonly used for dishwashing gloves and Halloween masks. When not bonded to fabric, neoprene is often in its default rubber state—no air has been added to turn it into a squishy foam. This dense material is also included in this section, even though it's not technically foam.

Wetsuit Material

Neoprene is extremely insulating, making it the perfect material for wetsuits. It's often coated with waterproofing; if your material is, you'll need to consider that coating when pressing and washing.

Neoprene may also have added spandex, which makes it easier to mold to the body when used as swimming gear. If you're sewing with a spandex neoprene, consider the stretch and use techniques to compensate for it.

Fabric Preparation and Care

If you will be washing your fabric-bonded neoprene, prewash it. Bonded neoprene can be machine washed cold or warm and dried on low heat, but it should be spot cleaned when possible to preserve the adhesive used in bonding.

Unbonded neoprene should be hand washed. Submerge it in cool soapy water, and then gently agitate it.

Pressing

Both bonded and unbonded neoprene can be lightly pressed under a parchment paper press cloth using low heat. Steaming is a safer option, though, because there's less risk of damaging your material or iron.

Folds and bubbly seam allowances may need to be sewn or glued down because the foam does resist creasing.

⚠ STAY SAFE!
Because neoprene is so insulating, it gets hot very fast. Be careful when touching neoprene that you've just pressed! •

Pattern Transfer/Marking

On the fabric side of bonded neoprene, use a marking tool relevant for that material; chalk and erasable pens are usually safe bets. On the reverse and on unbonded neoprene, chalk and metallic markers are easy to see and will not show through the opaque material.

Cutting

Unbonded neoprene is easy to cut: Use a rotary cutter, a craft knife, or a box cutter (pg 200) to get clean, smooth edges.

A rotary cutter is the best option for fabric-backed neoprene, because knives will catch on the yarns of the fabric, resulting in jagged edges. Do not use your fabric scissors; the foam will dull the blades.

The direction of stretch will usually determine your cutting layout. If your neoprene is not stretchy or the direction of stretch does not matter, use a puzzle-piece style layout.

Pinning and Alternatives

Neoprene is best held together with sewing clips; pins will leave permanent holes, which will weaken the material. This is particularly important when talking about unbonded versions, because they don't have the advantage of a strengthening layer (or two!) of bonded fabric. When making with the bonded version, ballpoint pins are an acceptable choice when clips aren't convenient.

Interfacing

When you're making with bonded neoprene with fabric on each side, nonwoven or woven fusible interfacing will bond easily to the fabric. Just be careful not to damage the material or hurt yourself during the fusing process.

If you're working with either single-sided bonded neoprene or unbonded neoprene, your best bet is to use a thicker version of the material instead of interfacing. If that's not an option, use a self-interfacing (pg 45) or sew in a woven or nonwoven commercial interfacing.

Sewing

Use a 100/16 denim needle, a 3.5mm zigzag stitch, and heavy-duty polyester thread when sewing with neoprene. A walking foot will help feed the substantial material through your material; you may also want to decrease the foot pressure to make more room for its thickness.

Because neoprene does not fray, seams and hems are easy to implement; the most difficult part of sewing with them is dealing with the bulk! For that reason, consider abutted (pg 171), lapped (pg 160), or plain seams with topstitched or glued seam allowances (pg 177). Leave your edges unhemmed, or overedge (zigzag, three- or four-thread overlock, or three-thread wrapped, pg 138) or bind (pg 73) them for a cleaner finish.

You can also use glue on neoprene materials. Contact cement (pg 204) works well on both the fabric side and the rubber or foam side; just remember to wear lung protection when working with that glue. 3M Neoprene High Performance Rubber and Gasket Adhesive 1300 (by 3M) is a contact cement specifically made for neoprene.

Tutorial Time: Using Contact Cement

Contact cement can be a bit tricky: It takes timing, and that timing can change with material, temperature, and humidity. It's one of the strongest and most versatile crafting glues though; it's worth it to learn its ins and outs!

1. Begin with clean and dry materials. Apply contact cement to both of the materials you intend to adhere. You want a thin layer with no drips or globs; this is most easily achieved with a silicone makeup brush or with a scrap of EVA foam.

2. Let the contact cement gas off for 10–15 minutes or until it's very slightly tacky. If you wait too long or want an extra-strong hold, at this point you can add another layer of glue and then let *that* layer sit.

3. Press your pieces together.

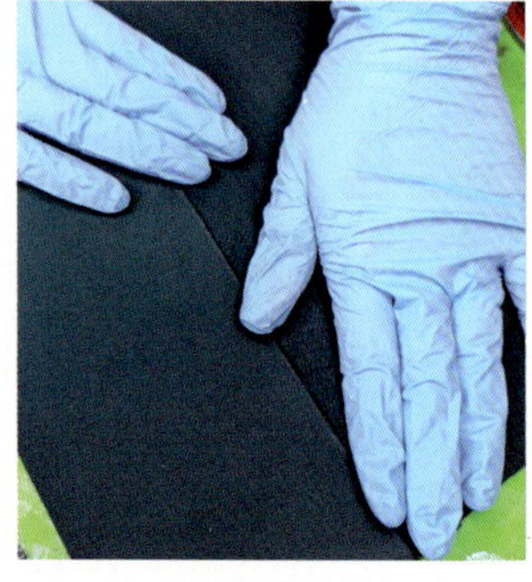

4. Contact cement needs pressure to adhere; press a seam or hem with a seam roller, or apply pressure with your fingers if creating an abutted seam (pg 171).

Don't forget! Contact cement is dangerous for your lungs and brain. Always work in a well-ventilated area and wear a respirator appropriate for fumes when working with it.

Sealing Your Seams

If you choose to create your neoprene project with contact cement, the seams may already be watertight. However, if you sew or use a different kind of glue, you'll need to seal your seams before you can trust your project in the water. This process is best done with glue; a product like Aquaseal NEO Neoprene Contact Cement (by GEAR AID) is specifically made for this task. Any contact cement will work, though; just spread your glue over your stitch line to seal the holes made during the sewing process.

Utility Materials

Utility materials are those that are sewn rarely or for very specific applications. Nonslip materials—think kitchen shelf liners—have inherent stickiness, which makes them tricky to send through a sewing machine. Tarps and plastic bags are unconventional sewing materials but are easy to get and generally behave nicely for the sewing process. Finally, some materials are used often in specific sewing subsections, like bag making, to add structure and rigidity to a project. Because they're thick and stiff, they can be tough to sew.

Backpack made with cork, which has been backed with fusible fleece

BAG BY JESSICA KAPITANSKI FROM *CREATE WITH CORK FABRIC* (C&T PUBLISHING)

Nonslip Materials

Nonslip materials can vary wildly, but they do share some sewing difficulties among them—chiefly, that their very nature causes them to stick as they pass through your machine!

Some nonslip materials consist of a base fabric (of any kind) either coated or dotted with a PVC or rubber coating, which gives it a grippy texture. Others are entirely made of the grippy material; they may be 100 percent PVC, for example, or a PVC/polyester blend. Some of these, such as classic cabinet liners, have many small holes, which further complicate sewing—they are essentially a netting of nonslip substance.

Fabric Preparation and Care

Nonslip materials should generally not be pretreated; the sticky spots are sensitive to heat, and the glue adhering them to the base fabric (if relevant) may lose its adhesion after repeated washing. Instead, spot clean.

If your nonslip material is machine washable, it's probably a variety with occasional sticky dots on a base fabric. Washing specifics will vary according to composition, but generally washing on a gentle cycle and laying flat to dry is a safe bet.

Pressing

Do not press nonslip material; it will melt. If necessary, press with very low heat and a baking paper press cloth. If your fabric's sticky dots are spread far enough apart, you may be able to press around them.

Faux chain mail shirt made of nonslip material, which has been painted silver and black

SHIRT BY MAKER FISHMEAL
Photo by Maker Fishmeal

1

2

1. Fabric-backed nonslip material
2. Netting nonslip material

Pattern Transfer/Marking

Nonslip materials on a fabric base can be marked with chalk or disappearing ink. If your nonslip material is particularly holey, consider tape or thread tracing instead.

Cutting

Do not use your fabric scissors on nonslip materials; the plastic in the grippy substance will dull your nice shears. A rotary cutter works well and will achieve a clean cut through the plastic grippy dots.

When laying out your pattern pieces for a nonslip project, don't forget to consider the orientation and/or pattern of the nonslip material. Are the dots in a grid and, if so, do you need to make sure the lines of your piece are parallel to that grid? If your non-fabric-backed nonslip material is in a netting orientation, do you want all your holes oriented the same way?

Also, consider the base material, if your nonslip is fabric-backed. Do your pattern pieces need to be cut out on the bias to drape properly? Do you need to consider the stretch of a knit base fabric before committing to pattern placement?

If none of these factors is relevant, cut using puzzle-piece style.

Pinning and Alternatives

Clips, glue, and tape are all options for pinning non-fabric-backed nonslip materials; because they are netting, pins may be tougher to use effectively. Clips, if left in for a long time, may leave a dent in raw nonslip material.

For fabric-backed options, tailor your choices to the base fabric (all-purpose pins for wovens, ballpoint pins for knits, etc.). Clips are always a safe choice.

Interfacing

Netting-style nonslip material will not generally need to be interfaced; if it does need to be stiffened or thickened, use another layer of self, add a sturdy netting fabric like organza, or create your own fabric-backed nonslip material by sewing your netting to a base fabric that has the properties you need for your project.

Fabric-backed nonslip should be interfaced according to its base fabric (woven, nonwoven, knit, stretch for knits). Remember that nonslip material does not tolerate heat well; use sew-in interfacing.

Sewing

Because of their very nature as nonslip materials, sewing these fabrics can be really tricky. They'll stick to your needle and sewing plate, making feeding them through the machine a huge pain. For both versions, a walking, nonstick, or roller presser foot will help the sticky material move evenly through the feed dogs. Reduce your presser foot pressure, too, to have less of a grip on the material.

Unfortunately, changing the presser foot probably won't be enough to prevent the material from getting stuck in your machine. Ultimately, you'll almost certainly have to sew between two layers of parchment or tissue paper (pg 155) and then tear that material away when you're done with construction.

When sewing with fabric-backed nonslip material, tailor your machine needle, thread, and stitch to your base material. However, definitely use a nonslip version of the machine needle that's best for your material. When using the netted version of nonslip, a 90/14 leather or microtex needle is best; again, definitely get a nonstick version of whichever you go with.

For both versions, use a 3.5mm straight or wide zigzag stitch and all-purpose or heavy-duty polyester thread.

When creating with fabric-backed nonslip material, seams and hems should be tailored to the base material. For the netted version, use plain (pg 66), abutted (pg 171), or lapped seams (pg 160). In both cases, seam allowances may need to be sewn or glued down, because this material can have substantial bulk.

The netted version of the material does not fray and, therefore, does not need to be hemmed. Single- and double-fold hems (pg 85) work, but the fold will be visible through the net of the material. Overedging (three-thread overlock or zigzag, pg 138) is not necessary but is possible; for a very clean finish, bind (pg 73) the raw edge.

Wallet made from plastic tarp-like food packaging, pressed and sewn

WALLET AND MODELING BY SHARON STAHL
Photo by Sharon Stahl

Tarps, Cling Wrap, and Plastic Bags

Tarps, cling wrap, plastic trash bags, and **single-use shopping bags** are surprisingly versatile materials and easy to work with. They're all made of the same kind of plastic: polyethylene (PE). PE materials are almost always used for utility purposes where their strong and waterproof natures can be taken advantage of.

Tarps are usually made from woven strips of PE, which means that they fray over time, but it also increases the strength of the material.

PEs are very sensitive to heat, which complicates the sewing process somewhat but also unlocks some fun and creative options.

✸ QUICK TIP!
Some packaging and shopping bags, most notably IKEA totes, are constructed like, and sew similarly to tarps, though they're often made of polypropylene instead of PE. Follow the guidelines for tarp if you want to sew your woven plastic materials. •

Fabric Preparation and Care

PEs do not need to be pretreated other than to remove chemicals from the manufacturing process. To wash them, machine wash cold and then hang dry. Delicate PEs, like cling wrap and regular disposable shopping bags, should be machine washed in a delicates bag or gently hand washed, because they can rip.

1. Plastic shopping bag
2. Trash bag
3. Cling wrap
4. Tarp

Pressing

Press PE projects with low heat and no steam. Never let the iron touch the material directly; it will melt and ruin your iron. Use a piece of baking paper as a press cloth, and keep the iron moving at all times to prevent damage to both your iron and your material.

Pattern Transfer/Marking

Dry-erase marker and chalk work to mark PE materials, though chalk may wipe off easier than you want for construction purposes. Make sure that your dry-erase marker will not stain your material before making any marks outside of the seam allowance.

Cutting

Use craft or heavy-duty scissors on PE materials; the plastic will dull fabric shears. Tarps can be cut in two layers, but lighter trash bags and shopping bags will wiggle around too much and should be cut in a single layer.

A rotary cutter is also a great option for cutting through tarp material. If you use one on lightweight PEs, though, make sure to weight your material very thoroughly (pg 111) to prevent slipping during the cutting process.

Unless a print requires otherwise, PE materials can be cut puzzle-piece style. Tarps do technically have a grain, but their weave is so flat and tightly woven that it will not affect drape.

Pinning and Alternatives

Pins leave permanent holes in PE. Instead, use clips or tape to secure your materials before sewing.

Interfacing

PE materials are best interfaced with self (pg 45) or thicker PE plastic materials. Because gluing is tricky and sewing holes are permanent, consider flatlining: Use tape to baste your multiple layers together and then treat them as one layer during the sewing step (pg 141). Using this strategy, the interfacing and fashion layers will all be connected with just one line of stitching.

A much better option, which does not use sewing at all, is to fuse two layers of PE (pg 210) into one to create a thicker, more substantial material.

Sewing

Sew thicker PE using a 90/14 microtex, leather, or universal machine needle, and thinner versions using a 60/8 microtex. They'll probably be fine with a standard machine foot, but a walking foot will help evenly feed the bulk of tarp material and the slipperiness of trash bags through your machine. Use polyester all-purpose or fine thread for trash bags and heavy-duty for tarps.

Because lightweight PEs don't fray and tarps fray slowly, seam options are wide and raw edges do not need protection. A plain (pg 66) or lapped (pg 160) seam works well for tarp; add French (pg 114) and welt (pg 165) for lighter-weight PEs. Consider pinking (pg 66) the raw edges of your tarp; because it's made of woven PE strips, it will fray eventually.

A single- or double-fold hem (pg 85) will provide a clean finish.

When crafting with PE, sewing is not your only option! Because the material is heat-sensitive, it can actually be fused to create seams, hems, and other "sewn" details without the need for either holes (which weaken the material) or glue (which struggles to adhere).

⚠ STAY SAFE!
Work in a well-ventilated area and always wear lung protection when heating plastic like PEs. Ensure that your filters are appropriate for vapors, not just particles. •

Tutorial Time: Fusing PEs

PE materials, because they're so sensitive to heat, can be fused with heat instead of sewn or glued.

Begin with your iron on low heat with no steam, and use a piece of baking paper as a press cloth.

Keeping the iron moving at all times, press over the connection you want to make. For a single-use plastic bag, the welding will happen quickly; for thicker materials, you'll need more heat and time. Practice on swatches to discover what the best strategy is for your material.

You can use this strategy with your PE face to face to completely combine them into a new material—essentially permanently self-interfacing—or you can fuse conventional seams and hems.

Structural Materials

Structural materials are used in conjunction with other textiles to give stiffness, thickness, or both.

Buckram is the original stiffening material. Historically, it was made from jute or cotton and then thickened with glue. It's a coarse, stiff fabric. Buckram can be shaped using both moisture and heat (although it's best activated with both, using steam), and it's even available in fusible form.

Modern alternatives to buckram abound, although the material is still used frequently in bookbinding and millinery.

Foam interfacing is interfacing with foam integrated; usually, it's very lightweight PU foam (pg 194) sandwiched between thin tricot, but it can also be found in naked foam form. It's available in both sewable and fusible forms; the fusible version may be single- or double-sided.

The Huntsman *(Monster Hunter)* quilted chest and arm padding made of linen and quilt batting with polyester dupioni piping

COSTUME BY WIGTALL AND WIGSMALL OF WIG-WIG COSPLAY, MODELING WIGTALL
Photo by Donald Dao/Don Dolce Photography

FOSSHAPE (by Wonderflex World) is a material with a texture similar to felt; it can be cut, sewn, and glued using similar techniques. FOSSHAPE comes in multiple thicknesses; the thinner ones (such as 300) are best for detailing, while the thicker varieties (such as 600) work well as a rigid base.

⚠ STAY SAFE!

When creating with structural materials, you'll often use a combination of heat and physical manipulation to achieve your desired shape. Always be careful when working with these materials; wear heat-resistant gloves. •

Kobracast (by Worbla) is made from a mesh fabric that's been infused with thermoplastic. It is thin, sticky, and stretchy. Kobracast can be used as a traditional interfacing, as an interlining to provide significant structure, or (when painted, for example) as the outer fashion fabric of a creation.

Both FOSSHAPE and Kobracast have thermoplastic elements, which means that once heated, they harden enough to support not only themselves, but also the weight of other textiles and materials.

Tutorial Time: How to Use FOSSHAPE

FOSSHAPE is still sewable after it has been activated, but you may find it easier to sew while it's flat. You can then stiffen and mold it after all your pieces have been connected.

Note that FOSSHAPE does shrink as it stiffens. For that reason, molding it on a base (such as a wig head) will help control the shrinkage. You may also consider creating your patterns slightly large to account for the shrink.

Once you have your FOSSHAPE ready, activate it with heat. A heat gun works well for this purpose, but a steamer results in a slower activation and, therefore, more control. With either, use a light touch and work slowly, manipulating the material as you work to achieve your desired shape.

Tutorial Time: How to Use Kobracast

Unlike FOSSHAPE, which hardens with heat, Kobacrast begins rigid and maintains that rigidity even after it has been activated. For that reason, it doesn't matter if you take advantage of its thermoplastic properties before or after sewing—just make sure it's completely cool when you send it through your machine.

1. Activate Kobacrast with steam, a heat gun, or an iron (using parchment paper as a press cloth).

2. Once it's pliable, carefully form it to your desired shape. When cool, it will be rigid but flexible with a memory; you can manipulate it out of shape, and it will pop back to its resting position.

Kobracast does include an adhesive; pieces easily stick to each other, although reinforcement (with glue or stitches) is best when adhering to a secondary material.

Kobracast can be activated even through layers of fabric. So, if your finished bag, for example, isn't quite the shape you were hoping for, iron it to reactivate the thermoplastic and shape it again.

When pressing open seams that include Kobracast, be sure to protect the body of your pieces (pg 72) so that you activate only the seam allowance portion of the Kobracast.

Quilt batting, also known as wadding, was historically made using cotton or wool, but it's also available in polyester. Batting's thickness is called a *loft;* polyester batting is available in multiple lofts, while cotton is generally a lower loft. Batting is used to create the signature stitched depressions in quilts (and to add weight and warmth), but it can also be used to add structure and thickness in other applications.

✱ QUICK TIP!

Some batting has a right side and a wrong side. Inspect your batting: The wrong side will have a bumpy texture that somewhat resembles a pilled sweater. If you're quilting, make sure to sew with the right side up so that less of the batting is pulled through the top of the quilt (a phenomenon called *bearding*). ●

Fabric Preparation and Care

You do not want to prewash your structural materials; heat and water will remove desired finishings and activate thermoplastics.

Pressing

Generally, do not press your structural materials until they're part of a completed project. In that case, use caution; heat may damage the material (in the case of polyester quilt batting and foam interfacing) or activate the moldability aspects (in the case of buckram, FOSSHAPE, and Kobracast).

Batting can be carefully pressed; if it's polyester or a polyester blend, start at low heat, using a press cloth and steam. If your batting is wool or cotton, press on medium or high heat, respectively.

To remove wrinkles from quilt batting and foam interfacing, tumble dry. To remove wrinkles from buckram, moisten it and manipulate the wrinkles flat. FOSSHAPE and Kobracast should not wrinkle, and the thermoplastic process will remove any imperfections in the material.

Pattern Transfer/Marking

Standard marking tools work well on all structural materials. Chalk and disappearing ink are fine temporary options. Pen and permanent marker make easy-to-see marks, which will be hidden once your structural material is contained within the project.

Tailor's tacks are particularly great for quilt batting and foam interfacing, because the thread can go through even very thick versions and then remain visible from both sides.

Cutting

Do not use your sewing shears on structural materials; the adhesives and plastics used to make them will dull your scissors.

Use a rotary cutter on quilt batting, foam interfacing, buckram, and FOSSHAPE; heavy-duty or craft scissors will work on those materials and on Kobracast.

Because they don't fold well, all of these materials should be cut in one layer. They can also generally be cut puzzle-piece style; batting and buckram have grains, but those will be applicable only in specific situations (such as when a quilt will be hanging on the wall). In those cases, cut on the grain.

Pinning and Alternatives

Sewing clips are best for almost all situations when working with structural materials; pins won't be visible through thick materials, will get stuck in adhesives and coatings, or both.

Glue basting (pg 99) is a great option for structural materials; because they'll likely be enclosed within another material, the risk of ruining the material with glue seepage is very low. Basting spray is great for FOSSHAPE, foam interfacing, and batting. Use a glue stick for buckram and tape for Kobracast.

Interfacing

Structural materials are generally used *as* interfacing. If you need them to be stiffer, consider a thicker version of the material or a different interfacing altogether. Buckram, Kobracast, and FOSSHAPE will become rigid after activation, while batting and foam interfacing provide support while remaining squishy. If you need rigidity, switch to one of the former, or self-interface (pg 45).

Sewing

Though structural materials share many similarities—chief among them, their purpose—sewing them varies greatly. The guidelines below will outline how to sew them on their own, but, of course, you'll usually be sewing them with another material! In that case, experimentation is needed. Start with the guidelines presented for your *other* material, knowing that you may need to increase your machine needle size, decrease presser foot pressure, switch to a walking foot, and/or increase your stitch length to find success. Take your time and swatch; find the tools and settings that work for your specific combination of materials.

Use an 80/12 universal machine needle to sew batting, FOSSHAPE, and foam interfacing and a 90/14 or 100/16 denim machine needle with buckram and Kobracast. A standard presser foot is best for Kobracast and buckram; a walking foot will work well with batting, foam interfacing, and FOSSHAPE because they're thicker materials. Use a 2.5–3.5mm straight stitch for all materials. Use all-purpose polyester thread for all structural materials; buckram may also benefit from heavy-duty polyester thread.

Generally, seams and hems will need to be chosen based on the textile with which you're combining your structural material.

If you're working just with a structural material, however, abutted seams (pg 171) are always an option; just make sure to reinforce the seam. You can use a plain seam (pg 66) with thinner battings, buckram, FOSSHAPE, and Kobracast, though the seam allowances will need to be secured (pg 177) to prevent a bubbling front. Lapped seams (pg 160) work well for Kobracast and buckram, because those are thinner materials.

✸ QUICK TIP!
If your batting, foam interfacing, or FOSSHAPE are getting pulled into your machine, sew using a tissue paper sandwich (pg 155) and then pull the paper away once your sewing is complete. •

Of all these structural materials, only uncoated buckram needs its raw edges protected; all the other materials do not fray. If your buckram is uncoated, treat it like canvas (pg 78). If you do want to cover edges, overedging (pg 138) and binding (pg 73) are options for all structural materials; use a four-thread overlock stitch for batting, buckram, and foam interfacing and a wide zigzag stitch for FOSSHAPE (which should not be serged due to its thermoplastic properties). A single- or double-fold hem (pg 85) will also work for buckram.

Hemming is not relevant for FOSSHAPE; its very stiff, plasticky composition does not require or take well to edge finishing.

Adhesive works very well on structural materials. Contact cement (pg 204) is an option for all of them. Hot glue works extremely well on batting, foam interfacing, and FOSSHAPE, because it can seep into the pores in the materials. Don't forget: FOSSHAPE and Kobracast have adhesive built-in, so glue and sewing *may* not be necessary.

Fabric Encyclopedia

The following section provides an easy lookup for the textiles included in this book. Remember: Always swatch test not only the obvious (pressing temperatures, marking tools) but also the not so obvious (needle choice, interfacing technique). Even within categories, fabrics can vary and require slightly or even vastly different treatment.

QUICK TIP!

In the encyclopedia, the following abbreviations are used for various types of plastic:

- **EVA:** Ethylene-vinyl acetate
- **PE:** Polyethylene
- **PP:** Polypropylene
- **PU:** Polyurethane
- **PVC:** Polyvinyl chloride

Rey longline underwire bra and Millie Panty made with copper and navy printed mesh and a deadstock designer lace fabric.

MODELLING BY HARMONY JOY, GARMENTS BY MADDIE KULIG (MADALYNNE INTIMATES)
Photo by Maddie Kulig (Madalynne Intimates)

Delicates (pg 126)

Athletic Mesh

A warp-knit mesh made of polyester and often used for apparel and athletic gear.

Athletic mesh, most often used for jerseys, is tough and thick and does not stretch.

Prewash: yes

Pressing: low heat with press cloth

Marking: chalk, disappearing ink

Machine needle: 80/12 jersey

Cutting layout: on the grain

Cutting tools: fabric shears, rotary cutter

Pins: sewing clips, tape, tearaway or water-soluble stabilizer

Interfacing: sew-in or fusible woven or nonwoven

Machine foot: standard, roller

Conventional machine stitch: 2.5mm straight or 1.5mm narrow zigzag

Serger stitch: three-thread overlock

Thread: all-purpose or heavy-duty polyester

Seams: plain (pg 66), flat-fell (pg 81)

Hems: single fold or double fold (pg 85), mock cover (pg 104), bound (pg 73), overedged (pg 138)

Need to finish raw edges: no

Raw edge finishing: overedged (pg 138), bound (pg 73)

Care: Machine wash cold and gentle. Tumble dry on low heat.

Structural Materials (pg 210)

Batting

A nonwoven material made of cotton, polyester, or wool and often used for structure and thickness.

Batting is a fluffy material often used to create the signature stitched depressions in quilts. It can also be used to add structure and thickness in other applications.

Prewash: no

Pressing: carefully and sparingly, according to fiber content (pg 36)

Marking: chalk, disappearing ink, regular marking tools

Machine needle: 80/12 universal

Cutting layout: puzzle piece

Cutting tools: craft or fabric shears, rotary cutter

Pins: sewing clips, long pins

Interfacing: self, thicker batting, or stiffer structural material

Machine foot: standard, walking; decrease pressure

Conventional machine stitch: 2.5–3.5mm straight

Serger stitch: four-thread overlock

Thread: all-purpose polyester

Seams: plain (pg 66), abutted (pg 171)

Hems: overedge (pg 138), bound (pg 73)

Need to finish raw edges: no

Raw edge finishing: topstitched (pg 177), overedged (pg 138)

Care: Hand wash or spot clean.

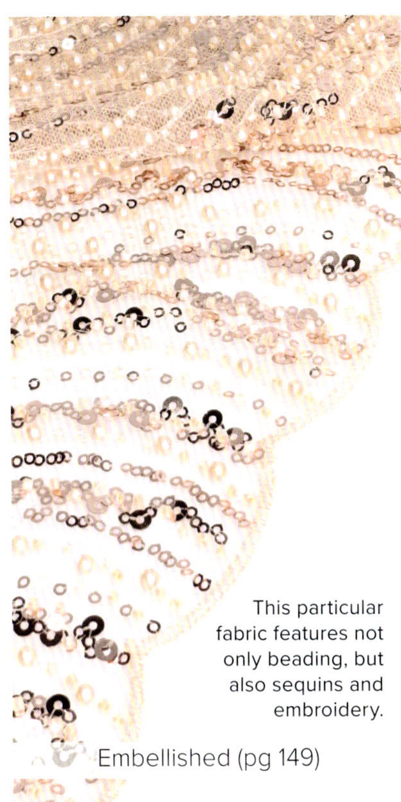

This particular fabric features not only beading, but also sequins and embroidery.

Embellished (pg 149)

Beading

An embellished fabric made of any base material with beading added, which is often used for apparel and special event garments.

Beading is any base fabric embellished with beads.

Machine needle, interfacing, serger stitch, thread, seams, hems, need to finish raw edges, and raw edge finishing: Refer to the encyclopedia entry for the base fabric.

Prewash: no

Pressing: do not iron beading directly; steam

Marking: chalk, tailor's tacks

Cutting layout: with nap, in a single layer

Cutting tools: craft or heavy-duty scissors, if cutting near beading; otherwise, refer to base fabric

Pins: refer to base fabric; do not pin through beads

Machine foot: walking; decrease pressure

Conventional machine stitch: 3.5mm straight

Care: Dry clean, hand wash, or spot clean. Lay flat to dry.

Felt, Boiled Wool, and Melton (pg 158)

Boiled Wool

A fulled knit fabric made of wool and often used for apparel and outerwear.

Boiled wool is made by fulling wool knit fabrics. It has a great body. It is wrinkle- and moisture-resistant.

Prewash: yes

Pressing: Press according to fiber content (pg 36) with a press cloth and steam.

Marking: chalk

Machine needle: 90/14 universal

Cutting layout: puzzle piece

Cutting tools: craft scissors, fabric shears, rotary cutter

Pins: all-purpose or long pins

Interfacing: sew-in or fusible woven or nonwoven

Machine foot: walking

Conventional machine stitch: 2.5mm straight; lengthen for thicker fabrics

Serger stitch: four-thread overlock

Thread: all-purpose cotton or polyester

Seams: lapped (pg 160), abutted (pg 171), plain (pg 66), overedged (pg 70)

Hems: single fold (pg 85), overedged (pg 138)

Need to finish raw edges: no

Raw edge finishing: topstitched (pg 177), overedged (pg 138)

Care: Machine wash cold and gentle. Lay flat to dry.

Textured Heavyweights (pg 86)

Bouclé

A plain-weave heavyweight woven made of acrylic, cotton, linen, polyester, silk, or wool and often used for apparel, outerwear, and upholstery.

Bouclé's looped curling and textured yarns creates a distinctive texture. It's warm but can be scratchy against the skin.

Prewash: yes

Pressing: Press from the wrong side on low heat using steam, a press cloth, and a plush fabric against the right side.

Marking: chalk, disappearing ink, tailor's tacks

Machine needle: 80/12 universal

Cutting layout: with nap, in a single layer

Cutting tools: fabric shears, rotary cutter

Pins: long pins, sewing clips

Interfacing: sew-in woven or nonwoven, batiste, organza

Machine foot: walking

Conventional machine stitch: 3mm straight

Serger stitch: three- or four-thread overlock

Thread: all-purpose cotton or polyester

Seams: plain (pg 66), overedged (pg 70), flat-fell (pg 81), welt (pg 165), reversible lapped (pg 88)

Hems: faced (pg 124), bound (pg 73), single fold (pg 85)

Need to finish raw edges: yes

Raw edge finishing: bound (pg 73), topstitched (pg 177), overedged (pg 138)

Care: Hand wash or dry clean.

Suiting and Shirting (pg 67)

Broadcloth

A plain-weave medium-weight woven made of cotton and often used for apparel.

Broadcloth is tightly woven and the most lightweight of the suiting fabrics; it is most commonly used for shirts. It is soft and smooth.

Prewash: yes

Pressing: high heat

Marking: chalk, disappearing ink, tailor's tacks

Machine needle: 80/12 universal

Cutting layout: on the grain

Cutting tools: fabric shears, rotary cutter

Pins: all-purpose pins

Interfacing: sew-in or fusible woven or nonwoven

Machine foot: standard

Conventional machine stitch: 2.5mm straight

Serger stitch: three- or four-thread overlock

Thread: all-purpose polyester

Seams: plain (pg 66), flat-fell (pg 81), overedged (pg 70)

Hems: double fold (pg 85), bound (pg 73), overedged (pg 138)

Need to finish raw edges: yes

Raw edge finishing: overedged (pg 138), bound (pg 73), topstitched (pg 177)

Care: Machine wash cold and gentle. Tumble dry.

Jacquards (pg 82)

Brocade / Jacquard

A jacquard heavyweight woven made of cotton, polyester, rayon, silk, or blends of those materials and often used for home decor, upholstery, apparel, outerwear, and bags.

Brocade, which is sometimes referred to as just jacquard, is heavy and luxurious. Often more than one color of yarn is used in the patterning process, creating a tapestry-like appearance.

Prewash: yes

Pressing: Press from the wrong side on medium heat, using steam, a press cloth, and a plush fabric against the right side.

Marking: chalk, disappearing ink, tailor's tacks

Machine needle: 80/12 universal

Cutting layout: on the grain

Cutting tools: fabric shears, pinking shears, rotary cutter

Pins: T-pins

Interfacing: sew-in or fusible nonwoven, batiste, organza

Machine foot: standard, walking

Conventional machine stitch: 2.5–3.5mm straight

Serger stitch: four-thread or wide three-thread overlock

Thread: all-purpose cotton or polyester

Seams: flat-fell (pg 81), plain (pg 66), overedged (pg 70)

Hems: faced (pg 124), single fold or wide double fold (pg 85), blind (pg 84)

Need to finish raw edges: yes

Raw edge finishing: bound (pg 73), overedged (pg 138)

Care: Silk is dry-clean only. For other fibers, machine wash warm or cold; then tumble dry on low heat.

Structural Materials (pg 210)

Buckram

A plain-weave structural material made of cotton or jute and often used for upholstery.

Buckram is a fabric that's been thickened with glue. It's a coarse, stiff material. Buckram can be shaped using both moisture and heat.

Prewash: no

Pressing: high heat with steam

Marking: chalk, disappearing ink

Machine needle: 90/14 or 100/16 denim

Cutting layout: on the grain

Cutting tools: rotary cutter, craft or heavy-duty scissors

Pins: sewing clips, T-pins, glue stick

Interfacing: self, thicker buckram

Machine foot: standard

Conventional machine stitch: 2.5–3.5mm straight

Serger stitch: four-thread overlock

Thread: all-purpose or heavy-duty polyester

Seams: plain (pg 66), abutted (pg 171), lapped (pg 160)

Hems: overedge (pg 138), single or double fold (pg 85)

Need to finish raw edges: no, unless uncoated

Raw edge finishing: topstitched (pg 177), overedged (pg 138)

Care: Machine wash cold and gentle. Lay flat to dry.

Nets (pg 128)

Burlap / Hessian

A plain-weave netting made of jute and often used for utility and crafting purposes.

Burlap, also known as hessian, is a rough, durable, open-weave fabric. Denser weave burlaps sew like heavyweight wovens, but many forms of burlap are extremely open weave.

Prewash: yes

Pressing: high heat with steam

Marking: chalk

Machine needle: 80/12 denim

Cutting layout: on the grain

Cutting tools: fabric shears, rotary cutter

Pins: sewing clips

Interfacing: starch

Machine foot: roller, walking

Conventional machine stitch: 2mm zigzag

Serger stitch: three- or four-thread overlock

Thread: all-purpose polyester

Seams: plain (pg 66), overedged (pg 70), flat-fell (pg 81)

Hems: bound (pg 73), overedged (pg 138), single fold (pg 85)

Need to finish raw edges: yes

Raw edge finishing: bound (pg 73), overedged (pg 138), topstitched (pg 177)

Care: Hand wash. Hang to dry.

Sheer (pg 107)

Cambric and Batiste

A plain-weave sheer made of cotton, linen, polyester, or wool and often used for apparel and home decor.

Cambric is a soft and fairly crisp fabric. Batiste, which is a particularly lightweight variety of cambric, has a slight sheen and is often printed. Either fabric may or may not be translucent.

Prewash: yes

Pressing: Press according to fiber content (pg 36) with a press cloth.

Marking: chalk, disappearing ink, thread tracing, tracing wheel

Machine needle: 70/10 universal

Cutting layout: on the grain, in a single layer

Cutting tools: fabric shears, rotary cutter

Pins: fine pins, hand-basting

Interfacing: sheer nonwoven sew-in, organza, self

Machine foot: straight stitch, walking

Conventional machine stitch: 2.5mm straight with straight stitch plate

Serger stitch: two- or thread-thread overlock

Thread: fine polyester, cotton, or silk

Seams: French (pg 114), overedged (pg 70), hairline (pg 122), plain (pg 66)

Hems: overedged (pg 138), rolled (pg 132), bound (pg 73), hairline (pg 122), double fold (pg 85)

Need to finish raw edges: yes

Raw edge finishing: bound (pg 73), overedged (pg 138)

Care: Machine wash warm or cold and gentle. Lay flat to dry.

Canvas and Denim (pg 78)

Canvas (Duck)

A plain-weave heavyweight woven made of cotton or linen and often used for apparel, outerwear, and adventure gear.

Duck canvas is a tighter weave than plain canvas, making it even stiffer and more durable. It is often treated with waterproofing.

Prewash: yes

Pressing: On high heat with steam unless waterproofed; in that case, press sparingly with a press cloth and low heat.

Marking: chalk, disappearing ink

Machine needle: 100/16 denim

Cutting layout: on the grain, in a single layer

Cutting tools: fabric shears, rotary cutter, heavy-duty scissors

Pins: T-pins, sewing clips

Interfacing: sew-in or fusible woven or nonwoven

Machine foot: standard; decrease pressure

Conventional machine stitch: 3.5mm straight

Serger stitch: four-thread or wide three-thread overlock

Thread: heavy-duty polyester

Seams: plain (pg 66), overedged (pg 70), flat-fell (pg 81), welt (pg 165)

Hems: wide double fold (pg 85), overedged (pg 138)

Need to finish raw edges: yes

Raw edge finishing: topstitched (pg 177), overedged (pg 138)

Care: Machine wash cold. Lay flat to dry.

Canvas and Denim (pg 78)

Canvas (Plain)

A plain-weave heavyweight woven made of cotton or linen and often used for bags and upholstery.

Canvas is usually very heavyweight, stiff, and durable, though it does come in versions light enough for suiting. It is often treated to be waterproof.

Prewash: yes

Pressing: On high heat with steam unless waterproofed; in that case, press sparingly with a press cloth and low heat.

Marking: chalk, disappearing ink

Machine needle: 90/14 denim

Cutting layout: on the grain, in a single layer

Cutting tools: fabric shears, rotary cutter

Pins: T-pins, sewing clips

Interfacing: sew-in or fusible woven or nonwoven

Machine foot: standard; decrease pressure

Conventional machine stitch: 3.5mm straight

Serger stitch: four-thread or wide three-thread overlock

Thread: heavy-duty polyester

Seams: plain (pg 66), overedged (pg 70), flat-fell (pg 81), welt (pg 165)

Hems: wide double fold (pg 85), overedged (pg 138)

Need to finish raw edges: yes

Raw edge finishing: topstitched (pg 177), overedged (pg 138)

Care: Machine wash cold. Lay flat to dry.

Thick Cardboard (pg 191)

Cardboard (Thick; > ~1mm)

A nonwoven material made of cellulose and often used for crafts and utility purposes.

Thick cardboard, like that used in shipping boxes, is sturdy enough to tolerate the holes made in sewing. It does not drape or behave like fabric, generally. It is almost always corrugated.

Prewash: no

Pressing: medium heat with no steam

Marking: chalk, regular writing tools

Machine needle: 90/14 leather, microtex, or universal

Cutting layout: on the grain (corrugation line), in a single layer

Cutting tools: box cutter

Pins: sewing clips, glue stick, tape

Interfacing: self or starch

Machine foot: standard

Conventional machine stitch: 3.5mm straight

Serger stitch: three-thread overlock

Thread: heavy-duty polyester

Seams: plain (pg 66), lapped (pg 160), abutted (pg 171)

Hems: overedge (pg 138), single fold (pg 85)

Need to finish raw edges: no

Raw edge finishing: topstitched (pg 177)

Care: Do not wash.

Thin Cardboard (pg 189)

Cardboard (Thin, < ~1mm)

A nonwoven material made of cellulose and often used for crafts and utility purposes.

Thin cardboard and thick scrapbooking are significantly sturdier than standard paper, making them much more resistant to tearing. However, they don't take curves or drape at all.

Prewash: no

Pressing: medium heat with no steam

Marking: chalk, regular writing tools

Machine needle: 60/8 universal

Cutting layout: puzzle piece

Cutting tools: craft scissors

Pins: sewing clips, glue stick, tape

Interfacing: self, thicker cardboard

Machine foot: standard

Conventional machine stitch: 3.5mm straight

Serger stitch: N/A

Thread: all-purpose polyester

Seams: plain (pg 66), lapped (pg 160), abutted (pg 171)

Hems: single fold (pg 85)

Need to finish raw edges: no

Raw edge finishing: topstitched (pg 177)

Care: Do not wash.

Lightweight Wovens (pg 71)

Challis

A plain-weave lightweight woven made of polyester, rayon, or wool and often used for apparel.

Challis, which is sometimes referred to as challie or chally, has a smooth, flowy drape. It can be textured but is often smooth and printed with floral patterns.

Prewash: yes

Pressing: Press according to fiber content (pg 36) with a press cloth.

Marking: chalk, disappearing ink, tailor's tacks

Machine needle: 70/10 universal

Cutting layout: on the grain, in a single layer

Cutting tools: rotary cutter

Pins: sewing clips or fine pins; pin densely

Interfacing: self, sew-in woven or nonwoven

Machine foot: standard

Conventional machine stitch: 2.5mm straight

Serger stitch: two- or thread-thread overlock

Thread: fine polyester, cotton, or silk

Seams: flat-fell (pg 81), French (pg 114), plain (pg 66), overedged (pg 70)

Hems: double fold (pg 85), bound (pg 73), rolled (pg 132)

Need to finish raw edges: yes

Raw edge finishing: bound (pg 73), overedged (pg 138)

Care: Machine wash cold and gentle. Hang to dry.

Lightweight Wovens (pg 71)

Chambray

A plain-weave lightweight woven made of cotton and often used for apparel.

Because of its combination of white and (often) light blue yarns, chambray looks a lot like denim but is significantly thinner and softer than that material.

Prewash: yes

Pressing: high heat with no steam

Marking: chalk, disappearing ink, tailor's tacks

Machine needle: 80/12 universal

Cutting layout: on the grain, in a single layer

Cutting tools: fabric shears, rotary cutter

Pins: sewing clips or fine pins; pin densely

Interfacing: self, sew-in or fusible woven or nonwoven

Machine foot: standard

Conventional machine stitch: 2.5mm straight

Serger stitch: two- or thread-thread overlock

Thread: fine polyester, cotton, or silk

Seams: flat-fell (pg 81), French (pg 114), plain (pg 66), overedged (pg 70)

Hems: double fold (pg 85), bound (pg 73), rolled (pg 132)

Need to finish raw edges: yes

Raw edge finishing: bound (pg 73), overedged (pg 138)

Care: Machine wash cold and gentle. Hang to dry.

Shinies and Sleeks (pg 116)

Charmeuse

A satin-weave shiny and sleek fabric made of polyester, rayon, or silk and often used for apparel.

Charmeuse has the classic shiny on one side, matte on the other satin structure. It is lightweight and drapey.

Prewash: if polyester, then yes

Pressing: low heat from the wrong side

Marking: chalk, disappearing ink, thread tracing, tracing wheel

Machine needle: 70/10 microtex

Cutting layout: on the grain, in a single layer

Cutting tools: fabric shears, rotary cutter

Pins: fine pins

Interfacing: sew-in or fusible nonwoven, batiste, self, organza

Machine foot: standard, walking

Conventional machine stitch: 2.5mm straight with straight stitch plate

Serger stitch: three-thread overlock

Thread: fine polyester, cotton, or silk

Seams: hairline (pg 122), plain (pg 66), overedged (pg 70)

Hems: overedged (pg 138), rolled (pg 132), bound (pg 73), horsehair braid (pg 124), hairline (pg 122), double fold (pg 85)

Need to finish raw edges: yes

Raw edge finishing: pinked (pg 66), seared if synthetic (pg 121)

Care: Machine wash warm or cold and gentle. Hang to dry.

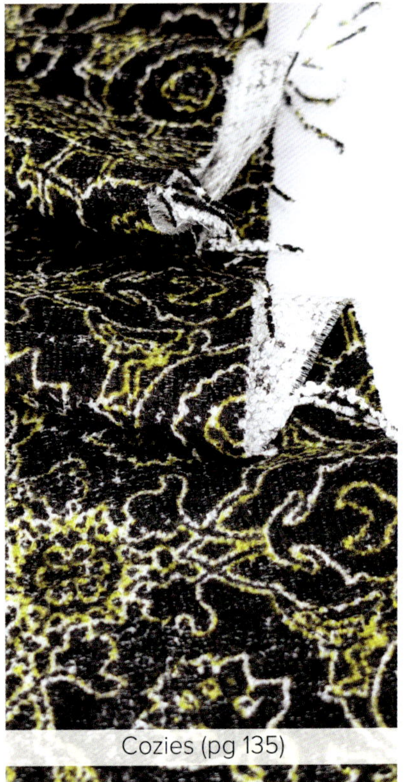
Cozies (pg 135)

Chenille

A knit or woven-with-pile cozy fabric made of cotton, polyester, rayon, silk, or wool and often used for upholstery, accessories, and linens.

Chenille is heavy but extremely soft, durable, and textured. Because of the way the pile is constructed, chenille has an iridescent quality.

Prewash: yes

Pressing: Press from the wrong side on low heat, using a press cloth and a plush fabric against the right side.

Marking: chalk on front or disappearing ink on reverse

Machine needle: 90/14 ballpoint or universal

Cutting layout: with nap

Cutting tools: fabric shears, rotary cutter

Pins: all-purpose pins; pin densely

Interfacing: tricot

Machine foot: walking; decrease pressure

Conventional machine stitch: 2.5mm straight; 2.5mm zigzag if stretchy

Serger stitch: three- or four-thread overlock

Thread: all-purpose polyester

Seams: plain (pg 66), overedged (pg 70), reversible lapped (pg 88)

Hems: overedged (pg 138), bound (pg 73), wide double fold (pg 85)

Need to finish raw edges: yes

Raw edge finishing: overedged (pg 138), bound (pg 73)

Care: May be dry-clean only. If not, hand wash or machine wash gentle; then tumble dry on low heat.

Sheers (pg 107)

Chiffon

A plain-weave sheer made of polyester or silk and often used for apparel.

Chiffon's twisted threads give it a slightly rough feel, but also add a shimmery finish. It has a soft hand and drape.

Prewash: yes

Pressing: low heat and a press cloth with no steam

Marking: chalk, disappearing ink, thread tracing, tracing wheel

Machine needle: 60/8 microtex

Cutting layout: on the grain, in a single layer

Cutting tools: fabric shears, rotary cutter

Pins: fine pins, hand-basting

Interfacing: sheer nonwoven sew-in, organza, self

Machine foot: straight stitch, walking

Conventional machine stitch: 2.5mm straight with straight stitch plate

Serger stitch: two- or thread-thread overlock

Thread: fine polyester, cotton, or silk

Seams: French (pg 114), overedged (pg 70), hairline (pg 122), plain (pg 66)

Hems: overedged (pg 138), rolled (pg 132), bound (pg 73), hairline (pg 122), double fold (pg 85)

Need to finish raw edges: yes

Raw edge finishing: bound (pg 73), overedged (pg 138)

Care: Silk is dry-clean only. For other fibers, machine wash warm or cold; then lay flat or tumble dry on low heat.

Velvet, Velveteen, and Corduroy (pg 139)

Corduroy

A woven piled fabric made of cotton, a cotton and polyester blend, or polyester and often used for apparel and upholstery.

In corduroy, the weft yarns are cut to create long ridges of pile, which run along the length of the fabric. Corduroy is durable.

Prewash: yes

Pressing: Press from the wrong side on low heat, using a press cloth and a plush fabric against the right side.

Marking: chalk on wrong side

Machine needle: 80/12 denim

Cutting layout: with nap

Cutting tools: fabric shears, rotary cutter

Pins: all-purpose pins, hand-basting

Interfacing: sew-in woven or nonwoven interfacing or tricot

Machine foot: roller, walking; decrease pressure

Conventional machine stitch: 2.5mm straight or zigzag

Serger stitch: three- or four-thread overlock

Thread: all-purpose or heavy-duty cotton or polyester

Seams: plain (pg 66), overedged (pg 70)

Hems: faced (pg 124), blind hem (pg 84), overedged (pg 138), single fold (pg 85)

Need to finish raw edges: yes

Raw edge finishing: overedged (pg 138), bound (pg 73)

Care: Machine wash cold and gentle. Hang to dry.

Cork (pg 169)

Cork

An adhered specialty fabric made of cork and often used for bags, upholstery, and accessories.

Thin cork adhered to a fabric backing is soft and flexible, durable, lightweight, and easy to clean. Thicker, unbacked cork is stiff and structured.

Prewash: no

Pressing: steam

Marking: chalk, leather marking tool

Machine needle: 80/12 microtex, topstitch, or universal

Cutting layout: puzzle piece, in a single layer

Cutting tools: craft scissors, rotary cutter

Pins: sewing clips, glue stick

Interfacing: fleece batting or foam

Machine foot: roller, nonstick

Conventional machine stitch: 2.5mm straight

Serger stitch: four-thread overlock

Thread: all-purpose or heavy-duty polyester

Seams: plain (pg 66), abutted (pg 171), lapped (pg 160)

Hems: overedged (pg 138), single fold (pg 85), bound (pg 73)

Need to finish raw edges: no

Raw edge finishing: topstitched (pg 177), overedged (pg 138), bound (pg 73)

Care: Spot clean.

Lightweight Wovens (pg 71)

Crepe de Chine

A plain-weave lightweight woven made of acetate, nylon, polyester, rayon, silk, or wool and often used for apparel.

Crepe de chine is delicate, is light- to medium-weight, and can be matte or have a light sheen.

Prewash: yes

Pressing: Press according to fiber content (pg 36) with a press cloth.

Marking: chalk, disappearing ink, tailor's tacks

Machine needle: 70/10 universal

Cutting layout: on the grain, in a single layer

Cutting tools: fabric shears, pinking shears, rotary cutter

Pins: sewing clips or fine pins; pin densely

Interfacing: self, sew-in woven or nonwoven

Machine foot: standard

Conventional machine stitch: 2.5mm straight

Serger stitch: two- or thread-thread overlock

Thread: fine polyester, cotton, or silk

Seams: flat-fell (pg 81), French (pg 114), plain (pg 66), overedged (pg 70)

Hems: double fold (pg 85), bound (pg 73), rolled (pg 132)

Need to finish raw edges: yes

Raw edge finishing: bound (pg 73), overedged (pg 138)

Care: Machine wash cold and gentle. Hang to dry.

Jacquards (pg 82)

Damask

A jacquard heavyweight woven made of cotton, linen, rayon, or silk and often used for home decor, upholstery, apparel, outerwear, and bags.

Damasks have a relatively dense weave for jacquards, making them strong and durable. Damasks have a distinctive texture and sheen. They are usually made with two colors of yarn, which makes them reversible.

Prewash: yes

Pressing: Press from the wrong side on medium heat, using steam, a press cloth, and a plush fabric against the right side.

Marking: chalk, disappearing ink, tailor's tacks

Machine needle: 80/12 universal

Cutting layout: on the grain

Cutting tools: fabric shears, rotary cutter

Pins: T-pins

Interfacing: sew-in or fusible nonwoven, batiste, organza

Machine foot: standard, walking

Conventional machine stitch: 2.5–3.5mm straight

Serger stitch: four-thread or wide three-thread overlock

Thread: all-purpose cotton or polyester

Seams: flat-fell (pg 81), plain (pg 66), overedged (pg 70)

Hems: faced (pg 124), single fold or wide double fold (pg 85), blind (pg 84)

Need to finish raw edges: yes

Raw edge finishing: bound (pg 73), overedged (pg 138)

Care: Silk is dry-clean only. For other fibers, machine wash warm or cold; then tumble dry on low heat.

Canvas and Denim (pg 78)

Denim

A twill-weave heavyweight woven made of cotton and often used for apparel and accessories.

Denim is strong and durable, but it frays. It is traditionally woven with dark warp yarns and white weft yarns, creating the distinctive color and pattern.

Prewash: yes

Pressing: high heat with steam

Marking: chalk

Machine needle: 110/18 denim

Cutting layout: may use with nap

Cutting tools: fabric shears, rotary cutter

Pins: T-pins, sewing clips

Interfacing: sew-in or fusible woven or nonwoven

Machine foot: standard

Conventional machine stitch: 3mm straight

Serger stitch: four-thread or wide three-thread overlock

Thread: heavy-duty polyester or cotton

Seams: plain (pg 66), overedged (pg 70), flat-fell (pg 81), welt (pg 165), reversible lapped (pg 88)

Hems: wide double fold (pg 85), overedged (pg 138)

Need to finish raw edges: yes

Raw edge finishing: topstitched (pg 177), overedged (pg 138)

Care: Machine wash cold. Tumble dry on low heat.

Canvas and Denim (pg 78)

Denim (Stretch)

A twill-weave light- to medium-weight woven made of a cotton and spandex blend and often used for apparel.

Denim can be blended with spandex to create stretch denim. Stretch denim is usually lighter weight than the traditional version, but it still has significant structure and support.

Prewash: yes

Pressing: low heat

Marking: chalk

Machine needle: 80/12 denim

Cutting layout: may use with nap

Cutting tools: fabric shears, rotary cutter

Pins: all-purpose pins

Interfacing: sew-in or fusible woven or nonwoven or tricot

Machine foot: standard

Conventional machine stitch: 2.5mm zigzag

Serger stitch: four-thread or wide three-thread overlock

Thread: all-purpose cotton or polyester

Seams: plain (pg 66), overedged (pg 70), flat-fell (pg 81), welt (pg 165)

Hems: wide double fold (pg 85), overedged (pg 138)

Need to finish raw edges: yes

Raw edge finishing: topstitched (pg 177), overedged (pg 138)

Care: Machine wash warm. Tumble dry on low heat.

Shinies and Sleeks (pg 116)

Dupioni

A plain-weave shiny and sleek fabric made of polyester, rayon, or silk and often used for apparel.

Dupioni has a distinctive slubby finish with a sheen. It has a crisp drape, is soft, and will fray easily and excessively.

Prewash: yes

Pressing: steam

Marking: chalk, disappearing ink, thread tracing, tracing wheel

Machine needle: 70/10 microtex

Cutting layout: on the grain, in a single layer

Cutting tools: fabric shears, pinking shears, rotary cutter

Pins: fine pins

Interfacing: sew-in or fusible nonwoven, batiste, self, organza

Machine foot: standard, walking

Conventional machine stitch: 2.5–3.5mm straight with straight stitch plate

Serger stitch: three-thread overlock

Thread: fine or all-purpose polyester, cotton, or silk

Seams: plain (pg 66), overedged (pg 70), French (pg 114)

Hems: overedged (pg 138), rolled (pg 132), bound (pg 73), horsehair braid (pg 124), hairline (pg 122), double fold (pg 85)

Need to finish raw edges: yes

Raw edge finishing: bound (pg 73), overedged (pg 138)

Care: Silk is dry-clean only. For other fibers, machine wash warm or cold; then lay flat or tumble dry on low heat.

Embroidery, Lace, and Eyelet (pg 153)

Embroidery

An embellished fabric made of any base material with embroidery added and often used for apparel.

In embroidery, a decorative element is added with stitches of thread or yarn to a base material.

Interfacing, serger stitch, thread, hems, need to finish raw edges, and raw edge finishing: Refer to the encyclopedia entry for the base fabric.

Prewash: no

Pressing: Do not iron embroidery directly; steam.

Marking: tailor's tacks

Machine needle: 80/12 denim

Cutting layout: with nap, in a single layer

Cutting tools: craft or heavy-duty scissors, if cutting through embroidery; otherwise, refer to base fabric

Pins: Refer to base fabric generally; do not pin through embroidery.

Machine foot: walking; decrease pressure

Conventional machine stitch: 3.5mm straight

Seams: refer to base fabric, lapped (pg 160)

Care: Spot clean, hand wash, or dry clean. Hang or lay flat to dry.

Thick Foam (pg 199)

EVA Foam (Thick; > ~4mm)

A foam made of EVA and often used for structure, thickness, and costuming.

Thick EVA foam, often sold as floor mats, is rigid but soft. It is durable and inexpensive.

Prewash: no

Pressing: remove wrinkles with a heat gun

Marking: chalk, metallic marking tools, regular writing tools

Machine needle: N/A

Cutting layout: puzzle piece, in a single layer

Cutting tools: box cutter

Pins: glue stick, tape

Interfacing: self, thicker foam

Machine foot: N/A

Conventional machine stitch: N/A

Serger stitch: N/A

Thread: N/A

Seams: abutted (pg 171)

Hems: beveled (pg 198)

Need to finish raw edges: no

Raw edge finishing: N/A

Care: Spot clean.

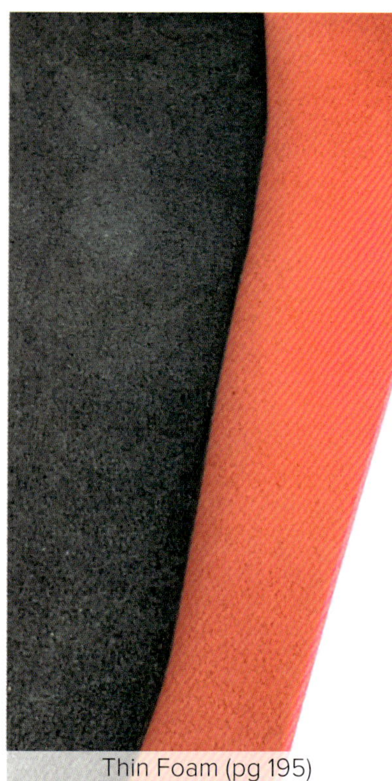

Thin Foam (pg 195)

EVA Foam (Thin; < ~4mm)

A foam made of EVA and often used for structure, thickness, and costuming.

Thin EVA foam, often called craft foam, is soft and flexible and has a small amount of stretch. It is durable and inexpensive.

Prewash: no

Pressing: Remove wrinkles with a heat gun.

Marking: chalk, metallic marking tools, regular writing tools

Machine needle: 100/16 denim

Cutting layout: puzzle piece, in a single layer

Cutting tools: box cutter, craft scissors, craft knife

Pins: sewing clips, glue stick, tape

Interfacing: self, thicker foam, sew-in woven or nonwoven

Machine foot: walking; decrease pressure

Conventional machine stitch: 4mm straight

Serger stitch: N/A

Thread: heavy-duty polyester

Seams: abutted (pg 171), lapped (pg 160), plain (pg 66)

Hems: single fold (pg 85), beveled (pg 198)

Need to finish raw edges: no

Raw edge finishing: topstitched (pg 177)

Care: Spot clean.

Embroidery, Lace, and Eyelet (pg 153)

Eyelet

An embellished fabric made of any base material with eyelets added and often used for detailing and intimates.

To create eyelet, also called cutwork, holes are cut into fabric and then reinforced with decorative stitching.

Cutting tools, serger stitch, hems, need to finish raw edges, and raw edge finishing: Refer to the encyclopedia entry for the base fabric.

Prewash: yes

Pressing: Press from the wrong side according to base fabric with a press cloth.

Marking: chalk, disappearing ink, tailor's tacks

Machine needle: 60/8 microtex, stretch, or universal

Cutting layout: on the grain, in a single layer

Pins: fine pins, hand-basting

Interfacing: fusible woven or nonwoven, used sparingly

Machine foot: walking; decrease pressure

Conventional machine stitch: 2.5mm straight

Thread: all-purpose polyester

Seams: refer to base fabric, lapped (pg 160)

Care: May be hand wash or dry-clean only. If not, machine wash cold; then hang or lay flat to dry.

Fabric Paper (pg 187)

Fabric Paper

A nonwoven material usually made of cellulose and often used for bags, accessories, and crafts.

Washable paper combines the textures and drapes of both paper and leather. It's often advertised as an eco-friendly alternative to faux leather.

Prewash: yes

Pressing: high heat

Marking: chalk, disappearing ink, washi tape, regular writing tool on reverse

Machine needle: 80/12 microtex

Cutting layout: puzzle piece

Cutting tools: craft scissors, rotary cutter

Pins: sewing clips, glue stick

Interfacing: woven fusible

Machine foot: standard

Conventional machine stitch: 3.5mm straight

Serger stitch: three-thread overlock

Thread: all-purpose polyester

Seams: plain (pg 66), lapped (pg 160), flat-fell (pg 81), welt (pg 165)

Hems: single or double fold (pg 85), decorative cut

Need to finish raw edges: no

Raw edge finishing: topstitched (pg 177)

Care: Machine wash warm. Lay flat to dry.

Faux Fur (pg 144)

Faux Fur

A knit or woven piled fabric made of acrylic, nylon, or polyester and often used for apparel, accessories, bags, and outerwear.

Faux fur is a pile fabric on a strong base textile; both the pile and the base fabric are almost always acrylic, polyester, or another synthetic material. Faux fur comes in a vast array of textures, colors, patterns, and pile length.

Prewash: no

Pressing: Tumble dry to remove wrinkles.

Marking: chalk, disappearing ink, regular writing tool on reverse

Machine needle: 80/12 denim or universal

Cutting layout: with nap, in a single layer

Cutting tools: box cutter, craft knife

Pins: long pins

Interfacing: do not

Machine foot: standard; decrease pressure

Conventional machine stitch: 3.5mm straight

Serger stitch: four-thread overlock

Thread: all-purpose polyester

Seams: plain (pg 66), flatlock (pg 147), abutted (pg 171)

Hems: single fold (pg 85), faced (pg 124)

Need to finish raw edges: no

Raw edge finishing: N/A

Care: Hand wash only if necessary. Hang to dry; then brush.

Stretch Vinyl (pg 178)

Faux Stretch Leather

A nonwoven vinyl made of polyester, PU, or PVC and often used for apparel.

Faux stretch leather is lightweight, very drapey, and stretchy. Generally, one side emulates leather or another texture, and the reverse is a matte fabric.

Prewash: no

Pressing: Steam or press from back on low heat with a press cloth.

Marking: dry erase on front, disappearing ink on reverse

Machine needle: 70/10 nonstick denim or microtex

Cutting layout: on the grain, in a single layer

Cutting tools: craft scissors, rotary cutter

Pins: sewing clips; clip densely

Interfacing: tricot

Machine foot: nonstick, roller, walking

Conventional machine stitch: 3mm zigzag

Serger stitch: three-thread overlock

Thread: all-purpose polyester

Seams: plain (pg 66), overedged (pg 70), flat-fell (pg 81)

Hems: overedge (pg 138), single fold (pg 85), mock cover (pg 104)

Need to finish raw edges: no

Raw edge finishing: overedge (pg 138), topstitched (pg 177)

Care: Spot clean.

Cozies (pg 135)

Faux Suede

A nonwoven cozy fabric made of polyester and often used for apparel, bags, upholstery, and accessories.

Faux suede, often referred to by the trade name Ultrasuede (by Toray Industries), emulates the fuzzy side of genuine suede but is on a nonwoven backing. It is thin, soft, smooth, and drapey.

Prewash: no

Pressing: Press from the wrong side on low heat, using a press cloth and a plush fabric against the right side.

Marking: chalk

Machine needle: 90/14 microtex

Cutting layout: with nap

Cutting tools: rotary cutter

Pins: glue stick, tape, sewing clips

Interfacing: sew-in woven or nonwoven

Machine foot: nonstick, roller, walking

Conventional machine stitch: 3mm straight

Serger stitch: three-thread overlock

Thread: all-purpose polyester

Seams: plain (pg 66), overedged (pg 70)

Hems: single fold (pg 85), overedged (pg 138), bound (pg 73)

Need to finish raw edges: no

Raw edge finishing: overedged (pg 138), topstitched (pg 177)

Care: May be dry-clean only. If not, hand wash or machine wash gentle; then tumble dry on low heat.

Felt, Boiled Wool, Melton (pg 158)

Felt

A nonwoven fabric made of acrylic, rayon, or wool and often used for apparel, crafts, and home decor.

Felt, which we may buy in sheets from the craft store or on typical fabric bolts, is a stiff and textured fabric with no grain. Wool felt is very warm and wrinkle-resistant; acrylic felt is inexpensive and accessible.

Prewash: yes

Pressing: Press according to fiber content (pg 36) with a press cloth.

Marking: chalk

Machine needle: 90/14 or 100/16 microtex or universal

Cutting layout: puzzle piece

Cutting tools: craft scissors, fabric shears, rotary cutter

Pins: all-purpose or long pins

Interfacing: sew-in or fusible woven or nonwoven

Machine foot: nonstick, walking

Conventional machine stitch: 2.5mm straight; lengthen for thicker fabrics

Serger stitch: four-thread overlock

Thread: all-purpose or heavy-duty polyester

Seams: lapped (pg 160), abutted (pg 171), plain (pg 66), overedged (pg 70)

Hems: single fold (pg 85), overedged (pg 138)

Need to finish raw edges: no

Raw edge finishing: topstitched (pg 177), overedged (pg 138)

Care: Machine wash cold and gentle. Lay flat to dry.

Nets (pg 128)

Fishnet

A warp-knit netting made of nylon or polyester blended with spandex and often used for apparel and intimates.

Fishnet is an extremely low-density stretchy knit with diamond-shaped holes.

Prewash: yes

Pressing: low heat with press cloth

Marking: safety pins, tailor's tacks

Machine needle: 70/10 jersey

Cutting layout: on the grain, in a single layer

Cutting tools: rotary cutter

Pins: sewing clips, tape, tearaway or water-soluble stabilizer

Interfacing: starch

Machine foot: standard, roller

Conventional machine stitch: 2mm straight

Serger stitch: three-thread overlock

Thread: all-purpose polyester

Seams: plain (pg 66), overedged (pg 70), French (pg 114)

Hems: bound (pg 73), rolled (pg 132), overedged (pg 138)

Need to finish raw edges: no

Raw edge finishing: overedged (pg 138), bound (pg 73)

Care: Hand wash cold or machine wash cold in delicates bag. Lay flat to dry.

Cozies (pg 135)

Flannel

A plain- or twill-weave cozy fabric made of acetate, acrylic, cotton, nylon, polyester, rayon, or wool and often used for apparel, accessories, and linens.

Flannel is soft and warm. It may or may not have a brushed nap.

Prewash: yes

Pressing: Press according to fiber content (pg 36) with steam.

Marking: chalk or disappearing ink

Machine needle: 90/14 universal

Cutting layout: with nap

Cutting tools: fabric shears, pinking shears, rotary cutter

Pins: all-purpose pins

Interfacing: sew-in woven or nonwoven

Machine foot: walking

Conventional machine stitch: 3mm straight

Serger stitch: three-thread overlock

Thread: all-purpose cotton or polyester

Seams: plain (pg 66), overedged (pg 70), flat-fell (pg 81)

Hems: overedged (pg 138), bound (pg 73), double fold (pg 85)

Need to finish raw edges: yes

Raw edge finishing: overedged (pg 138)

Care: Machine wash warm and gentle. Tumble dry on low heat

Cozies (pg 135)

Fleece / Polar Fleece

A knit or woven cozy fabric made of acrylic, polyester, or wool and often used for apparel, outerwear, and linens.

Fleece, commonly known as polar fleece, is soft, napped, and lightweight. It may have a low pile on just one side or on both.

Prewash: yes

Pressing: Press from the wrong side on low heat, using a press cloth and a plush fabric against the right side.

Marking: disappearing ink

Machine needle: 80/12 universal

Cutting layout: with nap

Cutting tools: fabric shears, rotary cutter

Pins: all-purpose or ballpoint pins; pin densely

Interfacing: tricot

Machine foot: nonstick, walking; decrease pressure

Conventional machine stitch: 2.5mm straight or zigzag

Serger stitch: three-thread overlock

Thread: all-purpose or heavy-duty polyester

Seams: plain (pg 66), overedged (pg 70)

Hems: single fold (pg 85), overedged (pg 138), bound (pg 73)

Need to finish raw edges: no

Raw edge finishing: overedged (pg 138), topstitched (pg 177)

Care: Machine wash warm. Tumble dry on low heat. Pills; turn inside out to wash.

Structural Materials (pg 210)

Foam Interfacing

A nonwoven material made of polyester or PU and often used for structure and thickness.

Foam interfacing is interfacing with foam integrated; usually, it's very lightweight PU foam sandwiched between thin tricot, but it can also be found in "naked" foam form. It's available in both sewable and fusible forms; the fusible version may be single- or double-sided.

Prewash: no

Pressing: do not

Marking: chalk, disappearing ink, regular marking tools

Machine needle: 80/12 universal

Cutting layout: puzzle piece, in a single layer

Cutting tools: rotary cutter, craft or heavy-duty scissors

Pins: sewing clips, long pins

Interfacing: self, thicker foam interfacing, stiffer structural material

Machine foot: standard, walking; decrease pressure

Conventional machine stitch: 2.5–3.5mm straight

Serger stitch: four-thread overlock

Thread: all-purpose polyester

Seams: abutted (pg 171)

Hems: overedged (pg 138), bound (pg 73)

Need to finish raw edges: no

Raw edge finishing: topstitched (pg 177), overedged (pg 138)

Care: Machine wash cold and gentle.

Structural Materials (210)

FOSSHAPE

A nonwoven material made of polyester and often used for structure.

FOSSHAPE (by Wonderflex World) is a material with a texture similar to felt that can be cut, sewn, and glued in similar ways as well. It is a thermoplastic; once activated, it becomes stiff and can support itself and other materials.

Prewash: no

Pressing: do not

Marking: chalk, disappearing ink, regular marking tools

Machine needle: 80/12 universal

Cutting layout: puzzle piece, in a single layer

Cutting tools: rotary cutter, craft or heavy-duty scissors

Pins: sewing clips, long pins

Interfacing: self, thicker FOSSHAPE

Machine foot: standard, walking; decrease pressure

Conventional machine stitch: 2.5–3.5mm straight

Serger stitch: N/A

Thread: all-purpose polyester

Seams: plain (pg 66), abutted (pg 171)

Hems: overedged (pg 138), bound (pg 73)

Need to finish raw edges: no

Raw edge finishing: topstitched (pg 177), overedged (pg 138)

Care: Hand wash or spot clean.

Stretch Velvet, French Terry, and Velour (pg 142)

French Terry

A weft-knit piled fabric made of cotton or rayon and often used for apparel and linens.

French terry has small loops on one side and low ribs on the other; either can be the right side. It is warm and absorbent. It has some natural stretch but also often has added spandex to increase its stretch and elasticity.

Prewash: yes

Pressing: Press from the wrong side on high heat, using steam, a press cloth and a plush fabric against the right side.

Marking: disappearing ink or chalk on the wrong side

Machine needle: 90/14 ballpoint

Cutting layout: with nap

Cutting tools: fabric shears, rotary cutter

Pins: ballpoint pins

Interfacing: tricot

Machine foot: walking

Conventional machine stitch: 1.5mm zigzag

Serger stitch: three-thread overlock

Thread: all-purpose polyester

Seams: plain (pg 66), overedged (pg 70)

Hems: overedged (pg 138), bound (pg 73), single fold (pg 85)

Need to finish raw edges: no

Raw edge finishing: pinked (pg 66), overedged (pg 138), bound (pg 73)

Care: Machine wash warm. Tumble dry.

Suiting and Shirting (pg 67)

Gabardine

A twill-weave medium-weight woven made of cotton, polyester, viscose, wool, or blends of those materials and often used for apparel and outerwear.

Gabardine is firmly woven and often smooth and shiny. It is dense and durable.

Prewash: yes

Pressing: Press according to fiber content (pg 36) with a press cloth.

Marking: chalk, disappearing ink, tailor's tacks

Machine needle: 90/14 universal

Cutting layout: with nap

Cutting tools: fabric shears, rotary cutter

Pins: all-purpose pins

Interfacing: sew-in woven or nonwoven

Machine foot: standard

Conventional machine stitch: 2.5mm straight

Serger stitch: four-thread overlock

Thread: all-purpose polyester

Seams: plain (pg 66), overedged (pg 70)

Hems: single fold (pg 85), mock cover (pg 104)

Need to finish raw edges: yes

Raw edge finishing: pinked (pg 66), overedged (pg 138), topstitched (pg 177)

Care: Varies by fiber content. Generally, hand wash or machine wash cold and gentle. Tumble or hang to dry.

Lightweight Wovens (pg 71)

Gauze (Fabric)

A typically plain-weave lightweight woven made of cotton, polyester, rayon, or silk and often used for apparel.

Gauze is lightweight, breathable, and delicately drapey. Within the gauze category, there's a vast array of both weight and weave density; some gauzes are thin enough to be veils, while others are more typical shirting fabric.

Prewash: yes

Pressing: Press according to fiber content (pg 36) with a press cloth.

Marking: chalk, disappearing ink, tailor's tacks

Machine needle: 70/10 universal

Cutting layout: on the grain, in a single layer

Cutting tools: fabric shears, rotary cutter

Pins: sewing clips or fine pins; pin densely

Interfacing: self, sew-in woven or nonwoven

Machine foot: standard

Conventional machine stitch: 2.5mm straight

Serger stitch: two- or thread-thread overlock

Thread: fine polyester, cotton, or silk

Seams: flat-fell (pg 81), French (pg 114), plain (pg 66), overedged (pg 70)

Hems: double fold (pg 85), bound (pg 73), rolled (pg 132)

Need to finish raw edges: yes

Raw edge finishing: bound (pg 73), overedged (pg 138)

Care: Machine wash cold and gentle. Hang to dry.

Gauze (Medical)

A plain-weave netting made of cotton, polyester, or rayon and often used for medical and utility purposes.

Medical gauze is strong and sturdy, but thin. Cheesecloth is a very loosely woven variety of gauze.

Prewash: yes

Pressing: high heat with steam

Marking: disappearing ink, tailor's tacks

Machine needle: 80/12 ballpoint

Cutting layout: on the grain

Cutting tools: fabric shears, rotary cutter

Pins: sewing clips, tape, tearaway or water-soluble stabilizer

Interfacing: starch

Machine foot: walking; decrease pressure

Conventional machine stitch: 3mm straight

Serger stitch: three- or four-thread overlock

Thread: all-purpose polyester

Seams: plain (pg 66), overedged (pg 70)

Hems: bound (pg 73), overedged (pg 138), single fold (pg 85)

Need to finish raw edges: yes

Raw edge finishing: bound (pg 73), overedged (pg 138), topstitched (pg 177)

Care: Machine wash cold. Tumble dry on low heat.

Nets (pg 128)

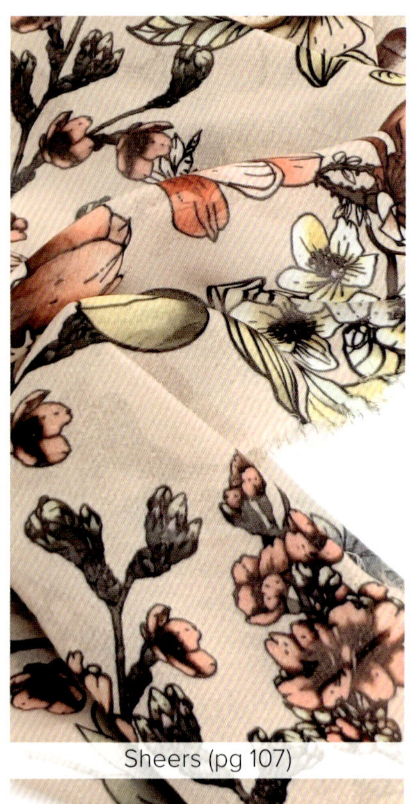
Sheers (pg 107)

Georgette

A plain-weave sheer made of polyester, silk, or viscose and often used for apparel.

Georgette's twists and alternating yarns in the weave give it a crepe texture. It has a matte finish and a soft hand and drape.

Prewash: yes

Pressing: low heat and a press cloth with no steam

Marking: chalk, disappearing ink, thread tracing, tracing wheel

Machine needle: 70/10 microtex or universal

Cutting layout: on the grain, in a single layer

Cutting tools: fabric shears, pinking shears, rotary cutter

Pins: fine pins, hand-basting

Interfacing: sheer nonwoven sew-in, organza, self

Machine foot: straight stitch, walking

Conventional machine stitch: 2.5mm straight with straight stitch plate

Serger stitch: two- or three-thread overlock

Thread: fine polyester, cotton, or silk

Seams: French (pg 114), overedged (pg 70), hairline (pg 122), plain (pg 66)

Hems: overedged (pg 138), rolled (pg 132), bound (pg 73), hairline (pg 122), double fold (pg 85)

Need to finish raw edges: yes

Raw edge finishing: bound (pg 73), overedged (pg 138)

Care: Silk is dry-clean only. For other fibers, machine wash warm or cold; then tumble dry on low heat.

Embellished (pg 149)

Glitter

An embellished fabric made of any base material with glitter added and often used for apparel, especially for performance and costuming.

Any base fabric can be embellished with glitter, which is adhered in a solid layer or in patterns.

For all tools and techniques (cutting tools, pins, interfacing, serger stitch, thread, seams, hems, raw edge finishing, and more): Refer to the encyclopedia entry for the base fabric.

Prewash: yes

Pressing: Steam or press from back on low heat with a press cloth

Marking: chalk, tailor's tacks

Machine needle: 80/12 stretch or universal

Cutting layout: on grain or with nap depending on specific glitter application, in a single layer

Cutting tools: craft scissors, rotary cutter

Machine foot: walking; decrease pressure

Conventional machine stitch: 3.5mm straight

Care: Refer to base fabric; generally, dry clean, hand wash, or spot clean only.

Sheers (pg 107)

Habutai Silk / China Silk

A plain-weave sheer made of silk and often used for apparel.

Habutai silk, also known as China silk, is fairly inexpensive compared to other genuine silks. Some habutais are sheer, while others are very slinky.

Prewash: yes

Pressing: Press according to fiber content (pg 36) with a press cloth.

Marking: chalk, disappearing ink, thread tracing, tracing wheel

Machine needle: 70/10 microtex

Cutting layout: on the grain, in a single layer

Cutting tools: fabric shears, rotary cutter

Pins: fine pins, hand-basting

Interfacing: sheer nonwoven sew-in, organza, self

Machine foot: straight stitch, walking

Conventional machine stitch: 2.5mm straight with straight stitch plate

Serger stitch: two- or three-thread overlock

Thread: fine polyester, cotton, or silk

Seams: French (pg 114), overedged (pg 70), hairline (pg 122), plain (pg 66)

Hems: overedged (pg 138), rolled (pg 132), bound (pg 73), hairline (pg 122), double fold (pg 85)

Need to finish raw edges: yes

Raw edge finishing: bound (pg 73), overedged (pg 138)

Care: Machine wash warm or cold and gentle. Tumble dry on low heat. Changes when washed, becoming softer.

Meshes (pg 126)

Illusion Mesh / Stretch Mesh

A warp-knit mesh made of nylon and spandex blends and often used for apparel, especially performance apparel.

Illusion mesh, sometimes called stretch mesh, is a fine and delicate fabric that is often used to create the illusion of bare skin.

Prewash: yes

Pressing: low heat

Marking: chalk, disappearing ink, thread tracing

Machine needle: 70/10 jersey

Cutting layout: on the grain, in a single layer

Cutting tools: fabric shears, rotary cutter

Pins: sewing clips, tape, tearaway or water-soluble stabilizer

Interfacing: self or starch

Machine foot: standard, roller

Conventional machine stitch: 2mm zigzag

Serger stitch: three-thread overlock

Thread: fine or all-purpose polyester

Seams: plain (pg 66), flat-fell (pg 81)

Hems: single or double fold (pg 85), mock cover (pg 104), bound (pg 73), overedged (pg 138)

Need to finish raw edges: no

Raw edge finishing: overedged (pg 138), bound (pg 73)

Care: Hand wash cold. Lay flat to dry.

Sturdy Knits (pg 91)

Interlock

A sturdy weft knit usually made of polyester or a polyester/spandex blend and often used for apparel.

Interlock is two layers of jersey knit together, which makes it a double knit. It is light- to medium-weight and soft with moderate stretch. It has fine ribs on both the right and wrong sides.

Prewash: yes

Pressing: low heat with a press cloth

Marking: chalk, disappearing ink

Machine needle: 70/10 ballpoint

Cutting layout: with nap

Cutting tools: fabric shears, rotary cutter

Pins: ballpoint pins

Interfacing: tricot

Machine foot: standard

Conventional machine stitch: 2.5mm straight or narrow zigzag

Serger stitch: narrow three-thread overlock

Thread: all-purpose polyester

Seams: plain (pg 66), overedged (pg 70), flatlocked (pg 147)

Hems: mock cover (pg 104), single or double fold (pg 85)

Need to finish raw edges: no

Raw edge finishing: overedged (pg 138)

Care: Machine wash. Tumble dry.

Stretch Knits (pg 95)

Jersey

A stretchy weft knit made of cotton, rayon, silk, wool, or blends of those materials and often used for apparel, especially athletic apparel.

Jersey ranges quite wildly in both weight and stretch, but most commonly is lightweight with medium stretch. Because it is a weft knit, the right side has V-shaped stitches and the wrong side shows the loops of the knit.

Prewash: yes

Pressing: low heat

Marking: chalk, disappearing ink, tailor's tacks

Machine needle: 70/10 ballpoint

Cutting layout: on the grain

Cutting tools: rotary cutter

Pins: ballpoint pins

Interfacing: tricot

Machine foot: standard, walking

Conventional machine stitch: 1.5mm zigzag

Serger stitch: three- or four-thread overlock

Thread: fine or all-purpose polyester

Seams: plain (pg 66), overedged (pg 70), twin needle (pg 50), flatlocked (pg 147)

Hems: overedged (pg 138), blind (pg 84), single or double fold (pg 85)

Need to finish raw edges: no

Raw edge finishing: overedged (pg 138), reinforced (pg 100) with zigzag, bound (pg 73)

Care: Machine wash cold. Tumble dry.

Structural Materials (pg 210)

Kobracast

A nonwoven material made of polyester and often used for structure and stability.

Kobracast (by Worbla) is made from a mesh fabric that has been infused with thermoplastic. It is thin, sticky, and stretchy. After activation, it is rigid and can support itself and other materials but still maintains some flexibility.

Prewash: no

Pressing: do not

Marking: chalk, regular marking tools

Machine needle: 90/14 or 100/16 denim

Cutting layout: puzzle piece, in a single layer

Cutting tools: craft or heavy-duty scissors

Pins: sewing clips, tape

Interfacing: self

Machine foot: standard

Conventional machine stitch: 2.5–3.5mm straight

Serger stitch: N/A

Thread: all-purpose polyester

Seams: plain (pg 66), abutted (pg 171), lapped (pg 160)

Hems: N/A

Need to finish raw edges: no

Raw edge finishing: N/A

Care: Spot clean.

Embroidery, Lace, and Eyelet (pg 153)

Lace

An embellished fabric made of cotton, linen, polyester, rayon, or silk and often used for detailing and intimates.

Lace is created by knotting or weaving yarns into an open, airy format.

Prewash: no

Pressing: Press from the wrong side according to fiber content (pg 36) with a press cloth.

Marking: tailor's tacks

Machine needle: 60/8 microtex or universal

Cutting layout: puzzle piece, in a single layer

Cutting tools: fabric or serrated shears, rotary cutter

Pins: fine pins, hand-basting

Interfacing: starch

Machine foot: walking; decrease pressure

Conventional machine stitch: 2.5mm straight

Serger stitch: two- or three-thread overlock

Thread: fine polyester

Seams: plain (pg 66), overedge (pg 70), lapped (pg 160)

Hems: edge of lace (pg 156), bound (pg 73), overedged (pg 138), single fold (pg 85)

Need to finish raw edges: no

Raw edge finishing: edge of lace (pg 156), bound (pg 73), overedged (pg 138)

Care: Dry clean or hand wash. Lay flat to dry.

Latex (pg 172)

Latex

A nonwoven specialty fabric made of rubber and often used for apparel, costuming, and intimates.

Latex rubber is made from the sap of a tree, which is processed into "sheets" that can be used as a textile. Latex is stretchy and usually shiny. It comes in different thickness, ranging from 0.2–1.0mm.

Prewash: no

Pressing: do not

Marking: gel pen

Machine needle: N/A

Cutting layout: puzzle piece, in a single layer

Cutting tools: rotary cutter

Pins: tape, sewing clips

Interfacing: do not

Machine foot: N/A

Conventional machine stitch: N/A

Serger stitch: N/A

Thread: N/A

Seams: lapped (pg 160)

Hems: single fold (pg 85)

Need to finish raw edges: no

Raw edge finishing: N/A

Care: Spot clean. Refresh with powder or oil.

Sheers (pg 107)

Lawn

A plain-weave sheer made of cotton, linen, polyester, or wool and often used for apparel and home decor.

Lawn is slightly heavier than most sheer fabrics. It is crisp and dense and mimics linen. It may or may not be translucent.

Prewash: yes

Pressing: Press according to fiber content (pg 36) with a press cloth.

Marking: chalk, disappearing ink, thread tracing, tracing wheel

Machine needle: 70/10 universal

Cutting layout: on the grain, in a single layer

Cutting tools: fabric shears, rotary cutter

Pins: fine pins, hand-basting

Interfacing: sheer nonwoven sew-in, organza, self

Machine foot: straight stitch, walking

Conventional machine stitch: 2.5mm straight with straight stitch plate

Serger stitch: two- or three-thread overlock

Thread: fine polyester, cotton, or silk

Seams: French (pg 114), overedged (pg 70), hairline (pg 122), plain (pg 66)

Hems: overedged (pg 138), rolled (pg 132), bound (pg 73), hairline (pg 122), double fold (pg 85)

Need to finish raw edges: yes

Raw edge finishing: bound (pg 73), overedged (pg 138)

Care: Machine wash warm or cold and gentle. Lay flat to dry.

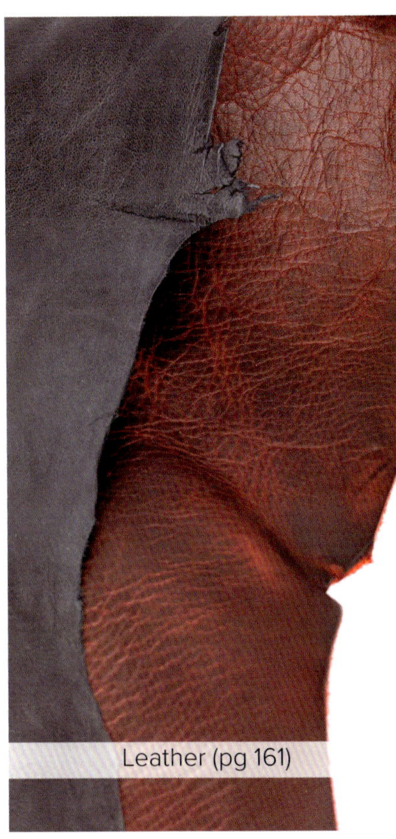

Leather (pg 161)

Leather

A nonwoven material made of hide and often used for apparel, bags, and accessories.

Leather is durable and soft and has a beautiful drape. It is insulating and breathable.

Prewash: no

Pressing: medium heat with a press cloth

Marking: chalk, leather marking tool, regular writing tools on reverse

Machine needle: 80/12 universal or 90/14 to 110/18 leather depending on thickness

Cutting layout: puzzle piece, in a single layer

Cutting tools: fabric or heavy-duty shears, rotary cutter

Pins: glue stick, tape, sewing clips

Interfacing: sew-in woven or nonwoven, organza, or fusible woven or nonwoven with caution

Machine foot: nonstick, roller, walking

Conventional machine stitch: 3mm

Serger stitch: N/A

Thread: heavy-duty polyester

Seams: plain (pg 66), lapped (pg 160), welt (pg 165), and flat-fell (pg 81)

Hems: single fold (pg 85)

Need to finish raw edges: no

Raw edge finishing: topstitched (pg 177), faced (pg 124), bound (pg 73)

Care: Hand wash or spot clean; then condition.

Non-Stretch Vinyls (pg 175)

Lightweight PU Laminate

An adhered vinyl made of cotton, linen, or polyester coated with PU and often used for bags, accessories, and home goods.

Lightweight PU laminates, commonly known as PU fabrics or PULs, are fabrics which have been coated with a clear layer of polyurethane, allowing the base fabric's pattern to show through the film. This protective layer makes them durable, waterproof, and very easy to clean.

Prewash: no

Pressing: low heat from the wrong side

Marking: disappearing ink or regular pens, chalk or dry-erase marker on right side, markers on wrong side

Machine needle: 80/12 universal

Cutting layout: puzzle piece, in a single layer

Cutting tools: craft scissors, rotary cutter

Pins: sewing clips, glue stick, fusible web tape

Interfacing: sew-in nonwoven, foam

Machine foot: nonstick, roller, walking; decrease pressure

Conventional machine stitch: 3mm straight or zigzag

Serger stitch: three- or four-thread overlock

Thread: all-purpose or heavy-duty polyester

Seams: plain (pg 66), welt (pg 165), flat-fell (pg 81), overedge (pg 70)

Hems: overedge (pg 138), single fold (pg 85), bound (pg 73)

Need to finish raw edges: no

Raw edge finishing: topstitched (pg 177)

Care: Machine wash hot. Tumble dry.

Easy Sewing (pg 64)

Linen Wovens

A medium-weight woven that is usually plain weave. It is made of linen or linen blend and often used for apparel, quilts, upholstery, and linens.

Linen wovens is an umbrella term for linen and linen-blend medium-weight woven fabrics. Linen wovens are durable, cool, and prone to wrinkling and fraying.

Prewash: yes

Pressing: high heat with no steam

Marking: chalk, disappearing ink, tailor's tacks

Machine needle: 70/10 or 80/12 universal

Cutting layout: on the grain

Cutting tools: fabric shears, rotary cutter

Pins: all-purpose pins

Interfacing: self, sew-in or fusible woven or nonwoven

Machine foot: standard

Conventional machine stitch: 2.5mm straight

Serger stitch: three- or four-thread overlock

Thread: all-purpose polyester

Seams: French (pg 114), flat-fell (pg 81), plain (pg 66), overedged (pg 70)

Hems: overedged (pg 138), double fold (pg 85), bound (pg 73)

Need to finish raw edges: yes

Raw edge finishing: bound (pg 73), overedged (pg 138)

Care: Machine wash warm and gentle. Hang to dry.

Felt, Boiled Wool, and Melton (pg 158)

Melton

A twill-weave fabric made of wool and often used for outerwear and bags.

Melton, a fulled twill wool, has a pronounced nap and is wrinkle- and moisture-resistant.

Prewash: yes

Pressing: Press according to fiber content (pg 36) with a press cloth and steam.

Marking: chalk

Machine needle: 80/12 microtex or universal

Cutting layout: puzzle piece, in a single layer

Cutting tools: craft scissors, fabric shears, rotary cutter

Pins: all-purpose or long pins

Interfacing: sew-in or fusible woven or nonwoven

Machine foot: walking

Conventional machine stitch: 2.5mm straight; lengthen for thicker fabrics

Serger stitch: four-thread overlock

Thread: all-purpose cotton or polyester

Seams: lapped (pg 160), abutted (pg 171), plain (pg 66), overedged (pg 70)

Hems: single fold (pg 85), overedged (pg 138)

Need to finish raw edges: no

Raw edge finishing: topstitched (pg 177), overedged (pg 138)

Care: Spot clean, dry clean, or hand wash.

Cozies (pg 135)

Microfiber

A knit or woven-with-pile cozy fabric made of nylon, polyester, or rayon and often used for apparel and home goods.

Microfiber fabrics are soft, lightly napped, very dense, and durable. They are soft and drape nicely. They make great fabrics for cleaning supplies and garments; they resist stains, are absorbent, and wick moisture.

Prewash: no

Pressing: Press from the wrong side on low heat, using a press cloth and a plush fabric against the right side.

Marking: disappearing ink on wrong side

Machine needle: 60/8 microtex

Cutting layout: with nap

Cutting tools: rotary cutter

Pins: all-purpose pins; pin densely

Interfacing: sew-in woven or nonwoven

Machine foot: walking; decrease pressure

Conventional machine stitch: 3mm straight

Serger stitch: three-thread overlock

Thread: all-purpose polyester

Seams: plain (pg 66), overedge (pg 70)

Hems: single fold (pg 85), overedged (pg 138), bound (pg 73)

Need to finish raw edges: no

Raw edge finishing: overedged (pg 138), topstitched (pg 177)

Care: Machine wash cold. Tumble dry on low heat.

Cozies (pg 135)

Minky

A warp-knit cozy fabric made of cotton or polyester and often used for apparel and toys.

Minky, a microfiber, is extremely soft, but also durable and easy to care for.

Prewash: no

Pressing: Press from the wrong side on low heat, using a press cloth and a plush fabric against the right side.

Marking: disappearing ink on wrong side

Machine needle: 90/14 microtex

Cutting layout: with nap

Cutting tools: rotary cutter

Pins: all-purpose pins; pin densely

Interfacing: sew-in woven or nonwoven

Machine foot: walking; decrease pressure

Conventional machine stitch: 3mm straight

Serger stitch: three-thread overlock

Thread: all-purpose polyester

Seams: plain (pg 66), overedge (pg 70)

Hems: single fold (pg 85), overedged (pg 138), bound (pg 73)

Need to finish raw edges: no

Raw edge finishing: overedged (pg 138), topstitched (pg 177)

Care: Machine wash cold. Tumble dry on low heat.

Easy Sewing (pg 64)

Muslin and Calico

A plain-weave medium-weight woven made of cotton and often used for apparel, mockups, and linings.

In the United States, muslin is the name for a form of unprocessed and undyed cotton; elsewhere this fabric is referred to as calico. Muslin/calico is densely woven, stiff, and coarse.

Prewash: yes

Pressing: high heat with no steam

Marking: chalk, disappearing ink, tailor's tacks

Machine needle: 80/12 universal

Cutting layout: on the grain

Cutting tools: fabric shears, rotary cutter

Pins: all-purpose pins

Interfacing: self, sew-in or fusible woven or nonwoven

Machine foot: standard

Conventional machine stitch: 2.5mm straight

Serger stitch: three- or four-thread overlock

Thread: all-purpose polyester

Seams: French (pg 114), flat-fell (pg 81), plain (pg 66), overedged (pg 70)

Hems: overedged (pg 138), double fold (pg 85), bound (pg 73)

Need to finish raw edges: yes

Raw edge finishing: bound (pg 73), overedged (pg 138)

Care: Machine wash warm or cold and gentle. Hang to dry.

Neoprene (pg 202)

Neoprene

An adhered foam made of neoprene or neoprene bonded to fabric and often used for athletic wear and adventure gear.

Most neoprene fabric is foam and fabric bonded together, which creates a spongy and flexible textile. It is strong and warm. Neoprene comes in a wide range of thicknesses, generally from 0.5mm up to 7mm, and may be bonded with fabric on either one or both sides—or neither!

Prewash: no

Pressing: low heat from the fabric side

Marking: chalk, disappearing ink

Machine needle: 100/16 denim

Cutting layout: on the grain, in a single layer

Cutting tools: craft scissors, rotary cutter

Pins: sewing clips

Interfacing: self, thicker foam, sew-in woven or nonwoven, fusible woven or nonwoven

Machine foot: walking; decrease pressure

Conventional machine stitch: 3.5mm zigzag

Serger stitch: three- or four-thread overlock

Thread: heavy-duty polyester

Seams: abutted (pg 171), lapped (pg 160), plain (pg 66)

Hems: overedged (pg 138), bound (pg 73)

Need to finish raw edges: no

Raw edge finishing: topstitched (pg 177), overedged (pg 138)

Care: Hand wash or machine wash cold or warm. Tumble dry on low heat.

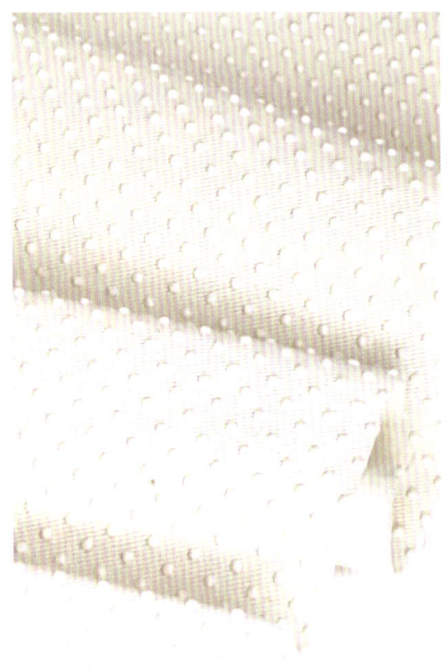

Nonslip Materials (pg 206)

Nonslip Materials (Fabric-Backed)

A utility material made of any base fabric with nonstick vinyl dots and often used for utility purposes and home goods.

Fabric-bonded nonslip materials are a base fabric (of any kind) either coated or dotted with a PVC or rubber coating, which gives it a grippy texture.

Interfacing, conventional machine stitch, thread, serger stitch, hems, need to finish raw edges, and raw edge finishing: Refer to the encyclopedia entry for the base fabric.

Prewash: no

Pressing: do not

Marking: chalk, tailor's tacks

Machine needle: tailor to base material

Cutting layout: on the grain, in a single layer

Cutting tools: craft scissors

Pins: sewing clips, tape

Machine foot: nonstick, roller, walking; decrease pressure

Seams: refer to base fabric, lapped (pg 160)

Care: Spot clean.

Nonslip Materials (pg 206)

Nonslip Materials (Netting)

A nonwoven utility material made of vinyl and often used for utility and home goods.

Netting nonslip fabrics are made entirely of a grippy material, creating a nonslip fabric that can be very difficult to sew with.

Prewash: no

Pressing: do not

Marking: chalk, tailor's tacks

Machine needle: 90/14 nonstick leather or microtex

Cutting layout: on the grain, in a single layer

Cutting tools: craft scissors

Pins: sewing clips, tape

Interfacing: do not

Machine foot: nonstick, roller, walking; decrease pressure

Conventional machine stitch: 3.5mm straight or zigzag

Serger stitch: three-thread overlock

Thread: all-purpose or heavy-duty polyester

Seams: plain (pg 66), abutted (pg 171)

Hems: single or double fold (pg 85), bound (pg 73)

Need to finish raw edges: no

Raw edge finishing: topstitched (pg 177)

Care: Spot clean.

Non-Stretch Vinyls (pg 175)

Oilcloth

An adhered vinyl made of duck or canvas coated with PVC and often used for bags, upholstery, and outerwear.

Oilcloth, also known as enameled cloth or American cloth, is duck or canvas coated with PVC.

Prewash: no

Pressing: low heat from the wrong side

Marking: dry erase on right side, disappearing ink on wrong side

Machine needle: 90/14 nonstick denim or microtex

Cutting layout: on the grain, in a single layer

Cutting tools: craft scissors, rotary cutter

Pins: sewing clips, glue stick, fusible web tape

Interfacing: sew-in nonwoven, foam

Machine foot: nonstick, roller, walking; decrease pressure

Conventional machine stitch: 3mm straight

Serger stitch: four-thread overlock

Thread: all-purpose or heavy-duty polyester

Seams: plain (pg 66), welt (pg 165), flat-fell (pg 81), lapped (pg 160)

Hems: overedge (pg 138), single fold (pg 85), bound (pg 73)

Need to finish raw edges: no

Raw edge finishing: topstitched (pg 177)

Care: Spot clean.

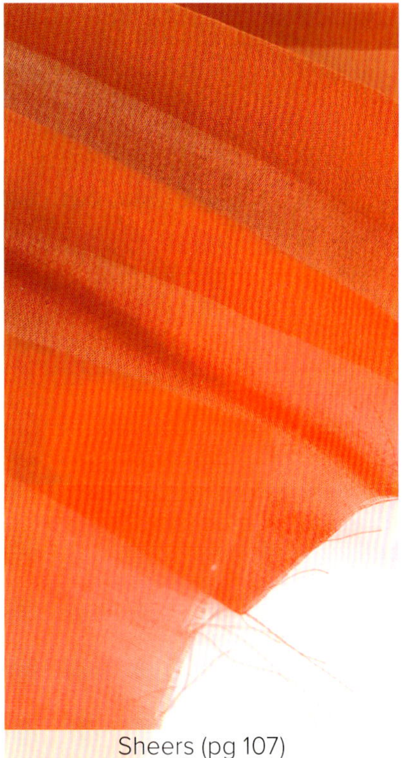

Sheers (pg 107)

Organdy

A plain-weave sheer made of cotton or polyester and often used for apparel and interfacing.

Organdy, the cotton version of organza, is a stiff and sheer netlike fabric that is now almost always polyester.

Prewash: yes

Pressing: low heat with press cloth

Marking: chalk, disappearing ink, thread tracing, tracing wheel

Machine needle: 70/10 microtex

Cutting layout: on the grain, in a single layer

Cutting tools: fabric shears, rotary cutter

Pins: fine pins, hand-basting

Interfacing: sheer nonwoven sew-in, organza, self

Machine foot: straight stitch, walking

Conventional machine stitch: 2.5mm straight with straight stitch plate

Serger stitch: two- or three-thread overlock

Thread: fine polyester, cotton, or silk

Seams: French (pg 114), overedged (pg 70), hairline (pg 122), plain (pg 66)

Hems: overedged (pg 138), rolled (pg 132), bound (pg 73), hairline (pg 122), double fold (pg 85)

Need to finish raw edges: yes

Raw edge finishing: bound (pg 73), overedged (pg 138)

Care: Machine wash warm or cold and gentle. Lay flat to dry.

Sheers (pg 107)

Organza

A plain-weave sheer made of polyester or silk and often used for apparel and as interfacing.

Organza, historically made from silk, is smooth, stiff, lightweight, and almost entirely transparent.

Prewash: generally, no

Pressing: Press according to fiber content (pg 36) with a press cloth.

Marking: chalk, disappearing ink, thread tracing, tracing wheel

Machine needle: 70/10 microtex

Cutting layout: on the grain, in a single layer

Cutting tools: fabric shears, pinking shears, rotary cutter

Pins: fine pins, hand-basting

Interfacing: sheer nonwoven sew-in, organza, self

Machine foot: straight stitch, walking

Conventional machine stitch: 2.5mm straight with straight stitch plate

Serger stitch: two- or three-thread overlock

Thread: fine polyester, cotton, or silk

Seams: French (pg 114), overedged (pg 70), hairline (pg 122), plain (pg 66)

Hems: overedged (pg 138), rolled (pg 132), bound (pg 73), hairline (pg 122), double fold (pg 85)

Need to finish raw edges: yes

Raw edge finishing: bound (pg 73), overedged (pg 138)

Care: Silk is dry-clean only. For other fibers, machine wash warm or cold; then tumble dry on low heat.

Standard Paper (pg 185)

Paper (Standard Weight: Construction Paper, Printer Paper, and Wrapping Paper)

A nonwoven material made of cellulose and often used for crafts and utility purposes.

Standard paper is opaque or nearly so, resists tearing, and is much easier to sew than lightweight papers.

Prewash: no

Pressing: medium heat with no steam

Marking: chalk, regular writing tools

Machine needle: 60/8 universal

Cutting layout: puzzle piece

Cutting tools: craft scissors

Pins: sewing clips, glue stick, tape

Interfacing: fusible woven or nonwoven

Machine foot: standard

Conventional machine stitch: 3.5mm straight

Serger stitch: N/A

Thread: fine polyester

Seams: plain (pg 66), lapped (pg 160), flat-fell (pg 81), welt (pg 165), reinforced (pg 100)

Hems: single or double fold (pg 85), decorative cut

Need to finish raw edges: no

Raw edge finishing: topstitched (pg 177)

Care: Do not wash.

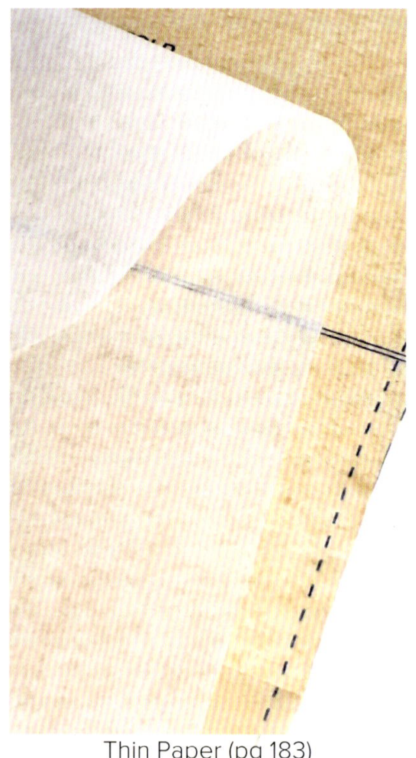

Thin Paper (pg 183)

Paper (Thin: Wrapping Tissue, Crepe Paper, and Origami)

A nonwoven material made of cellulose and often used for crafts and utility purposes.

Washi (origami), tissue, classic crinkly sewing pattern paper, and crepe paper are extremely delicate and often translucent.

Prewash: no

Pressing: low heat with no steam

Marking: chalk, regular writing tools

Machine needle: 60/8 universal

Cutting layout: puzzle piece

Cutting tools: craft scissors

Pins: sewing clips, glue stick, tape

Interfacing: fusible woven or nonwoven

Machine foot: standard; increase pressure

Conventional machine stitch: 3.5mm straight

Serger stitch: N/A

Thread: fine polyester

Seams: plain (pg 66), lapped (pg 160), flat-fell (pg 81), French (pg 114), reinforced (pg 100)

Hems: single or double fold (pg 85), decorative cut

Need to finish raw edges: no

Raw edge finishing: topstitch (pg 177)

Care: Do not wash.

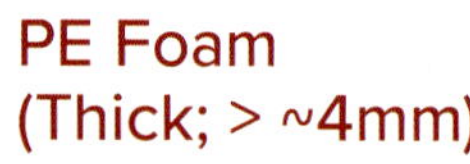

Thick Foam (pg 199)

PE Foam (Thick; > ~4mm)

A foam made of PE and often used for structure and thickness.

PE foam is less dense and rigid than EVA foam, which makes it a better squishy cushion and can make it easier to work with. PE foam has a scratchy texture.

Prewash: no

Pressing: Remove wrinkles with a heat gun.

Marking: chalk, metallic marking tools, regular writing tools

Machine needle: N/A

Cutting layout: puzzle piece, in a single layer

Cutting tools: box cutter

Pins: sewing clips, glue stick, tape

Interfacing: self, thicker foam

Machine foot: N/A

Conventional machine stitch: N/A

Serger stitch: N/A

Thread: N/A

Seams: abutted (pg 171)

Hems: beveled (pg 198)

Need to finish raw edges: no

Raw edge finishing: N/A

Care: Spot clean.

Thin Foam (pg 195)

PE Foam (Thin; < ~4mm)

A foam made of PE and often used for structure and thickness.

Thin PE foam is squishy, scratchy, and not very durable. It can be translucent.

Prewash: no

Pressing: Remove wrinkles with a heat gun.

Marking: chalk, metallic marking tools, regular writing tools

Machine needle: 100/16 denim

Cutting layout: puzzle piece, in a single layer

Cutting tools: box cutter, craft scissors, craft knife

Pins: sewing clips, glue stick, tape

Interfacing: self, thicker foam, sew-in woven or nonwoven

Machine foot: walking; decrease pressure

Conventional machine stitch: 4mm straight

Serger stitch: N/A

Thread: heavy-duty polyester

Seams: abutted (pg 171), lapped (pg 160), plain (pg 66)

Hems: single fold (pg 85), beveled (pg 198)

Need to finish raw edges: no

Raw edge finishing: topstitched (pg 177)

Care: Spot clean.

Tarps, Cling Wrap, and Plastic Bags (pg 208)

Plastic Trash Bags, Shopping Bags, and Cling Wrap

A nonwoven material made of PE and often used for utility purposes.

Plastic trash and shopping bags and cling wrap are lightweight, waterproof, and very sensitive to heat. They can be entirely transparent or completely opaque.

Prewash: no

Pressing: do not

Marking: chalk, dry-erase marker

Machine needle: 60/8 microtex

Cutting layout: puzzle piece

Cutting tools: craft scissors

Pins: sewing clips, tape

Interfacing: self, thicker PE

Machine foot: standard

Conventional machine stitch: 3.5mm straight

Serger stitch: N/A

Thread: all-purpose polyester

Seams: plain (pg 66), lapped (pg 160), French (pg 114), welt (pg 165)

Hems: single or double fold (pg 85)

Need to finish raw edges: no

Raw edge finishing: N/A

Care: Hand wash cold. Hang to dry.

Sturdy Knits (pg 91)

Ponte

A sturdy weft knit made of acrylic, cotton, polyester, nylon, or viscose and often used for apparel.

Ponte, which is often referred to as just "double knit," is structured, sturdy, and easy to work with.

Prewash: yes

Pressing: low heat with a press cloth

Marking: chalk, disappearing ink

Machine needle: 70/10 ballpoint

Cutting layout: on the grain

Cutting tools: fabric shears, rotary cutter

Pins: ballpoint pins

Interfacing: tricot

Machine foot: standard

Conventional machine stitch: 2.5mm straight or narrow zigzag

Serger stitch: narrow three-thread overlock

Thread: all-purpose polyester

Seams: plain (pg 66), overedged (pg 70), flatlocked (pg 147)

Hems: mock cover (pg 104), single or double fold (pg 85)

Need to finish raw edges: no

Raw edge finishing: overedged (pg 138)

Care: Machine wash. Tumble dry.

Suiting and Shirting (pg 67)

Poplin

A plain-weave medium-weight woven made of cotton, polyester, rayon, silk, or wool and often used for apparel.

Poplin is very densely woven and, therefore, strong and crisp. It has a slight sheen and very fine ribbing.

Prewash: yes

Pressing: press according to fiber content (pg 36)

Marking: chalk, disappearing ink, tailor's tacks

Machine needle: 80/12 universal

Cutting layout: on the grain

Cutting tools: fabric shears, rotary cutter

Pins: all-purpose pins

Interfacing: sew-in or fusible woven or nonwoven

Machine foot: standard

Conventional machine stitch: 2.5mm straight

Serger stitch: four-thread overlock

Thread: all-purpose polyester

Seams: plain (pg 66), overedged (pg 70)

Hems: single fold (pg 85), mock cover (pg 104)

Need to finish raw edges: yes

Raw edge finishing: pinked (pg 66), overedged (pg 138), topstitched (pg 177)

Care: Varies by fiber content. Generally, hand wash or machine wash cold and gentle. Tumble or hang to dry.

Meshes (pg 126)

Power Mesh

A warp-knit mesh made of nylon or polyester blended with spandex and often used for accessories and detailing.

Power Mesh is strong and stretchy. It's sturdy and lightweight.

Prewash: yes

Pressing: low heat

Marking: chalk, disappearing ink, thread tracing

Machine needle: 80/12 jersey

Cutting layout: on the grain, in a single layer

Cutting tools: fabric shears, rotary cutter

Pins: ballpoint pins, sewing clips, tearaway or water-soluble stabilizer

Interfacing: self or starch

Machine foot: standard, roller

Conventional machine stitch: 2mm zigzag

Serger stitch: three-thread overlock

Thread: all-purpose polyester

Seams: plain (pg 66), flat-fell (pg 81)

Hems: single fold or double fold (pg 85), mock cover (pg 104), bound (pg 73), overedged (pg 138)

Need to finish raw edges: no

Raw edge finishing: overedged (pg 138), bound (pg 73)

Care: Machine wash cold and gentle. Lay flat to dry.

Meshes (pg 126)

Powernet

A warp-knit mesh made of nylon or polyester blended with spandex and often used for apparel, especially athletic apparel.

Powernet has a very tight weave, giving it the strength to support and compress. It is durable and stretchy and may be almost entirely opaque.

Prewash: yes

Pressing: low heat

Marking: chalk, disappearing ink, thread tracing

Machine needle: 80/12 jersey

Cutting layout: on the grain, in a single layer

Cutting tools: fabric shears, rotary cutter

Pins: ballpoint pins, sewing clips

Interfacing: self or starch

Machine foot: standard, roller

Conventional machine stitch: 2mm zigzag

Serger stitch: three-thread overlock

Thread: all-purpose polyester

Seams: plain (pg 66), flat-fell (pg 81)

Hems: single fold or double fold (pg 85), mock cover (pg 104), bound (pg 73), overedged (pg 138)

Need to finish raw edges: no

Raw edge finishing: overedged (pg 138), bound (pg 73)

Care: Machine wash cold and gentle. Lay flat to dry.

Easy Sewing (pg 64)

Quilting Cotton

A plain-weave medium-weight woven made of cotton and often used for apparel, quilts, and linings.

Quilting cotton, because it's made specifically for quilters, has a huge amount of pattern and style diversity. It does not have a great drape compared to other medium-weight wovens but will soften with repeated washes.

Prewash: yes

Pressing: high heat with no steam

Marking: chalk, disappearing ink, tailor's tacks

Machine needle: 80/12 universal

Cutting layout: on the grain

Cutting tools: fabric shears, rotary cutter

Pins: all-purpose pins

Interfacing: self, sew-in or fusible woven or nonwoven

Machine foot: standard

Conventional machine stitch: 2.5mm straight

Serger stitch: three- or four-thread overlock

Thread: all-purpose polyester

Seams: French (pg 114), flat-fell (pg 81), plain (pg 66), overedged (pg 70)

Hems: pinked (pg 66), single or double fold (pg 85), mock cover (pg 104), overedged (pg 138), bound (pg 73)

Need to finish raw edges: yes

Raw edge finishing: bound (pg 73), overedged (pg 138), pinked (pg 66)

Care: Machine wash warm or cold. Tumble dry on low heat.

Stretch Knits (pg 95)

Ribbing

A stretchy weft knit made of cotton, polyester, rayon, or wool and often used for apparel and as binding.

Ribbing is named after the obvious ribs on both sides of the fabric. It is a double knit and extremely stretchy. It is often sold in a form ready to be used to finish the neckline and sleeve opening for other knit fabrics, although it can also be found as a regular-width fabric.

Prewash: yes

Pressing: Press gently along ribs with low heat, or steam.

Marking: chalk, tailor's tacks

Machine needle: 80/12 ballpoint

Cutting layout: on the grain

Cutting tools: rotary cutter

Pins: sewing clips, tape

Interfacing: tricot

Machine foot: walking

Conventional machine stitch: 2.5mm zigzag

Serger stitch: three- or four-thread overlock

Thread: all-purpose polyester

Seams: plain (pg 66), overedged (pg 70), twin needle (pg 50), flatlocked (pg 147)

Hems: overedged (pg 138), blind (pg 84), single or double fold (pg 85)

Need to finish raw edges: no

Raw edge finishing: overedged (pg 138), reinforced (pg 100) with zigzag, bound (pg 73)

Care: Hand wash or machine wash cold and gentle. Lay flat to dry.

Shinies and Sleeks (pg 116)

Sateen

A satin weave shiny and sleek fabric made of cotton and often used for apparel, lining, and linens.

Sateen, unlike other satin fabrics, is commonly matte. It is lightweight with a delicate drape. It is often combined with spandex to create stretch cotton sateen.

Prewash: yes

Pressing: medium to high heat and steam from the wrong side

Marking: chalk, disappearing ink, thread tracing, tracing wheel

Machine needle: 80/12 microtex

Cutting layout: on the grain, in a single layer

Cutting tools: fabric shears, rotary cutter

Pins: fine pins

Interfacing: sew-in or fusible nonwoven, batiste, self, organza

Machine foot: standard, walking

Conventional machine stitch: 2.5–3.5mm straight with straight stitch plate

Serger stitch: three-thread overlock

Thread: all-purpose cotton or polyester

Seams: hairline (pg 122), plain (pg 66), overedged (pg 70)

Hems: overedged (pg 138), rolled (pg 132, bound (pg 73), horsehair braid (pg 124), hairline (pg 122), double fold (pg 85)

Need to finish raw edges: yes

Raw edge finishing: pinked (pg 66), seared if synthetic (pg 121)

Care: Machine wash warm or cold and gentle. Tumble dry on low heat.

Shinies and Sleeks (pg 116)

Satin—Duchesse, Crepe-Backed, and "Lining"

A satin-weave shiny and sleek fabric made of polyester, silk, or viscose and often used for apparel, lining, and linens.

Crepe-backed satin has one shiny side with a crepe reverse. Duchesse satin is medium-weight with a slightly duller finish and firmer hand than a classic satin-weave fabric. Many satin fabrics are sold as just "satin" or "satin lining"—those fabrics are usually similar to either duchesse or crepe-backed satin.

Prewash: yes

Pressing: low to medium heat and steam from the wrong side

Marking: chalk, disappearing ink, thread tracing, tracing wheel

Machine needle: 80/12 microtex

Cutting layout: on the grain, in a single layer

Cutting tools: fabric shears, rotary cutter

Pins: fine pins

Interfacing: sew-in or fusible nonwoven, batiste, self, organza

Machine foot: standard, walking

Conventional machine stitch: 2.5–3.5mm straight with straight stitch plate

Serger stitch: three-thread overlock

Thread: all-purpose cotton or polyester

Seams: hairline (pg 122), plain (pg 66), overedged (pg 70)

Hems: overedged (pg 138), rolled (pg 132), bound (pg 73), horsehair braid (pg 124), hairline (pg 122), double fold (pg 85)

Need to finish raw edges: yes

Raw edge finishing: pinked (pg 66), seared if synthetic (pg 121)

Care: Silk is dry-clean only. For other fibers, machine wash warm or cold; then tumble dry on low heat.

Sturdy Knits (pg 91)

Scuba Knit

A sturdy weft knit made of nylon or polyester and often used for apparel.

Scuba knit is a thick knit that's extremely warm with a full drape and a slight sheen.

Prewash: no

Pressing: low heat

Marking: chalk, disappearing ink

Machine needle: 70/10 ballpoint

Cutting layout: on the grain

Cutting tools: fabric shears, rotary cutter

Pins: sewing clips

Interfacing: sew-in nonwoven

Machine foot: walking; decrease pressure

Conventional machine stitch: 3mm straight

Serger stitch: three- or four-thread overlock

Thread: all-purpose or heavy-duty polyester

Seams: plain (pg 66), flatlocked (pg 147)

Hems: bound (pg 73), mock cover (pg 104), overedged (pg 138)

Need to finish raw edges: no

Raw edge finishing: overedged (pg 138), topstitched (pg 177)

Care: Machine wash warm or cold. Tumble dry on low heat.

Embellished (pg 149)

Sequin (Sewn)

An embellished fabric made of any base material with sequins sewn on and often used for apparel, especially for special occasions and performance.

Sewn sequin-embellished fabrics are any base fabric with sequins sewn to the surface.

Interfacing, machine needle, serger stitch, thread, seams, hems, need to finish raw edges, and raw edge finishing: Refer to the encyclopedia entry for the base fabric.

Prewash: no

Pressing: Do not iron sequins directly; steam.

Marking: chalk, tailor's tacks

Cutting layout: with nap, in a single layer

Cutting tools: craft or heavy-duty scissors, if cutting through sequins; otherwise, refer to base fabric

Pins: Tailor to base fabric; do not pin through sequins.

Machine foot: walking; decrease pressure

Conventional machine stitch: 3.5mm straight

Care: Dry clean, hand wash, or spot clean. Lay flat to dry.

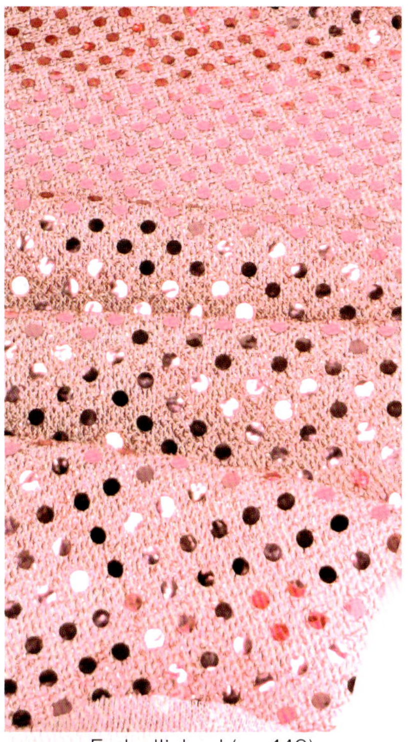

Embellished (pg 149)

Sequin (Adhered)

An embellished fabric made of any base material with sequins adhered and often used for apparel, especially for special occasions and performance.

Adhered sequin-embellished fabrics are any base fabric with sequins glued to the surface.

Interfacing, serger stitch, thread, seams, hems, need to finish raw edges, and raw edge finishing: Refer to the encyclopedia entry for the base fabric.

Prewash: no

Pressing: Steam or press from back on low heat with a press cloth.

Marking: chalk, tailor's tacks

Machine needle: 80/12 microtex or stretch or refer to base fabric

Cutting layout: with nap, in a single layer

Cutting tools: craft or heavy-duty scissors, if cutting through sequins; otherwise, refer to base fabric

Pins: Refer to base fabric; do not pin through sequins.

Machine foot: walking; decrease pressure

Conventional machine stitch: 3.5mm straight

Care: Dry clean, hand wash, or spot clean. Lay flat to dry.

Shinies and Sleeks (pg 116)

Shantung

A plain-weave shiny and sleek fabric made of silk and often used for apparel.

Shantung is lightly slubby and is crisp with a great drape. It is lightweight and frays dramatically.

Prewash: yes

Pressing: low to medium heat with a press cloth

Marking: chalk, disappearing ink, thread tracing, tracing wheel

Machine needle: 75/11 microtex

Cutting layout: on the grain, in a single layer

Cutting tools: fabric shears, pinking shears, rotary cutter

Pins: fine pins

Interfacing: sew-in or fusible nonwoven, batiste, self, organza

Machine foot: standard, walking

Conventional machine stitch: 2.5–3.5mm straight with straight stitch plate

Serger stitch: three-thread overlock

Thread: fine or all-purpose polyester, silk, or cotton

Seams: plain (pg 66), overedged (pg 70), French (pg 114)

Hems: overedged (pg 138), rolled (pg 132), bound (pg 73), horsehair braid (pg 124), hairline (pg 122), double fold (pg 85)

Need to finish raw edges: yes

Raw edge finishing: bound (pg 73), overedged (pg 138)

Care: Machine wash cold and gentle. Lay flat to dry.

Leather (pg 161)

Suede

A nonwoven material made of hide and often used for apparel, bags, and accessories.

Suede is a specific finish applied to leather, which gives it a pleasant fuzzy nap. It is generally less durable and harder to clean than other leather finishes but is softer.

Prewash: no

Pressing: Press from the wrong side on medium heat, using a press cloth and a plush fabric against the right side.

Marking: chalk, leather marking tool, regular writing tools on reverse

Machine needle: 80/12 universal or 90/14 to 110/18 leather depending on thickness

Cutting layout: with nap, in a single layer

Cutting tools: fabric or heavy-duty shears, rotary cutter

Pins: glue stick, tape, sewing clips

Interfacing: sew-in woven or nonwoven, organza, or fusible woven or nonwoven with caution

Machine foot: nonstick, roller, walking

Conventional machine stitch: 3mm

Serger stitch: N/A

Thread: heavy-duty polyester

Seams: plain (pg 66), lapped (pg 160), welt (pg 165), and flat-fell (pg 81)

Hems: single fold (pg 85)

Need to finish raw edges: no

Raw edge finishing: topstitched (pg 177), faced (pg 124), bound (pg 73)

Care: Hand wash or spot clean; then condition the reverse (non-textured side).

Sweater Knits (pg 102)

Sweater Knit

A weft knit made of acrylic, cotton, wool, or blends of those materials and often used for apparel.

Sweater knits can be medium- to heavyweight, are napped, and ravel considerably and immediately. They are unstable and loosely woven.

Prewash: yes

Pressing: as little as possible on the lowest heat possible

Marking: tailor's tacks

Machine needle: 90/14 ballpoint

Cutting layout: with nap, in a single layer

Cutting tools: fabric shears, rotary cutter

Pins: sewing clips

Interfacing: tricot

Machine foot: walking

Conventional machine stitch: 2.5mm narrow zigzag

Serger stitch: three- or four- thread overlock

Thread: all-purpose polyester

Seams: plain (pg 66), overedged (pg 70)

Hems: mock cover (pg 104), double fold (pg 85)

Need to finish raw edges: no

Raw edge finishing: overedged (pg 138), reinforced (pg 100) with zigzag

Care: Hand wash. Lay flat to dry.

Cozies (pg 135)

Sweatshirting / Sweatshirt Fabric / Sweatshirt Fleece

A weft-knit cozy fabric made of cotton, fleece, polyester, or wool and often used for apparel and accessories.

Sweatshirt fleece, which may also be referred to as sweatshirting, is cozy and warm but bulky. One side is brushed and napped and the other is smooth.

Prewash: yes

Pressing: Press from the smooth side on low heat, using a press cloth and a plush fabric against the napped side.

Marking: disappearing ink

Machine needle: 90/14 ballpoint

Cutting layout: on the grain on smooth side, or with nap on napped side

Cutting tools: fabric shears, rotary cutter

Pins: ballpoint pins; pin densely

Interfacing: tricot

Machine foot: nonstick, walking; decrease pressure

Conventional machine stitch: 2.5mm straight or zigzag

Serger stitch: three-thread overlock

Thread: all-purpose or heavy-duty polyester

Seams: plain (pg 66), overedge (pg 70)

Hems: single fold (pg 85), overedged (pg 138), bound (pg 73)

Need to finish raw edges: yes

Raw edge finishing: overedged (pg 138), topstitched (pg 177)

Care: Machine wash warm. Tumble dry on low heat. Pills; turn inside out to wash.

Stretch Knits (pg 95)

Swimsuit Fabric / Spandex

A stretchy knit made of nylon or polyester blended with spandex and often used for athletic wear, costuming, and intimates.

Swimsuit fabric, often referred to as just spandex or Lycra, is lightweight among the stretchy knits. It is extremely stretchy in all directions.

Prewash: yes

Pressing: low heat with a press cloth

Marking: chalk, disappearing ink

Machine needle: 75/11 microtex

Cutting layout: on the grain

Cutting tools: rotary cutter

Pins: ballpoint pins, sewing clips

Interfacing: tricot

Machine foot: roller

Conventional machine stitch: 1.5mm narrow zigzag

Serger stitch: three- or four-thread overlock

Thread: all-purpose polyester

Seams: plain (pg 66), overedged (pg 70), twin needle (pg 50), flatlocked (pg 147)

Hems: overedged (pg 138), blind (pg 84), single or double fold (pg 85)

Need to finish raw edges: no

Raw edge finishing: overedged (pg 138), reinforced (pg 100) with zigzag, bound (pg 73)

Care: Machine wash cold. Lay flat to dry.

Shinies and Sleeks (pg 116)

Taffeta

A plain-weave shiny and sleek fabric made of nylon, polyester, or silk and often used for apparel and home decor.

Taffeta is light- to medium-weight and is structured and stiff but delicate. It is smooth with a distinctive sound and sheen.

Prewash: yes

Pressing: Press from the wrong side on low heat using a press cloth.

Marking: chalk, disappearing ink, thread tracing, tracing wheel

Machine needle: 80/12 microtex or universal

Cutting layout: on the grain, in a single layer

Cutting tools: fabric shears, rotary cutter

Pins: fine pins, hand-basting

Interfacing: sew-in or fusible nonwoven, batiste, self, organza

Machine foot: standard, walking

Conventional machine stitch: 2.5–3.5mm straight with straight stitch plate

Serger stitch: three-thread overlock

Thread: fine or all-purpose polyester, silk, or cotton

Seams: hairline (pg 122), plain (pg 66), overedged (pg 70)

Hems: overedged (pg 138), rolled (pg 132), bound (pg 73), horsehair braid (pg 124), hairline (pg 122), double fold (pg 85)

Need to finish raw edges: yes

Raw edge finishing: pinked (pg 66), seared if synthetic (pg 121)

Care: Silk is dry-clean only. For other fibers, machine wash warm or cold; then tumble dry on low heat.

Tarps, Cling Wrap, and Plastic Bags (pg 208)

Tarp

A nonwoven utility material made of PE and often used for utility purposes and adventure gear.

Many tarps are made of woven strips of PE, which gives them strength but also allows them to fray over time. Tarp is strong, waterproof, and sensitive to heat.

Prewash: no

Pressing: do not

Marking: chalk, dry-erase marker

Machine needle: 90/14 leather, microtex, or universal

Cutting layout: puzzle piece

Cutting tools: craft or heavy-duty scissors

Pins: sewing clips, tape

Interfacing: do not

Machine foot: walking

Conventional machine stitch: 3.5mm straight

Serger stitch: N/A

Thread: heavy-duty polyester

Seams: plain (pg 66), lapped (pg 160)

Hems: single or double fold (pg 85)

Need to finish raw edges: no

Raw edge finishing: pinked (pg 66)

Care: Machine wash cold. Hang to dry.

Faux Fur (pg 144)

Teddy Fur

A knit or woven piled fabric made of acrylic, nylon, or polyester and often used for apparel, outerwear, and toys.

Teddy fur is a long-pile fabric on a strong base; it has a shorter pile than faux fur. The pile and base fabric can be different fibers but are almost always acrylic, polyester, or another synthetic material. It comes in a wide variety of colors, patterns, and textures.

Prewash: no

Pressing: Tumble dry to remove wrinkles.

Marking: chalk, disappearing ink, regular writing tool on reverse

Machine needle: 80/12 universal

Cutting layout: with nap

Cutting tools: box cutter, craft knife

Pins: long pins

Interfacing: starch

Machine foot: standard; decrease pressure

Conventional machine stitch: 3.5mm straight

Serger stitch: four-thread overlock

Thread: all-purpose polyester

Seams: plain (pg 66), flatlock (pg 147), abutted (pg 171)

Hems: single fold (pg 85), faced (pg 124)

Need to finish raw edges: no

Raw edge finishing: N/A

Care: Hand wash only if necessary. Hang to dry; then brush.

Tissue Lamé (pg 166)

Tissue Lamé

A knit or woven fabric made of cotton, nylon, or silk yarns woven with gold, silver, copper, or mylar yarns and often used for apparel and detailing.

Tissue lamé is an extremely lightweight shiny metallic fabric. Lamé frays and runs like wild. Exposed metallic yarns can be very scratchy.

Prewash: no

Pressing: low heat and no steam from back with a press cloth

Marking: chalk, disappearing ink

Machine needle: 70/10 microtex, metallic, or ballpoint

Cutting layout: with nap, in a single layer

Cutting tools: new craft scissors, fabric shears, rotary cutter

Pins: sewing clips

Interfacing: sew-in or fusible nonwoven, batiste, organza

Machine foot: standard

Conventional machine stitch: 2.5–3.5mm straight

Serger stitch: N/A

Thread: all-purpose polyester

Seams: French (pg 114), flat-fell (pg 81)

Hems: rolled (pg 132)

Need to finish raw edges: yes

Raw edge finishing: rolled (pg 132)

Care: Dry clean.

Cozies (pg 135)

Towel Terry

A knit or woven-with-pile cozy fabric made of cotton and often used for linens.

Towel terry's protruding loops create an absorbent and soft surface on both sides. It is warm and cozy but frays and sheds.

Prewash: yes

Pressing: Press from the wrong side on high heat, using steam, a press cloth, and a plush fabric against the right side.

Marking: disappearing ink

Machine needle: 100/16 ballpoint

Cutting layout: with nap

Cutting tools: fabric shears, rotary cutter

Pins: long ballpoint pins

Interfacing: sew-in woven

Machine foot: walking; decrease pressure

Conventional machine stitch: 3mm straight or zigzag

Serger stitch: three- or four-thread overlock

Thread: all-purpose or heavy-duty polyester

Seams: plain (pg 66), overedged (pg 70), reversible lapped (pg 88)

Hems: overedged (pg 138), bound (pg 73), wide double fold (pg 85)

Need to finish raw edges: yes

Raw edge finishing: overedged (pg 138), bound (pg 73)

Care: Machine wash warm. Tumble dry.

Sturdy Knits (pg 91)

Tricot

A sturdy warp knit made of cotton, nylon, polyester, rayon, or silk and often used for activewear and as a stabilizer for other knits.

Tricot is densely knitted and doesn't have much natural stretch. It's soft, but sturdy. Tricot can have a sheen or a matte finish and can be sheer but is not always.

Prewash: yes

Pressing: low heat

Marking: chalk, disappearing ink

Machine needle: 70/10 ballpoint

Cutting layout: on the grain

Cutting tools: fabric shears, rotary cutter

Pins: ballpoint pins; pin densely

Interfacing: sew-in nonwoven

Machine foot: walking

Conventional machine stitch: 2.5mm straight or zigzag

Serger stitch: narrow three-thread overlock

Thread: all-purpose polyester

Seams: plain (pg 66), overedged (pg 70), flatlocked (pg 147)

Hems: mock cover (pg 104), single or double fold (pg 85)

Need to finish raw edges: no

Raw edge finishing: overedged (pg 138)

Care: Machine wash warm or cold. Tumble dry.

Nets (pg 128)

Tulle / Bobbinet / Crinoline

A woven netting made of cotton, nylon, polyester, or silk and often used for home decor, petticoats, and tutus.

Tulle is a very strong and lightweight netting. The very common nylon version is strong and inexpensive; silk tulle, its traditional makeup, is soft and much less stiff. Bobbinet is a specific kind of tulle woven on a special machine, which gives it hexagonal holes. Crinoline is extremely stiff. All three can be used as a structural material for lightweight fabrics.

Prewash: no

Pressing: low heat with press cloth

Marking: marker, safety pins, thread tracing

Machine needle: 70/10 universal

Cutting layout: puzzle piece

Cutting tools: rotary cutter

Pins: sewing clips, tape, tearaway or water-soluble stabilizer

Interfacing: starch

Machine foot: roller

Conventional machine stitch: 2mm straight or zigzag

Serger stitch: three-thread overlock

Thread: all-purpose polyester

Seams: plain (pg 66), overedged (pg 70), French (pg 114)

Hems: bound (pg 73), rolled (pg 132), overedged (pg 138)

Need to finish raw edges: no

Raw edge finishing: overedged (pg 138), bound (pg 73)

Care: Hand wash cold. Lay flat or hang to dry.

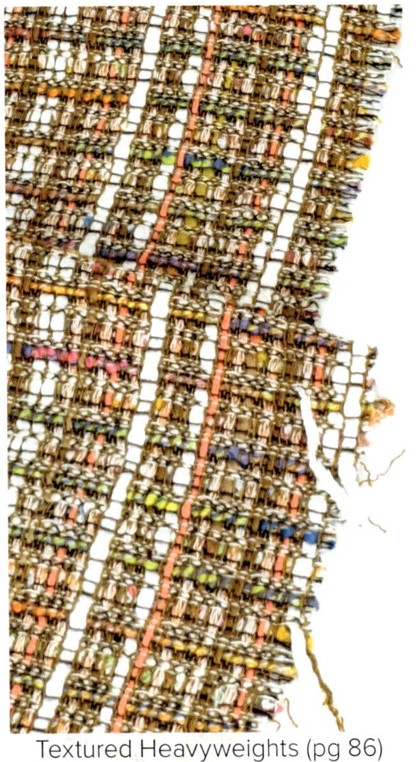

Textured Heavyweights (pg 86)

Tweed

A plain- or twill-weave heavyweight woven made of polyester or wool and often used for apparel and outerwear.

Tweed is a category term for heavyweight, rough, and durable woolens. Because the wool fibers that make the fabric are fairly unprocessed, tweeds are textured, scratchy, and nubby.

Prewash: yes

Pressing: Press according to fiber content (pg 36) with a press cloth.

Marking: chalk, disappearing ink, tailor's tacks

Machine needle: 80/12 universal

Cutting layout: with nap

Cutting tools: fabric shears, rotary cutter

Pins: all-purpose pins, sewing clips

Interfacing: sew-in or fusible woven or nonwoven

Machine foot: standard

Conventional machine stitch: 3mm straight

Serger stitch: three- or four-thread overlock

Thread: heavy-duty polyester or cotton

Seams: plain (pg 66), overedged (pg 70), flat-fell (pg 81), welt (pg 165), reversible lapped (pg 88)

Hems: faced (pg 124), bound (pg 73), single fold (pg 85)

Need to finish raw edges: yes

Raw edge finishing: bound (pg 73), topstitched (pg 177), overedged (pg 138)

Care: Spot clean, dry clean, or hand wash.

Suiting and Shirting (pg 67)

Twill / Chino

A twill-weave medium-weight woven made of cotton or wool and often used for apparel and outerwear.

Twill, also known as chino, is durable with a nice drape. It is one of the heavier suiting and shirting fabrics.

Prewash: yes

Pressing: Press according to fiber content (pg 36) with a press cloth.

Marking: chalk, disappearing ink, tailor's tacks

Machine needle: 90/14 universal or denim

Cutting layout: with nap

Cutting tools: fabric shears, rotary cutter

Pins: all-purpose pins

Interfacing: sew-in woven or nonwoven

Machine foot: standard

Conventional machine stitch: 2.5mm straight

Serger stitch: three- or four-thread overlock

Thread: all-purpose or heavy-duty polyester

Seams: plain (pg 66), flat-fell (pg 81), overedged (pg 70)

Hems: double fold (pg 85), bound (pg 73), overedged (pg 138)

Need to finish raw edges: yes

Raw edge finishing: overedged (pg 138), bound (pg 73), topstitched (pg 177)

Care: Machine wash warm or cold. Hang to dry.

Fabric Paper (pg 187)

Tyvek

A nonwoven material made of PE and often used for bags, accessories, utility purposes, and crafts.

Tyvek (by DuPont) is an extremely sturdy and rip-resistant material that you may know from festival wristbands and foot race bibs. Tyvek comes in different forms, and may be more fabric-like (Tyvek interfacing) or paper-like (Tyvek envelopes).

Prewash: yes

Pressing: low heat between layers of baking paper

Marking: chalk, disappearing ink, washi tape, regular writing tool on reverse

Machine needle: 80/12 microtex

Cutting layout: puzzle piece

Cutting tools: craft scissors, rotary cutter

Pins: sewing clips, glue stick

Interfacing: self, starch

Machine foot: standard

Conventional machine stitch: 3.5mm straight

Serger stitch: three-thread overlock

Thread: all-purpose polyester

Seams: plain (pg 66), lapped (pg 160), flat-fell (pg 81), welt (pg 165)

Hems: single or double fold (pg 85), decorative cut

Need to finish raw edges: no

Raw edge finishing: topstitched (pg 177)

Care: Machine wash warm. Lay flat to dry.

Thick Foam (pg 199)

Upholstery Foam (PU) (Thick; >~4mm)

A foam made of PU and often used for structure and thickness.

Upholstery or cushion foam is a low-rigidity form of foam; it's squishy and very flexible. It's often described by its density and thickness.

Prewash: no

Pressing: steam

Marking: chalk and regular writing tools

Machine needle: N/A

Cutting layout: puzzle piece, in a single layer

Cutting tools: box cutter

Pins: sewing clips, glue stick, tape

Interfacing: self, thicker foam

Machine foot: N/A

Conventional machine stitch: N/A

Serger stitch: N/A

Thread: N/A

Seams: abutted (pg 171)

Hems: beveled (pg 198)

Need to finish raw edges: no

Raw edge finishing: N/A

Care: Spot clean or hand wash.

Thin Foam (pg 195)

Upholstery Foam (PU) (Thin; < ~4mm)

A foam made of PU and often used for structure and thickness.

Thin upholstery foam is soft, squishy, and flexible. Because of its relatively low rigidity, it has more drape than other thin foams.

Prewash: no

Pressing: steam

Marking: chalk and regular writing tools

Machine needle: 100/16 denim

Cutting layout: puzzle piece, in a single layer

Cutting tools: box cutter, craft scissors, craft knife

Pins: sewing clips, glue stick, tape

Interfacing: self, thicker foam, sew-in woven or nonwoven

Machine foot: walking; decrease pressure

Conventional machine stitch: 4mm straight

Serger stitch: three-thread overlock

Thread: heavy-duty polyester

Seams: abutted (pg 171), lapped (pg 160), plain (pg 66)

Hems: overedge (pg 138), single fold (pg 85), beveled (pg 198)

Need to finish raw edges: no

Raw edge finishing: topstitched (pg 177)

Care: Spot clean or hand wash.

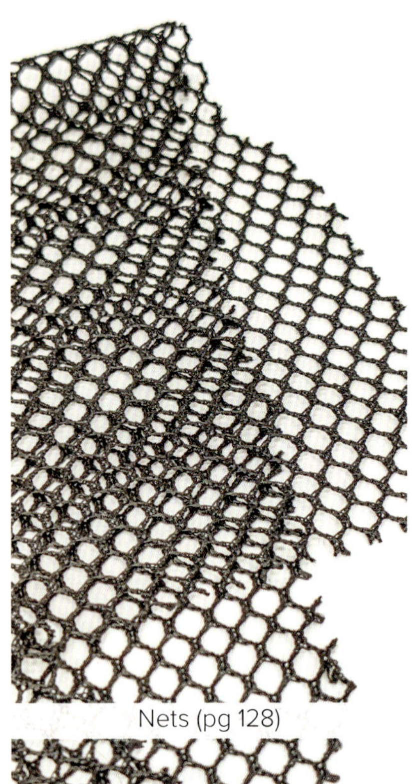

Nets (pg 128)

Utility Netting

A knit or nonwoven netting made of nylon and often used for detailing and utility purposes.

Utility netting is a catch-all term for the fabric used in laundry baskets, tent screens, and backpacks; of course, it can also be used for garment-making, especially to provide airflow in athletic apparel. Utility nettings are durable and easy to care for.

Prewash: yes

Pressing: low heat with press cloth

Marking: safety pins, tailor's tacks

Machine needle: 70/10 jersey

Cutting layout: puzzle piece, in a single layer

Cutting tools: rotary cutter

Pins: sewing clips, tape, tearaway or water-soluble stabilizer

Interfacing: starch

Machine foot: standard, roller

Conventional machine stitch: 2mm straight

Serger stitch: three- or four-thread overlock

Thread: all-purpose polyester

Seams: plain (pg 66), overedged (pg 70), flat-fell (pg 81)

Hems: bound (pg 73), overedged (pg 138), single fold (pg 85)

Need to finish raw edges: no

Raw edge finishing: bound (pg 73), overedged (pg 138), topstitched (pg 177)

Care: Machine wash cold or warm in a delicates bag. Lay flat to dry.

Easy Sewing (pg 64)

Utility Nonwoven (Reusable Shopping Bag Material)

A nonwoven medium-weight material made of PP and often used for utility purposes.

Utility nonwovens are the material reusable shopping bags and many medical gowns and masks are made of. Utility nonwovens are durable and do not fray and are, therefore, easy to sew with.

Prewash: yes

Pressing: low heat

Marking: chalk, disappearing ink

Machine needle: 80/12 universal

Cutting layout: puzzle piece

Cutting tools: craft scissors, rotary cutter

Pins: sewing clips

Interfacing: self, sew-in or fusible woven or nonwoven

Machine foot: standard

Conventional machine stitch: 2.5mm straight

Serger stitch: three- or four-thread overlock

Thread: all-purpose polyester

Seams: plain seam (pg 66), overedged (pg 70)

Hems: single or double fold (pg 85), overedged (pg 138)

Need to finish raw edges: no

Raw edge finishing: bound (pg 73), overedged (pg 138), pinked (pg 66)

Care: Machine wash warm or cold. Tumble dry on low heat.

Stretch Velvet, French Terry, and Velour (pg 142)

Velour

A knit piled fabric made of cotton and often used for apparel, upholstery, and home decor.

Velour, the knit version of velvet and velveteen, has a dense pile with a nap. It is shinier and softer than velvet.

Prewash: yes

Pressing: Press from the wrong side on low heat, using a press cloth and a plush fabric against the right side.

Marking: disappearing ink on wrong side

Machine needle: 90/14 ballpoint

Cutting layout: with nap, in a single layer

Cutting tools: rotary cutter

Pins: ballpoint pins; pin densely

Interfacing: sew-in woven or nonwoven interfacing or tricot

Machine foot: roller, walking

Conventional machine stitch: 2.5mm zigzag

Serger stitch: three-thread overlock

Thread: all-purpose polyester

Seams: plain (pg 66), flat-fell (pg 81), overedged (pg 70)

Hems: faced (pg 124), blind hem (pg 84), overedged (pg 138)

Need to finish raw edges: yes

Raw edge finishing: overedged (pg 138), bound (pg 73), pinked (pg 66)

Care: Machine wash cold and gentle. Lay flat or tumble dry on low heat.

Velvet, Velveteen, and Corduroy (pg 139)

Velvet

A woven piled fabric made of acetate, cotton, linen, nylon, polyester, rayon, silk, or viscose and often used for apparel, upholstery, and home decor.

Velvet is a dense short pile with a luxurious drape. It is very soft, napped, and often lustrous.

Prewash: yes

Pressing: Press from the wrong side on low heat, using a press cloth and a plush fabric against the right side.

Marking: disappearing ink on wrong side

Machine needle: 70/10 microtex

Cutting layout: with nap, in a single layer

Cutting tools: rotary cutter

Pins: all-purpose pins, hand-basting

Interfacing: sew-in woven or nonwoven interfacing or tricot

Machine foot: roller, walking

Conventional machine stitch: 2.5mm straight or zigzag

Serger stitch: three- or four-thread overlock

Thread: all-purpose cotton or silk

Seams: plain (pg 66), overedged (pg 70)

Hems: faced (pg 124), blind hem (pg 84), overedged (pg 138)

Need to finish raw edges: yes

Raw edge finishing: overedged (pg 138), topstitched (pg 177), pinked (pg 66)

Care: May be dry-clean only. If not, machine wash cold and gentle; then lay flat or tumble dry on low heat.

Stretch Velvet, French Terry, and Velour (pg 142)

Velvet (Stretch)

A knit piled fabric made of acetate, cotton, linen, nylon, polyester, rayon, silk, or viscose blended with spandex and often used for apparel.

Stretch velvet is velvet with spandex added to give stretch. Stretch velvet is sometimes significantly more lightweight than velvet.

Prewash: yes

Pressing: Press from the wrong side on low heat, using a press cloth and a plush fabric against the right side.

Marking: disappearing ink on wrong side

Machine needle: 70/10 stretch

Cutting layout: with nap, in a single layer

Cutting tools: rotary cutter

Pins: ballpoint pins; pin densely

Interfacing: sew-in woven or nonwoven interfacing or tricot

Machine foot: roller, walking

Conventional machine stitch: 2.5mm zigzag

Serger stitch: three-thread overlock

Thread: all-purpose polyester

Seams: plain (pg 66), flat-fell (pg 81), overedged (pg 70)

Hems: faced (pg 124), blind hem (pg 84), overedged (pg 138)

Need to finish raw edges: yes

Raw edge finishing: overedged (pg 138), bound (pg 73), pinked (pg 66)

Care: Machine wash cold and gentle. Lay flat or tumble dry on low heat.

Velvet, Velveteen, and Corduroy (pg 139)

Velveteen

A woven piled fabric made of cotton, polyester, or rayon and often used for apparel and home decor.

Velveteen, the cotton version of velvet, is stiffer, more durable, and less shiny than velvet. Like velvet, it has a thick, dense pile and a nap.

Prewash: yes

Pressing: Press from the wrong side on low heat, using a press cloth and a plush fabric against the right side.

Marking: disappearing ink on wrong side

Machine needle: 70/10 microtex or stretch (if stretch fabric)

Cutting layout: with nap, in a single layer

Cutting tools: rotary cutter

Pins: all-purpose pins, hand-basting

Interfacing: sew-in woven or nonwoven interfacing or tricot

Machine foot: roller, walking

Conventional machine stitch: 2.5mm straight or zigzag

Serger stitch: three- or four-thread overlock

Thread: all-purpose cotton or polyester

Seams: plain (pg 66), overedged (pg 70)

Hems: faced (pg 124), blind hem (pg 84), overedged (pg 138)

Need to finish raw edges: yes

Raw edge finishing: overedged (pg 138), bound (pg 73)

Care: Machine wash cold and gentle. Lay flat or tumble dry on low heat.

Clear and Tinted Vinyl (pg 180)

Vinyl (Clear and Tinted)

A nonwoven vinyl made of PU and often used for bags, upholstery, and outerwear.

Clear vinyl is either entirely clear or tinted. It is usually fairly heavyweight and rigid and needs special consideration due to its translucency.

Prewash: no

Pressing: do not

Marking: dry-erase marker

Machine needle: 90/14 nonstick leather or microtex

Cutting layout: puzzle piece, in a single layer

Cutting tools: craft scissors, rotary cutter

Pins: sewing clips

Interfacing: do not

Machine foot: nonstick, roller, walking; decrease pressure

Conventional machine stitch: 3mm straight

Serger stitch: four-thread overlock

Thread: all-purpose or heavy-duty polyester

Seams: plain (pg 66), lapped (pg 160), flat-fell (pg 81)

Hems: single or double fold (pg 85)

Need to finish raw edges: no

Raw edge finishing: topstitched (pg 177)

Care: Spot clean.

Non-Stretch Vinyls (pg 175)

Vinyl (Heavyweight PU)

An adhered or nonwoven vinyl made of PU or a PU blend and often used for apparel, upholstery, and bags.

Heavyweight PU vinyls have some natural elasticity and drape much better than PVC vinyls. They are often matte and when used as faux leather have a more natural (and, therefore, convincing) appearance. They're less durable than PVC vinyls and also more expensive.

Prewash: no

Pressing: low heat from the wrong side

Marking: disappearing ink or regular pens, chalk or dry-erase marker on the right side, markers on the wrong side

Machine needle: 90/14 nonstick leather or microtex

Cutting layout: puzzle piece, in a single layer

Cutting tools: craft scissors, rotary cutter

Pins: sewing clips, glue stick, fusible web tape

Interfacing: sew-in nonwoven, foam

Machine foot: nonstick, roller, walking; decrease pressure

Conventional machine stitch: 3.5mm straight

Serger stitch: four-thread overlock

Thread: all-purpose or heavy-duty polyester

Seams: plain (pg 66), welt (pg 165), flat-fell (pg 81), lapped (pg 160)

Hems: overedge (pg 138), single fold (pg 85), bound (pg 73)

Need to finish raw edges: no

Raw edge finishing: topstitched (pg 177)

Care: Spot clean.

Non-Stretch Vinyls (pg 175)

Vinyl (PVC)

An adhered or nonwoven vinyl made of PVC or a PVC blend and often used for apparel, upholstery, and bags.

PVC vinyls are often shiner and stiffer than PU vinyls. In faux leather form, they often appear less realistic. They're more durable than PU vinyls and are, therefore, better suited for outdoor and heavy-use upholstery.

Prewash: no

Pressing: low heat from the wrong side

Marking: disappearing ink or regular pens, chalk or dry-erase marker on right side, markers on wrong side

Machine needle: 90/14 nonstick leather or microtex

Cutting layout: puzzle piece, in a single layer

Cutting tools: craft scissors, rotary cutter

Pins: sewing clips, glue stick, fusible web tape

Interfacing: sew-in nonwoven, foam

Machine foot: nonstick, roller, walking; decrease pressure

Conventional machine stitch: 3.5mm straight

Serger stitch: four-thread overlock

Thread: all-purpose or heavy-duty polyester

Seams: plain (pg 66), welt (pg 165), flat-fell (pg 81), lapped (pg 160)

Hems: overedge (pg 138), single fold (pg 85), bound (pg 73)

Need to finish raw edges: no

Raw edge finishing: topstitched (pg 177)

Care: Spot clean.

Sheers (pg 107)

Voile

A plain-weave sheer made of cotton, polyester, or wool and often used for apparel and home decor.

Voile is very lightweight and ranges from semi-sheer to sheer. It is soft and smooth.

Prewash: yes

Pressing: Press according to fiber content (pg 36) with a press cloth.

Marking: chalk, disappearing ink, thread tracing, tracing wheel

Machine needle: 70/10 microtex

Cutting layout: on the grain, in a single layer

Cutting tools: fabric shears, rotary cutter

Pins: fine pins, hand-basting

Interfacing: sheer nonwoven sew-in, organza, self

Machine foot: straight stitch, walking

Conventional machine stitch: 2.5mm straight with straight stitch plate

Serger stitch: two- or thread-thread overlock

Thread: fine polyester, cotton, or silk

Seams: French (pg 114), overedged (pg 70), hairline (pg 122), plain (pg 66)

Hems: overedged (pg 138), rolled (pg 132), bound (pg 73), hairline (pg 122), double fold (pg 85)

Need to finish raw edges: yes

Raw edge finishing: bound (pg 73), overedged (pg 138)

Care: Machine wash cold and gentle. Lay flat to dry.

Further Reading

The following materials were incredible references for this book; check them out to learn more!

12 Essential Seams (a CreativeSpark course), by Shannon and Jason

Create with Cork Fabric, by Jessica Sallie Barrera (C&T Publishing)

Creative Cosplay, by Amanda Haas (C&T Publishing)

Essential Serger Reference Tool, by Katrina Walker (C&T Publishing)

Essential Sewing Reference Tool, by Carla Hegeman Crim (C&T Publishing)

Evelyn Wood's YouTube Channel at **youtube.com/@Evelyn__Wood**

Kraft-tex Creations, by Lindsay Conner (C&T Publishing)

Level Up! Creative Cosplay, by Amanda Haas (C&T Publishing)

Making Bags, A Field Guide, by Jessica Sallie Barrera (C&T Publishing)

McCall's Essential Guide to Sewing, by Brigitte Binder, Jutta Kühnle, Karin Roser (Sixth&Spring Books)

Projects in Leather, by Tony Laier and Kay Laier (Fox Chapel Publishing)

Sew Luxe Leather, by Rosanna Clare Gethin (David & Charles)

Sewing Knits from Fit to Finish, by Linda Lee (Quarry Books)

Sewing Machine Magic, by Steffani Lincecum (Quarry Books)

Sewing with Leather and Suede, by Sandy Scrivano (Lark Books)

Successful Serging, by Beth Baumgartel (Quarry Books)

Singer: The Complete Photo Guide to Sewing, 3rd Edition, by Nancy Langdon (Quarry Books)

The Hero's Closet, by Gillian Conahan (Abrams Books)

The Mood Guide to Fabric and Fashion, by Mood Designer Fabrics (STC Craft/A Melanie Falick Book)

The SCHMETZ ABC Pocket Guide, by SCHMETZ

The Sewport Fabrics Directory at **sewport.com/fabrics-directory**

Sewing Lingerie, by the Editors of Cy DeCosse Incorporated (Cy DeCosse Inc.)

The Ultimate Thread Guide, by Becky Goldsmith (C&T Publishing)

Threads Sewing Guide, edited by Carol Fresia (Taunton Press)

Cotton Fabrics at **thefabricofourlives.com/cotton-fabrics**

Upholstery: A Complete Course, by David James (GMC Publications)

We All Sew at **weallsew.com**

About the Author

Annye Driscoll believes that cosplay brings joy, that making is an incredible form of creative self-expression, and (most important!) that everyone can cosplay. Annye focuses on highly detailed craftsmanship, and they're willing to spend a year on a cosplay to get it right. They have won multiple best-in-show awards, are a repeat finalist for Riot Games' State Farm x LCS cosplay contest, and have been published by *Entertainment Weekly* and *Marvel Becoming*.

Annye lives in Ohio with their husband, cats, horse, and school of fancy guppies. Their first book, *The Ultimate Glue Guide,* was published by C&T Publishing in 2024.

You can find Annye on the internet as **@MakerFishmeal**

Photo by Abigail Davidson